ADVANCE PRAISE

"Your prose is engaging. Like the brush of silk on skin, the author-narrator becomes a character..... a theatrical crossing of thresholds of perception. I enjoyed it. I want to read more."

— WILLIAM YANKES, DOCTORATE IN LITERATURE,
ESTABLISHED POLITICAL JOURNALIST AND AUTHOR

"A complete treat! I found myself transported back to our farm, full of emotions. Such a brilliant view into preserving our past. A picture-perfect American postcard of our country's youth. A precious treasure that reminds me of the heartwarming stories from my growing-up years."

— RUBY TENNANT, NATUROPATHIC DOCTOR,
FAMILY HERBALIST, NATURAL HEALTH EDUCATOR
AND CONSULTANT

LOVE AT FIRST FIGHT
HEARTWARMING STORIES OF LIFE AND LOVE

JEFFREY HUGHES NAYLOR

WINTERWOLF PRESS

Books may be purchased by contacting the publisher at:

Winterwolf Press

8635 West Sahara Avenue, #425

Las Vegas, NV 89117

www.WinterwolfPress.com

Info@WinterwolfPress.com

Interior formatting by Christine Contini

Cover design © 2024 by Winterwolf Press

DEDICATION

To the best friend I have ever known, Jeramie Benson Naylor, my wife.
Truest, unconditional, and eternal love.

Jeffrey and Jeramie Naylor

CONTENTS

EDITOR'S PREFACE

My dad often retold this story about when Grandma tried to learn to drive, how the car jerked, how her and Grandpa's heads bobbled, Grandpa yelling watch out, Grandma bursting into tears, and Grandma finally throwing her hands up in the air and exiting the vehicle.

My brothers and sister all laughed as Daddy told us this story because he found such humor in it and could barely get through it without howling himself.

And the bit Dad casually tossed in at the end about his younger siblings (Grandpa and Grandma had 17 total) who stood all huddled in the window, watching with tears streaming down their faces...

"But why did they cry?" I asked every time. And every time the answer changed. One time he said it was because they had never seen Grandma give up, another time he said they thought Grandpa was killing Grandma. For me, the story was funny and worth a great big knee slap, but for Dad's younger siblings, sometimes there was a tragic tale of the world ending.

Then one day on a long car trip, with a broken radio and four kids of my own and with nothing to do, I thought I would pull out some of Dad's old stories to give us all something to think about.

What a trip it turned out to be, and a new generation of story retells was born.

I couldn't always remember the details of the stories shared by my father, and sometimes even when telling my own I think I made up new endings just like he did. But even still today, when we hop in the car, the grandkids remind me that their parents said I had all the family stories, and what about "the time you nearly kicked a one-legged pigeon, Grandma? Tell us that one again!"

There is something that aligns in your heart when you hop around your head in your memories, to and fro, here and there, adding up bits and pieces that inspire a vision.

Even 50 years later, you feel you are standing in the middle of family events watching all the characters move around you as if they exist at this present moment in their activities. Life becomes timeless and transcendent, and your traditions survive as ever-present.

Each of Jeffrey's stories has a way of opening the minds and hearts of its readers, inspiring a deeper understanding of how to live and live joyfully with all others around you, and to see others as vulnerable, reminding us to be inclusive of all people in whatever you do.

I love that these stories are parts of the author's life, how he reveals where truths were learned and applied and now, shared. Thank you, Jeffrey, for the many smiles I encountered during my involvement with this book.

There is something that happens when you read a collection of family tales. You bond with the material, and the characters, more and more. You leave the book feeling as if you are taking it with you instead of putting it down as finished. This is how I feel right now as I take a deep breath and roll again in my thoughts through the shares of this book. Powerful shares.

Certainly, I am giving my dad a copy of this book to inspire him, as I know it will inspire others, to carry on your example and share stories of joy, humor, sorrows, and tears. Such love and joy to be shared even in the tears.

Thank you for your generous gift. I feel I know your family as I know my own.

-Christine Contini
Senior Editor at Winterwolf Press

LOVE AT FIRST FIGHT
OR HOW MY MAMA MET MY DADDY

Most everybody has a story to tell about how their parents first met. My mama met my daddy while traveling on a bumpy country road in a squatty, yellow school bus headed for town.

Both were raised on farms that were at opposite ends of Haywood County, Tennessee. It was the same county that raised Tina Turner in Nutbush. When she passed away in May 2023, the media talked about Nutbush like it was a place on another planet. I've been to Nutbush many times; on one side of the road is Nutbush, and on the other side is Naylor Cemetery!

Mama and Daddy both grew up during the depression and knew all about toughing it out and doing without frills. Consequently, they didn't travel around very often and had the opportunity to meet one another for the first time when the little bus came to take them to high school. The elementary schools (grades 1 through 8) were community-based; however, there was one high school for whites only located in the county seat of Brownsville.

Unfortunately, I feel obligated to add that, due to segregation, Mama and Daddy would have never crossed social paths with someone like

Tina Bullock Turner, who attended the all-black Carver High School, also in Brownsville. I am thankful that the world has changed for the better.

Though they were the same age, Mama was one school year behind Daddy due to childhood illnesses. The year was 1942, and their world was pure-hearted and rustic. The trip to high school was on one of those "standing room only" buses that seemed to make a million-zillion stops at every dusty crossroads.

It wasn't too long after Mama had joined this circuit riding crew that she noticed that this strange looking guy always occupied a bench completely by himself—coming and going! She began to ask questions as to how this guy always rode first class while everybody else rode coach.

"Don't mess with him," everybody warned. "He'll beat the stuffing out of anybody who does."

And so Mama said, "We'll see about that!"

She gathered more information and planned for the day when old Mr. Crenshaw's bus route would be thrown into open rebellion.

Many of her friends told her she was a fool to try anything and to leave them out of whatever she tried. One thing was for certain: she would be wise to never touch his cap because he had a thing for this particular one (not unlike a lot of teenagers today).

This only increased the salivating juices of her mischievous conspiracy. She thought it might turn out to be her ace in the hole.

The Bible says, "It is appointed unto us once to die." As far as Mama's friends were concerned, her time had come on the day she announced that her plot had congealed.

"Voncille, you're not going to try and sit by him, are you?" One of her friends asked.

"Maybe," Mama sugared out with that southern, squeaky, practically unfathomable chirp people say she once used for a voice.

"But you ain't going to bother his cap, are you?" they begged.

But as fearful as they were for Mama's survival, they were equally confident that if anything could salvage the situation, it would be the indomitable spirit that had driven her to take this challenge at sanity's edge.

They used to say my grandpa was a gullible man. Just tell him he couldn't do something, and he'd try to do it, no matter the odds. Tell him that something outlandish had happened, and he'd believe it. He was a born sucker for the unbelievable, the impossible, and the preposterous.

But I like to think that Grandpa was a visionary. He needed and expected more pizzazz from life. The depressed world around him offered a lackluster existence, and he chased after things filled with challenge and excitement to make it all worthwhile.

His daughter possessed the same "Zip-a-Dee-Doo-Dah" kind of attitude, and I like to think his grandson does too.

Wherever she got it from, Mama always inspired me with her "take the highest hill" outlook on life, and her school bus insurrection was not the first or the last time that she would attempt the impossible.

Every time I would see one of my kids swing higher, kick harder, and scream louder than all the other kids on our block, I would think to myself, "It's got to be in the genes."

Daddy, however, was the flip side of that emotional coin and would never respond to the dictates of his emotions without tremendous outside pressure.

A quiet man by disposition, he projected his strength through his expressions. His steely blue eyes were set deep in their sockets and elicited respect and awe from all who met him. Or fear.

Mama once told me that while he was serving on a trans-Atlantic transport ship during WWII, some of the men were so taken with Daddy's strange eyes that they convinced themselves he was evil and vowed to throw him overboard if they had the chance. Thankfully, they never did, and the thousands of lives touched during his seven decades as a minister are better off for it.

Intimidation by appearance wasn't the only thing that scared

Haywood County boys and girls away from Daddy's bench on that squatty yellow bus.

It took more than two of the biggest boys at school to hold him down, and if he ever got loose, they were doomed because he was also the fastest boy in the county. During his freshman year, in the spring of 1942, he won second place in the one-mile run for the state of Tennessee. Yes, it was the one-mile race. This was before the world of sports forced us all to try and learn metrics. It wasn't until 1980 that the National Federation of State High Schools switched off the past and jumped into the futuristic sounding world of metrics!

The oldest of three boys, Daddy grew up working before dawn cracked the horizon until late-night lanterns spent their oil. All throughout my growing-pain days, I used to hear him talk about "burning the midnight oil" for twenty-eight hours a day.

His mama died when he was twelve, necessitating that he skip puberty and help raise his younger brothers. His quantity of strength combined with his quality of appearance inspired the young folks of Brownsville to stay out of his way.

Also, it didn't hurt that dear old Uncle Joe Naylor was the meanest, toughest Superintendent of Schools that Haywood County ever had or would have for the next thirty years. So, Daddy had muscle and clout!

And so, the fateful day arrived, posing the indomitable against the insurmountable, and everybody should have known that in such an absurd and unprecedented battle, the most logical winner would be none other than—MAMA.

She would wait until the bus was headed home, and she would wait a little longer until the more familiar surroundings of her upbringing would give her the edge in battle.

Home turf gives meaning to morale.

Patiently, she kept her head turned toward the windows, watching the narrow strips of white cottages fade behind her, and she waited and waited for the sight of her daddy's freshly plowed cotton rows, thick and black.

The serpentine road that led around the boundless acres of Grandpa's farm would provide her with enough distance to complete the coup d'état. In case he countered with a coup de grâce of his own, she'd almost be home, making it easier for the family to claim her body.

Responding to that same spontaneous surge that thrusts soldiers into battle, she jumped up and, in one broad gait, placed herself beside the forbidden bench and promptly sat down.

As they simultaneously turned to look at each other, they stared in mutual disbelief that what they saw...was what they saw.

Since Daddy's sacred territory had been invaded, he delivered the first salvo. "You need to get up," he announced, piercing her sharply with his steely blues.

"I don't have to, and you can't make me," my mother bitterly screeched. The shoving match ensued, in which Mama quickly realized she could not win and, therefore, was left with only one option: steal his precious cap!

As quick as she could squeal and scratch herself to the top of his head, she grabbed his cap and tossed it out the window. With this treasonous act, Daddy's great emotional control disappeared.

Down into the rubbery aisle went Mama, with Daddy's deathly grip around her neck.

Ring the bells! The revolution had arrived. Teenagers of any generation love a good fight, and this fight was a doozy. The din of their enthusiasm was deafening as they squealed and screamed right along with the embattled foes.

Old Mr. Crenshaw brought the squatty little bus to a furious and dusty halt. He deputized two big seniors to help him stop my daddy, the monster, from his mania.

If anybody had known about mouth-to-mouth resuscitation, they would have tried it because my mama appeared lifeless as she lay on the rubbery floor of the bus.

The bloodthirsty crew grew quiet at the spectacle, and even Daddy stopped his fervid struggle. Mama broke the stillness with a beaming smile as she surprisingly popped her eyes open while simultaneously revealing the stolen cap from behind her back.

With an unnerving shrill of a laugh, she tossed it in Daddy's face, jumped back onto his private bench, and condescendingly invited him to join her on this seat, now made for two. Such perspicuity was more than he could handle, and with a sheepish concession, he acquiesced to defeat.

My unpredictable mama never again wanted to sit on Daddy's bench during her high school career and chose not to speak to him for the next seven years. He went on to fight in a war that tempered his soul. She blossomed into a radiant flower that aptly augmented the beauty of her cunning.

And when they next met, they realized the surging magnetism they had for one another and wilted in the face of its power as it drew them inconceivably but inevitably together.

Seventy-five years ago, on a star-bright June night, the indomitable and the insuperable became inseparable.

Eighteen-year-old Jack Naylor

EVEN WHEN IT RAINED

My ears still ring with the loud, humming sound of the "cotton 'gin" that sat beside our house in the early sixties. "Gin" is a southern abbreviation for 'engine.' It is the machine or more appropriately, the engine, that separates the seeds from the white, fully formed stuff that our clothes were made of in those days. It was either cotton or wool before the emergence of synthetics became available to the public in the early 1950's. Wool? Ouch!

In the meadowy village of Charleston, Tennessee, cotton-picking season came during the late summer and early autumn. So, the old 'gin toiled endlessly during the day and through the night, trying to keep up with the harvest. Every night I somehow learned to sleep peacefully to the 'gin's rhythmic serenade.

It's difficult to imagine, but our school was dismissed for the entire month of October so that the children could help their parents harvest the crop.

Most children had to pick cotton just to help their parents "make ends meet," so to speak. I'm positive that my father could have used the money had he decided to hire us out to the cotton farmers, but such was never the case.

"No, you don't need to work," my father would announce. "The church provides for our needs."

Yes, indeed! They provided us with living quarters in the spacious red brick parsonage sitting next to the educational buildings of the church, all the food we could eat with seasonal "poundings," and a full-time salary just above the poverty line.

A ritual called "the pounding" came at the beginning of every new season. A special day planned well in advance would bring in church members from far and near, with their trucks loaded down with boxes and sacks full of food.

They'd set it all out in the church dining hall, like a celestial feast prepared for a king. Canned and frozen goods complemented countless hams, turkeys, beefsteaks, and lamb chops by the sackful. Eventually, one Christmas, their Christmas present to Mama and Daddy was a giant freezer to help them keep up with their frozen gifts! "Merry Christmas...here's your freezer!"

After every "pounding," we'd have a great feast of thanksgiving, which would end with the children chasing lightning bugs in the dark of night. I remember it being so dark that we were afraid of venturing too far from the comforting doors of the sacred house of the Lord Jehovah. They were safe! Us? Maybe not! It was unclear. So, we trusted the Almighty.

We would spend hours looking for white comets to streak across the Tennessee night amidst a sky filled with millions of stars that boggled the mind. Where have all the stars gone? I wonder about that nowadays, as my night sky is so full of light pollution that I can hardly see anything except UPS jets angling one after the other to successfully land at the Mohammed Ali International Airport in nearby Louisville, Kentucky. Oops, I got jerked into the present. Back to the past!

While we counted stars, wished for comets, and captured lightning bugs, the strong, robust looking farmers formed a human chain from the church to the parsonage, transferring the bounty that was to last us until next season.

Cotton-picking time for me and my sister was fun. We reasoned that since we didn't have to go to school, we'd contract out on our own with my father's church-going farmers. We were sure to make some quick cash to waste on the emergent sixties' junk we would later find in the treasure aisles of the Ben Franklin Five and Dime store over in the bustling metropolis of Covington. (Seriously, listen to me, all of you guys calling yourselves Generation X, Millennials, Generation Z, and Alpha Zen, it really was possible to buy something for five and ten cents.)

Church farmers eagerly hired up the preacher's kids, but we did not pick much cotton, and what we did pick was just tolerated. Often, church members invited us to pick cotton out of the kindness of their hearts. I suppose that through the influence of our father, the minister, they thought they might be eligible for a few extra stars in their heavenly crown.

Here it was in 1961, and most of the other children had little choice in this matter of picking cotton, but the preacher's kids were sent invitations, as if it were the social event of the season. Nevertheless, they invited us, and we went "a-picking."

I can't remember their names, but there was one well-to-do cotton family, good Baptists, who would guarantee me and my sister an opportunity to make some cotton money after a good, soaking summertime thunderstorm.

Now, it's important to know the context of this deal because nobody picked cotton when it rained. Why? You've got to understand that the cotton absorbed the water, thus weighing more. And what fiduciarily trained farmer would pay a field hand to pick waterlogged cotton? Why, he'd be paying mostly for water.

I was always amazed that when it rained, Old Mr. Forgotten-Name was on the phone with my father. He had sent the hired hands home, and the cotton was dripping wet. "Bring your kids over here, preacher, and let 'em pick all they want."

I thought that was great! Looking forward to these opportunities was the highlight of my cotton-picking career, and when they were long in coming, I'd get all down in the dumps about it.

At the time, I was convinced that it was because he liked us and wanted to do something special for us. Maybe he thought it was a sly way of giving the preacher's family a little extra help without making us feel beholden to him. I'm not so sure why he did it.

I imagine the poverty of those around me would have been a greater justification for that farmer's charity than mine.

The tragedy of their situation should have earned them a chance to pick cotton of their situation should have earned them a chance to pick cotton, **even when it rained**, not me.

It's hard to explain what the mood was like in that small rural town when it was time to pick cotton. Necessity and urgency hung around like the taskmasters of almost a century before. It was as if the survival of the whole human race depended on those West Tennessee farmers to get the cotton picked and ginned.

Years later, when I returned to Charleston as a man, I saw the effects of modernity. The little hub of our village, once thriving with the energy of a living, breathing entity, had practically disappeared. Cars barely slowed down as they zipped along.

Deserted stood the cotton gin.

Barren and forsaken stood the two little country stores.

In ruins, the bricks of my old schoolhouse crumbled like the medieval abbeys of the English countryside.

Standing on the vacant spot that had been the source of my education for five years, loneliness enveloped me. *"School days, school days,"* the little jingle echoed from deep within my memories.

All that remained were the Baptist and Methodist churches, separated by the graveyard, which had more than doubled in size. Polished granite statues spread out across the green hillside as silent witnesses to the community that once thrived here.

Seeing these last pieces of my past—this ghostly trio of two weathered churches standing sentinel around a pasture for the dead —was a harsh reality.

But before I end up making you cry about that, I need to say a little about the art of cotton-picking, even though I admit we never did it quite right. Some farmers had monstrous new machines called combine harvesters that did the picking with only the aid of drivers and haulers. This was expensive, and only the wealthiest could afford such a luxury.

Then there were the farmers, who had one small combine and a considerable number of field workers. Generally, field hands were recruited from some of the poor whites and nearly all the community's blacks.

Last were the farmers who picked their own cotton by hand with the aid of family members and a few extra, poorly paid field hands.

Most of my father's church members fell into that middle category, with a few wealthy families and a few dirt-poor families on either side to keep our fragile society in balance.

We would choose a cotton sack that the host farmer had given us before we went to the fields. Professional pickers usually provided their own sacks, but most chose the free company sack—courtesy of the suspicious company we all worked for.

Sacks varied in length depending on a body's pulling power. Mine was sort of limited due to the consumerist nature of my commitment. A six-foot sack was about all I could count on pulling, or in my case, dragging.

Near the mouth of the sack, there was a sling that fit over my neck and shoulder. Walking down the cotton rows, I would pull the sack behind me, all the while stuffing it full of the soft white cotton. You might figure that after a while of picking, the sack would become quite a burden to pull for little people like me.

Fitted like a mule in his harness, I plunged into the fields, always with a great spirit of determination to pick more cotton than anybody else.

All around me were scores of black laborers bending low, moving steadily and rhythmically, easing their burden while singing the hymns of heaven. The fellowship and the singing made it all seem a bit like church. In my blinded innocence, I had no concept of the suffering they incurred.

It was beyond the realm of my childhood comprehension that theirs was an unbearable task. Black women tugged effortlessly at huge serpentine sacks. They marched out of make-shift homes by the hundreds to pick cotton from dawn to dusk to earn barely enough to recoup the cost of the day. Nowadays, I see just how heavy and complex their burden was in 1960s America.

Once filled, the cotton sacks were weighed immediately in the field. A chart was used to keep a record of each person's harvest, with the day's tally figured correctly, of course. Good white Baptists kept track of the figures for the poor blacks, who couldn't add up the quantities of the cotton tally very well.

At the end of the day, folks were paid right on the spot. Sometimes it was enough to go to Mr. Robert's country store and buy a pound of rag bologna, a stack of saltine crackers, and a 16-ounce RC Cola stuffed with salty goobers. Cotton-picking drains the salt out of a fella. Salted goobers really help more than you know.

I wonder now what they thought of little white children picking cotton until they got tired, stopping to play, and then picking until they wanted to play again.

I wonder now what they thought of us starting at noon, finishing at four, and getting paid for a little more than we picked.

I wonder now what they thought of being paid the same or even less for their cotton when my cotton always had part of the prickly hull tossed in to weigh down the sack a little more.

If they had done the same, they would have been told to leave the field or cull the hulls again before having their sack weighed. Mine was never rejected for the same reasons.

I wonder now what they thought of the mockery that was made of their hard, earnest labor for survival.

Retrospect is a master of paradoxes.

Remembering the stuff of yesteryear enables us to recall fond moments that make us feel nurtured and whole. It also makes us feel ashamed for not knowing how ugly our ignorance is.

I don't know whether it's because of naiveté or piety that I recognize the shame of that distant time. Maybe I'm too harsh in my recollections. I mean, after all, what was a nine-year-old supposed to know about such things? How was I supposed to recognize their misery? It had so many faces in those days. It had been around for as long as anyone could remember.

Maybe nobody could recognize it. Maybe they didn't mind the dehumanized social status yoked tightly around their dignity.

Yeah, I know that's a lie.

Truly, old-man retrospect is odd, but at least he gives me a chance to say, "I'm sorry. I'm sorry for not knowing. I'm sorry for all my ignorance."

Whatever pain and heartbreak they suffered, it stood as a reproach to the generations that allowed it to go on unchecked. It is an even greater reproach to those who still give life to the stinking, rotting corpse of racism.

To my child's mind, however, it was a wonderful time. The vision of that past lingers dimly in the flickering images of so many years ago. But they are there.

The cool breeze of October's air comes to life when I remember the bitter sting of those crisp, bright mornings, the baby blue hues that streaked across the afternoon sky, and the cotton 'dust' floating thick and lazy in the late evening sunset.

Life crawled across the fertile fields, like swarming ants around the red pyramids that marked their colonies. Hordes of cotton pickers scattered across the land, singing songs about Jesus.

It was pure heaven.

It was only human.

It was good.

It was wrong.

It was then.

Now, it's gone.

There's a lesson in all of this if I think about it, and it probably goes something like: if I *get* to do something that others *have to do* (and that means that I didn't respect what it meant to be there), then any benefit I might've received is as if I shouldn't have done it at all.

Jeffrey and his sister Victoria

LGBTQIA+ AND THE BOY WHO WOULD BE A BULL

When I was a little boy, people used to always ask me, "What do you want to be one day?" No one ever asked "who" you wanted to be, but "what." Often, however, my behavior radicalized itself sufficiently enough to express rather violently exactly what I thought I could be—not one day, but at that very little boy moment.

Once, I wanted to be a bull. It was a cut-and-dry desire. I simply wanted to be a bull. I believed with all my heart that I could become a bull. Well, that was when I was about 4 years old, so I didn't have a lot of life experience that would have allowed me to realize that becoming a bull might not be quite the thing for a human boy to aspire to.

For millennia, people have struggled with the notion of identity, striving to become something of worth and value.

In mid-April 2023, Tommy Lee, the famous Mötley Crüe rock and roll artist, posted a video from the podcast of the political and social commentator Liz Wheeler. She was reporting how weird it is that people have grown so particular about "who" and "what" they want to be in these bizarre times.

In this *Brave New World* of the 21st century, people are constantly aligning themselves with the identity stream of LGBTQAI+. It looks like the letters will continue to stream longer and longer until they realistically might include the entire alphabet.

Maybe in the future, kids could learn to read by reciting the alphabet all jumbled up (it's a thought). How would Big Bird teach that on Sesame Street? (That's an even crazier thought.)

Tommy Lee's video highlighted Wheeler's report that suggested some people now want to identify themselves as blind or vision impaired. To be taken seriously, some people have taken measures to blind themselves permanently to be labeled "disabled." Some (courageously or shortsightedly) noble humans have chosen to wear the new mantle of "trans-abled" in describing this behavior, taking their cue from those who have campaigned to be identified as transgender or transracial.

Thus, Liz presented us with some unusual examples of transabled people, including a most bizarre example of someone wanting to identify with the sight-impaired community. You're not going to believe what some of these aspirants have done to themselves to lengthen the alphabet stream.

Normally, society understands that someone identifies as part of the blind community because they were born blind, became blind because of an unexpected, horrible accident, or became blind because of the ravages of disease or exposure to different real-world irritants.

Others become sight-impaired after birth because of situations they encounter that leave them blind or partially blind. I have the greatest respect for, love for, and tremendous admiration for people who identify themselves as blind or sight impaired.

It's simply impossible to mention this community without remembering the marvelous life of someone like Helen Keller. There are others who have become accomplished musicians, writers, politicians, etc., people like the musician Ray Charles, the poet Homer, or the hymnist Fanny J. Crosby.

Most people are unaware that Harriet Tubman, the great underground railroad conductor, was vision impaired. The list is long and glorious, but for the most part, the average vision-impaired person is the person that moves among us without calling attention to themselves, treading the same daily walk as we all dread—er—I mean tread.

Wheeler reported that recently, a woman from North Carolina expressed her desire to be identified as "trans-abled blind" after pouring drain cleaner into her eyes, thus leaving her sightless forever.

This isn't the only person taking drastic measures so that they might be identifiable as "trans-abled." It appears to be an undercurrent epidemic. These attempts to change a person's identity designation do not end with people purposefully becoming blind. There are other suspect individuals attempting to hijack American culture.

In his attempt to be identified as "trans-abled disabled," one man in Great Britain decided to cut off his arm. Something I would have never heard as a kid is, "I want to be identified as disabled when I grow up, so I'll cut off my arm."

A Chicago man posted a notice on Craig's List for a full-time nanny because he wants to be identified as a baby and needs somebody to regularly change his diapers. Well, if that's anything, it's downright creepy. Yet, these people are making legitimate appeals to join the "trans" communities to be legitimized as "unique."

Well, Liz's report goes on and on, detailing a veritable grocery list of these new waves of identity crises. If a child wants to identify as an adult, does that mean they can choose to buy liquor? An exasperated Wheeler pouted, "Where does this all end?"

Tommy Lee and Liz Wheeler take their arguments far beyond what I am thinking about here in this simple story of my yesteryears. But the thing that first caught my attention about their gripes was the fact that Tommy Lee's post had been *attacked* by media swarms, forcing him to take it down.

Have people really become so obsessed with accepting infinite expressions of identity that they would rather approve of a man wanting to be identified as a six-year-old girl than encourage him to seek help in accepting his own human nature?

I used to be a kid, and kids would play with a big stick, pretending to be blind as they grew up. But no kid grows up saying, "I want to be blind when I grow up." It's not because the visually impaired community is evil or bad, but because most people don't believe they could face the challenges that blind people face. Well, I think almost everybody believes that, at least until they are faced with the challenge.

When we were kids, we loved to play as "grown-ups" or dress up in mommy's or daddy's clothes, but that doesn't mean we wanted to permanently identify as adults in our eight-year-old bodies. The first part of that sentence is normal; the last part is absurd.

Before dozens of *Avengers* heroes overtook the imaginations of children everywhere, kids used to love playing Superman or Tarzan.

I used to dream of being Tarzan. I remember the day that eleven of us decided we wanted to become the famous vine-swinging jungle king in Mr. Crabtree's little forest far behind Phelan Elementary School in Charleston, Tennessee, where we lived.

The plot was hatched when, quite surprisingly, we learned one early morning that Mr. Hall, our principal, would be absent all day. Mr. Hall was a tall, lanky stick of a man who walked solidly on the ground where he ambled. Partially bald and wearing a string tie and Woodrow Wilson circular eyeglasses, Mr. Hall's stature and soft, deep voice demanded respect.

When he monitored the halls during school hours, looking for the delinquents among us, you could hear the pounding of his feet on the buckling tiles that lined the hallways. It was no joke to us kids that Mr. Hall could clearly and principally be heard patrolling the halls. Principally because he was the principal (I couldn't resist, sorry!) So, when we heard those sounds, if we weren't where we were supposed to be, we needed to run!

On this particularly beautiful spring morning, the absent sounds of his feet removed the fears of our escapades and enabled us to dare ourselves with antics that would immortalize us in the eyes of our less capable classmates.

Bobby McIntyre was the ringleader of our newly inspired group of rebels. He was always the instigator—our leader! At eleven years old, he was the local anomaly, standing almost six feet tall but appearing somewhat gaunt and bent a bit, which would one day be recognized as scoliosis.

Maybe those folks should have known what his condition was because, as far back as 400 BCE, Hippocrates understood what this disease was, but it wasn't a popular term in the medical world until the 19th and early 20th centuries.

Understandably, nobody around Charleston could've told you what Bobby McIntyre had. We just called it a crooked back. That's kind of prosaic, I realize, but in the mid-20th century on planet Earth, country people were calling things the only way they knew how. I guess today someone would want to imply that Bobby McIntyre was spinally "trans-abled" on the "sagittal plane." (I discovered that very smart-sounding term recently in the 21st century.)

But back in the mid-20th century, we all wished to swing among the trees just like Tarzan and bellow ferociously with his echoing yell. Man, we really worked on that yell, becoming hoarse in the process. And to top it all off, everyone tried to become hoarser than anyone else, as if there was a prize for who could lose their voice the fastest.

Mr. Crabtree's little forest was covered with climbing vines that were growing and leeching off the boxelders, black walnuts, and chestnut oaks that crowded the woods. Just like the fake Hollywood jungles that Tarzan the movie star swung in, our forest was full of climbing vines that were strong, slim, and long enough to enable us to swing confidently from tree to tree.

The only catch to this scenario was that we were not allowed to walk off school property during school time, and the woods were most definitely not school property.

Never tell a pubescent kid he's not supposed to do something he really enjoys, because that's an absolute challenge for him to figure out a way to do it. We had secretly fled the playground area during lunch—out of sight of the two other teachers and the obviously "stupid" substitute filling in for Mr. Hall.

Okay, I must digress for pedagogical purposes (take a moment and look that one up if you need to). To digress is like pulling off at the rest stop on the interstate just to think.

Just think: Phelan Elementary only had three teachers for grades 1-8. In addition to being the principal, Mr. Hall was responsible for teaching the 7th and 8th graders, who orbited far outside of our pubescent universe.

I mean, as an eleven-year-old the only contact I ever had with a 7th or 8th grader was the day Hattie McIntyre aggressively ambushed me by running up and kissing me smack on the lips during lunch. She burst out laughing, as did her roving "gang" of skirts. They only did it to embarrass me.

Obviously, as you will soon understand, I felt a moral duty to tell Mr. Hall what they had done, and if I remember correctly, they each got two swats from the "Colonel."

The "Colonel" was the private property of Mr. Hall, who named it after his old farm hinny that had once almost kicked the life out of him. In case you're wondering, a hinny is an old southern word for M-U-L-E. I guess Mr. Hall figured that since his mule had such a kick, it would be a good name for his paddle.

So, that was the name written on the six-inch-wide, two-foot-long piece of oak with a knapped handgrip on one end. The entire "paddle" was covered with half-dollar-sized holes, giving it extra SWOSH power! I think it probably hurt those girls more than giving me a kiss was worth.

Incidentally, that was my first kiss, but I don't think it counts since it was so painful for fifty percent of the participants.

Now, if you can shake off that random story and catch up with Bobby McIntyre, who ferociously led the rebellion into the woods so that we could all become the Tarzans of our dreams, at the border line where the school ceased to be the school and the forest became enemy territory, I hesitated. I was the preacher's kid.

The Baptist Church was exactly across the street, alongside the parsonage where I lived with the preacher and his mighty spouse— my mama! Both, I feared, could be watching us with binoculars from either the church or the parsonage, snooping on their son, the potential slacker.

Thus, I reasonably decided I did not identify enough with being Tarzan to risk rousing the ire of my parents. I continued to hesitate at the border and positioned myself comfortably to watch the others. In the process of their swinging and yelling, Bobby soon grew bored of the repetitiveness of it all and came up with the brilliant idea of smoking the tiny offshoots of the vines—the twigs.

Cutting them swiftly into little cigarette-sized thingamajigs, everyone across the sacred borderline decided to participate. But not me; I stood firmly at the border's edge, observing and salivating.

In short order, everyone else was smoking, I guess, just like Tarzan, when suddenly, for inexplicable reasons unbeknownst to any of us, the forest appeared to be on fire. After all these years, it has never occurred to me how they lit those woodland cigarettes.

As the smoke billowed up and out across the landscape, moving heavily towards the school building, everyone scattered like ants and ran back to the school building to find a place to hide, including me! What had we become, idiots? The smoke was obviously going to attack the school. Why were we hiding in the school building?

Gradually, I noticed that no one was reporting the fire. Bobby McIntyre, the leader, was nowhere in sight. Since I had not crossed the border nor smoked a vine, I felt no dishonor, fear, or guilt when I decided to inform the substitute principal that the back woods were on fire, moving fast to burn down the school! The poorly prepared sub was frantic, and assigning blame was the least of his worries. His only concern was calling for help.

Help was already on the way! Our fire department was a

regional, volunteer group of men who were used to fighting small forest fires and very rarely a few house fires. Somebody had already called them and once called, they were there in moments since the fire station was less than five miles from the school on the same highway.

Volunteers were mainly farmers and laborers who quickly assembled with a fevered urgency, as if the church itself were burning to the ground. Away from their labors they ran, dismounting their tractors and leaving their fields within seconds of hearing the five-story-tall alarm sound off loudly and with an ear-piercing effect.

The fire in the woods was more smoldering than it was burning. Ten boys smoking vine twigs disguised as cigarettes had produced an unusual amount of smoke and very little fire. It turns out that a burning little vine twig smolders with lots more smoke than a regular tree twig.

Nonetheless, the valorous volunteer farmer-firefighters extinguished the smoldering vines and left it for the teachers to figure out what had caused the tiny conflagration.

The "rebellious ten" did not confess anything having to do with a forest fire, nor did they admit to having been anywhere near Mr. Crabtree's woods. The two regular teachers were too harried and busy with the rest of the students to conduct a thorough investigation, and the substitute for Mr. Hall remained dubiously in the dark about most things throughout the entire day. It appeared the day would end with no indictments, no convictions, and no punishments.

Mr. Hall returned the next day without a report or any clue that something nefarious had happened in his kingdom whilst he was absent. As the preacher's son, and thus the acting moral compass for the entire student body, I felt it my duty once more to update Mr. Hall about the villainous activities that had happened in his absence.

I mean, the entire day had been unbelievably and deviously exciting, but I figured since I had not stepped across the sacred borderline, I was without guile. What eleven-year-old boy in my position would not be anxious and eager to describe such a debacle?

And so, I waited for the arrival of Mr. Hall's truck in the church parking lot across the street. That's where Daddy, the preacher, allowed all the teachers to park, far away from the school and students who might do their cars innocent harm. After all, they were all members of the church. Ours was one big, happy, circular world.

I ran to meet Mr. Hall before he could barely cross the road and began my tease by asking if he had heard about the fire. He stopped dead in his tracks in the middle of the road. As his face flushed redder and redder, the more I recounted in fanciful detail the entire event from start to finish. I really felt bad about being a rat that day. But not then; later, like forty years later.

Needless to say, indictments were made, convictions declared, and punishments delivered, with Mr. Hall serving as jury, judge, and executioner. The paddle was the only thing burning up the school that day. Ouch! I still feel bad about that.

It was in such a world of my childhood that I often dreamed of being Tarzan, Superman, or that caped guy that fought off the mole people—seemingly any character who could transform me for a little while and allow the boy inside of me to take flight, grow, and prosper. But I didn't remain mesmerized by those comic book characters, nor did I ever desire, as I grew older, to become transformed into their personalities.

It is a fact of life that humans, for the most part, must learn to accept and love themselves as they are and not attempt to morph into something that is unnatural to them. It seems a bit ridiculous that someone would aspire to be identified as Tarzan. Who would want that? Yet, it isn't any more ridiculous than someone aspiring to be identified as a cat, like the lady in Georgia who wanted to be a cat and have her own litter box.

When I became an adult, I put away childish things! And ridiculous things, I might add. That doesn't mean I can't accept people who identify with certain established categories in our culture. I can understand the string of letters that are listed as LGBTQAI+. They are identifications that define groups of people that have existed since the beginning of humanity but were perhaps not recognized by different cultures.

Yet, the further we go with this alphabet soup, the further our culture will decline into ridiculous nonsense. When will we ever evolve with enough wisdom to simply accept everyone for who they are without needing to create identifying labels or hijacking the alphabet?

I remember quite vividly that day when I was four years old and tried to identify with the animal community by trying out my "bull-ness." Wearing my cowboy costume, complete with cowboy hat and boots, emboldened my desire to make my move.

Removing my fancy hat, I paced back as far as I could from the brick wall at the back of our house. It was critically important to get a good running start, for I knew that if I had more space to build up my speed, I would more powerfully slam into that brick wall, blasting a hole three times as wide as my head. (The three times accounts for the damage caused by the imaginary, invisible horns.)

I guess I never wondered why my parents never tried to stop me. "Weren't they worried about the damage I would do to our house?" I pondered. But nope, they did not, and I announced that I was ready to declare my new identity with the force of the biblical whirlwind that Daddy always preached about.

Stomping and feigning, finally I took off like a bullet, running as fast as a four-year-old can run, which is pretty darn fast in the mind of any preschooler—just ask one!

Today, almost seven decades later, I still sport a small bump on the left side of my forehead as the mark of my fearless attempt to become a bull. For years, it looked more like a small horn was growing out of my head, an ironic thing for a preacher's kid whose daddy might preach about the devil from time to time.

On that memorable day sixty-five years ago, I did not become a bull, but forever after I would be known as the bullheaded boy! And still today, I would say that beyond identifying as a heterosexual male, I can identify as the orneriest, most bullheaded person my wife and kids know!

Neither Tarzan nor Bull am I, but I am truthfully a genuine lover of all humans, no matter what they choose to be.

REVENGE OF THE GRANDPARENTS

Sometimes the things kids do to us parents make us pause to ponder. For children, play is work, and I suppose they feel like they are doing us a favor when they're driving us insane.

But for the most part, they subject us to tests of endurance that should be banned by law. I remember the days when it appeared that some of our little children should no longer be allowed to live in the same house with the rest of us. What to do? But I had learned from the best and could recite the veritable sayings that had been burned into my memory.

"You want to live in a barn?" Mama used to ask. I like the sound of that and often try it out on my own kids. But I could never be too harsh on the little devils; after all, I put my own parents through the same ordeal almost sixty millennia ago.

I'm sure that my sister (Victoria—The Queen) and I are the direct cause of a physiological distortion that developed in my mother as she responded over the years to our antics. In response to our shenanigans, my mama would rant and rave and get the *bug eye*.

The *bug eye* was an evil bulge that expanded and projected from the deepest portals of Mama's eye sockets. Along with this otherworldly control device located in her head were the reach and action of Mama's fingers.

In the movie *Goonies*, one little inventive boy named Data uses a homemade device to foil the crooks who were chasing him and his little gang of cherubs. He called them the "pinchers of hell." All the baby boomers' kids know about the Goonies, as do even some of the Gen Xers and millennials.

He Huy Quan, who played the role of Data, finally won the Academy Award for Best Supporting Actor in 2023. But Data's pinchers of hell would've been no match against the "pinchers of mama."

I realize how exasperating it must have been to be capable of altering Mama's physiology with the games of our psychology.

Our parents loved us dearly, and I'm glad that I don't have to write one of those childhood persecution books. We'd get punished, but nothing like some of the nightmarish memories I read about in one of those tell-all books of the 1980s, like *Mommy Dearest*.

My "Mommy" was the dearest and sweetest mama anybody could ever hope to have. Nevertheless, I still put her through the wringer. But she knew how to get into my soul!

One Sunday, she wanted to take a group picture of our family with some friends at church. I turned around backward just as she pushed the button on the old, boxy camera. That picture hung framed in our house for a while, with me conveniently missing.

Mama had cut me out. If I was going to pose backwards, then I didn't exist. She got out her sewing scissors and promptly clipped me out.

My mother always excelled at coming up with little tricks of justified humiliation. She really seemed to take great pride in displaying the picture with the "cut-out boy."

"Oh, have you seen this recent picture we took?" She'd ask any visitors loudly enough to make sure I could hear her.

The nasty ordeal reached critical mass one day, and I started begging her to get rid of it. She did. There was truly no joy for her when she whipped my soul this way. It was just another one of her classic lessons that burned a powerful new understanding into my growing conscience.

Birthday parties were gala affairs when I was little. Mama would work overtime making party paraphernalia and creating games and special prize packages.

One time I got mad because I didn't win one of the silly birthday prizes on my own birthday. Mama had placed penny treats in little paper sacks to give to the kids. She fixed it so that the kids thought they had won a small sack of prizes. Mama took special care to make sure everyone had won a sack before the party was over.

Of course, I didn't know anything about Mama's egalitarian gift-giving strategies and so when the first winners were announced and I wasn't one of them, I got so mad that I ran away to hide in the woods. I moped around like an old mule for about thirty minutes, thinking I'd be sadly missed by everyone and upon my return, I would be welcomed back wholeheartedly.

Hmm...I guess to believe that such a thing was a possibility means you don't fully have an accurate picture of Mama. Mama had two sides to her gregarious personality, which meant that almost always, there was only one side that I ever wanted to see. Naturally, like any mother, her good side was always preferable to her bad side. Her bad side didn't mean that she was hurtful; it simply meant justice was coming and I probably earned whatever it was!

When I got back from pouting in the woods, I discovered that she had sent everybody home and had popped all the balloons. Wow, that was fast!

"If you are going to go sulking in the woods, then you don't exist. If you don't exist, then why the heck am I throwing you a party for?" She seemed to ask sarcastically, which for me signaled the coming of a dark cloud.

She had sent all the kids packing and wouldn't even let them leave presents for the AWOL birthday boy. All for the price of a trinket in a little paper sack. I had sold my soul to the devil of greed.

If my behaviors often conjured forth the lesser angels of Mama's nature, I could just as adroitly drive Daddy to the proverbial edge. Being the local preacher, he had a reputation to uphold, which I had a way of pulling down periodically.

I remember one event that happened during our annual church revival time. It could have been a career-ending event if Daddy hadn't stepped up and made everything work out for the benefit of everyone before my devilish deeds were discovered.

It had never entered my mind that the public address system inside the sanctuary could be altered to publicly address the outside world. I had always wondered why this huge electronic mystery, stuffed up under the pulpit, had so many strange buttons. It sure was fun flipping them up and down. How was I supposed to know how to reset every single one of them?

Daddy was busy getting dressed for revival services one evening, so I seized my chance to sneak into the church and play with the microphones.

He was far away in the parsonage (the preacher's house) next door—way back in the bathroom—with the door shut. I could steal a few moments without getting caught. What did it matter that our house stood ten feet from the side door of the church?

And so, I began swatting switches, singing loudly with my very best evangelical voice, and preaching all kinds of pious, eleven-year-old indictments when Daddy appeared at the side door. It was obvious he had come straight from the bathroom with no delay or detour.

It blew my mind that he would come into the sanctuary of the VERY LIVING GOD with his T-shirt on and looking like a rabid dog on top of it all! Shaving cream was caked on his face, and I was amazed that he still had the razor in his hands.

"Didn't I realize that I was inundating the whole blessed community with my stage show?" He demanded to know as he dragged his bedeviled son out of the holy chamber. He could've slit my throat bloody open with that long razor blade. I got a red bottom instead. It wasn't child abuse. It was justice!

Wiggling and giggling in church were mortal sins for a preacher's kid. Mama's silent pinchers proved highly effective when those uncontrollable waves of defiance rolled over me, making me do the wiggle-giggle. She'd come after me, dragging me up to the second pew (the appointed pew of the preacher's wife), totally cutting off any blood circulation, and forcing me to sit beside her.

Daddy's sermons seemed to last forever on those days.

Occasionally, she would have to take her turn operating the nursery, and oh boy, I thought I had hit the jackpot on those days and felt like I could get away with almost anything. With Daddy stuck up behind the pulpit, all caught up in his fiery oratory, I ruled supreme on the back seat.

I mean, how could he stop me if he was way up there at the front of the building, busily chastising the saints? What I learned, much to my regret, was that this man knew how to chew gum and walk at the same time—just like us kids.

I got too bold for my own good one time. (That's always a favorite parental admonition—doing something too much for your own good.) My buddies and I were sitting in the back row, having so much silent fun that we were dripping tears all over the wooden pews with our giggles. Confident that he couldn't possibly see us, we hadn't even looked up to see if he was still up there.

Being unobservant cost me a lot that day. Boy, ain't (southern for "isn't") that the truth, whatever year you're living in! I hadn't realized that the congregation of two hundred had hushed into a kind of deadly silence. Out of nowhere, he swooped down on me and unhinged me from my wayward ways.

Every eye was fixed on me in holy condemnation or so it felt. Maybe some of them felt a little sorry for me because my cheeks still showed the stains of some of those left-over happy, but sinful tears. It kind of looked like repentance. I bowed my head to add to the part.

He took me by the hand and escorted me all the way to the FRONT PEW (a virtual no-man's land—the church prison). Taking me by the shoulders, he positioned me firmly in my seat. Then he pointed his finger stiffly and downward at me just once, without saying a word. It was like I was the disobedient dog, and he was teaching me to "sit."

Getting back behind the pulpit, he picked up where he had left off, like nothing had happened, until he got to the part about sinners, judgment, and repentance. There seemed to be a little more oomph in his voice during that part of his sermon.

I'm sure he was looking right at me and most likely jabbing his finger in my direction. But I can't say for sure because, like a good dog, I kept my head bowed.

I remember doing about three million things to torment my parents. But wait! My kids did the same thing to me. Well, not the same things exactly; they had their own newly published editions of *How to Torment Your Parents*.

Sometimes I thought my parents got too much of a kick out of watching me shed tears of blood over the shenanigans of my darling rogues.

I won't name names. Just facts! For a couple of years, one little sweetheart enjoyed bringing up Daddy's and Mommy's strange behavior, which he discovered late one night when he burst unannounced into our bedroom. His eyes only recorded a few fleeting seconds, and even though we were securely under the blankets, he had seen enough to fuel his imagination. Don't laugh! Such is the least of every parent's guilt.

Over the next two years, he managed to make some colorful statements in public. Eventually, the formidable force of that ever-persuasive thing called parental power convinced him that it was in his best interest to delete those stories from his toolbox of conversation topics. That is, if he wanted to live.

Driving through Illinois one summer, we stopped to eat just off the interstate. One dear, precious second-born child screamed out, "Is he dead yet?" as they were carrying this poor fella out on a stretcher. We were sitting at a nice, big family-style table at the local Bob Evans restaurant.

"Enjoy your meal, folks!" Yeah, right! That will be easy with two hundred condemning eyes burning holes in our table. It felt a little like church for some reason. "Is he dead yet?" That is exactly what you want your eight-year-old to ask publicly for those being hauled off in an ambulance.

There are more! How about one of those interruptions when Daddy's telling a harmless white lie to a neighbor?

EXAMPLE: "We'd love to get together sometime, Mr. Smith," I might have said a hundred thousand times. "But Daddy, I thought you said we didn't like the Smiths." One (pick any "one") of my six kids might have said this a hundred times. In front of all the Smiths we have ever known.

I get all brain-cracked in situations like this. Honesty clears a room really fast.

There's a category for this kind of *faux pas*. It doesn't have a name other than what Mama would call "dad-burn ruination." It sounds good to me, whatever the heck it means.

The kids' charades come galloping down on me sometimes, even after they have become "so-called" grown-ups, but I can learn to live with them. Well, I'll try. But, oh, the things they do.

Kicking the dog.

Pulling the cat's whiskers and his tail.

Performing jumping jacks on my bed at 5:00 a.m.

Hiding leftover fish sandwiches under their sheets.

Breaking grandma's heirloom dishes.

Projectile vomiting at the table in a fancy restaurant, a feat accomplished by all six of them at one time or another.

Tots peeing in the neighbor's yard because they're too lazy to come into the house and too scared to do it in our yard.

Providing illustrative artwork, especially for my collector's First Edition books.

Running naked as a jaybird out the front door in broad daylight.

Being poignantly rude when the boss stops by.

Unplugging the computer in the middle of an unsaved twenty-page manuscript. Obviously, much to my chagrin, this was before the era of auto-save.

All these things can be forgiven. That is, if they are treated with appropriate sedatives.

It's all part of growing up, right?

You're all probably thinking in cadence with me now, remembering the shenanigans of your own kids. We're all thinking that somebody should compile a book containing all the tricks of our offspring.

Once I spotted a tiny article in the newspaper about two little girls whose babysitter had punished them by running them through a ten-second cycle in the family dryer. What a mess! The state police were involved, and it appeared to be a nasty affair.

I certainly don't endorse using such measures to punish children. As I read the article, it was obvious that the sitter wasn't much more than a child herself. She lost control. They wouldn't go to bed, and so she resorted to power tactics. A dare became a double dare, and well, there you go!

A small picture of the little girls showed them gathered around the dastardly machine in which they had twirled. They looked happy enough. All their eyes beamed with mischief.

I know the look. I'm an expert.

While I've never threatened my kids with time-outs in the dryer, I have thought of getting in there myself sometimes just to hide from the mania that often overwhelms our house.

I think I know how to repay my kids for all their wicked ways. It could happen anytime now; I won't wait much longer, but revenge (yay!) will soon be mine now that I have become a grandparent and they have become the newly ordained adults.

I have got this thing all worked out to the last detail, and now I only wait for the special occasion to put things in motion. It's really a simple plan.

Here's how it will work: I'll begin with some benign little gesture like: "Go out to dinner, kids, and have a nice time, and I'll watch the grandbabies for you."

That will be my first move. They'll leave happily with full confidence that everything will be better than fine with Dad in charge.

While they're gone, we're going to have school. We'll call it the school of... hmm... the school of "Grandma's dad-burn ruination."

The class curriculum will concern learning how to do the following:

1. set alarm clocks for some healthy 5:00 a.m. bed-jumping, (with a special emphasis on jumping really, really, really high).

2. hide food so that it can't be found for days, (and by the time it is found, it will have begun to mutate into a different life form).

3. scatter clean AND dirty clothes all over the house in such a way that it will be easier to wash them all over again rather than try and figure out which ones are clean.

4. put feet up on the furniture after running barefoot outside.

5. smear ketchup on the wall in the foyer, curving dramatically around the corner.

6. And last but most important, scream and holler like demons.

Nothing destructive, mind you, just good old-fashioned family chaos. That will be sweet revenge for grandparents everywhere.

"Have a nice life, kids."

THE COTTON GIN
MURDERS

The old man who owned the cotton gin in Charleston, Tennessee, never smiled much. Loaded wagons rolled into his gin every day—all day and all night.

Twenty yards and a tall, thick hedge of sycamores were all that stood between my bedroom wall and the weighing platform at the cotton gin.

Harvesting and *ginning* the cotton crop were at the center of this little community's heart from August through October. Because we lived so close to the cotton gin, my own life was caught up in the middle of this tense urgency.

At harvest time, the gin became a mini-universe, buzzing with the never-ending sounds of haste. The slightly raised windows in my room made me a nocturnal witness to the perseverance of that great machine as it did, unceasingly, whatever it did to the soft white stuff from the fields.

The day and night hum of the cotton gin bolstered everyone's confidence that our little valley was prosperous and secure.

I know all about cotton ginning nowadays. I thought I knew

about it then, but the machine that seemed to sing was more of a mystery to me, if anything.

Within our community, it was like a pivot of kindred pride—an icon that gave purpose to our corporate existence.

Cotton ginning had been around since way back in 1793, when a Massachusetts-born fellow by the name of Eli Whitney immigrated to Georgia to tutor the children of wealthy plantation owners.

Most of the sea-island type of cotton was grown near the coast, which was where most of the cotton business was. King Cotton hadn't been born in the South yet, but thanks to Mr. Whitney, this would soon change.

The sea-island variety wasn't the only kind of cotton available. The short-staple, green-seeded cotton showed promise of growing almost anywhere in the South's fertile belt.

But the blossoming cotton was filled with pesky little seeds that were all sticky and gooey. (The first cotton candy)?

Plantation owners found it to be a slow and almost punitive effort to get the stuff to market. Using valuable slave labor to spend countless hours picking out the tiny, sticky cotton seeds was proving to be the death knell for the spreading of the cotton culture.

Eli Whitney, on the other hand, had one of those "light bulb" moments and came up with a way to replace human labor. His new-fangled engine, or "gin," as it came to be called, pumped vitality into the lifeblood of the cotton economy. Soon, cotton became king throughout the South. Now don't blame poor Eli for everything that happened after 1793. Someone else would have invented the contraption sooner or later.

Technology is not the bane of humanity. Humanity is the bane of technology.

When I was in the fourth grade, I made a miniature replica of Mr. Whitney's engine and later received rave reviews from the local PTA. Back then, the Parent-Teacher Organization was called an Association. I like association better. Organization sounds too... hmm, well, too organized.

In Charleston, Tennessee, our small village culture backed the idea of the great cotton gin with as much passion as a Babylonian fertility cult. If the gin was running, folks knew that our world would remain on its axis.

Old Mr. Crabtree owned the gin and was respected as the local Atlas, whose job it was to keep the axis of the cotton world in balance.

Forever running, forever humming! Stay vigilant, mighty Atlas! Alas, the cotton gin forever stands! What a burden! No wonder he never smiled.

Crusty and wrinkle-faced like a Shar-Pei puppy, Mr. Crabtree was not the kind of man little boys could talk with easily. Little boys like to rattle on about every subject they can get out of their mouth in one swift, unconnected breath.

This kind of conversation unnerved Mr. Crabtree. Even though he had once spoken the *little boy's language* fluently, the constricting demands of the adult world of the cotton business had made him forget how.

I'd try to talk to him, but he never was able to translate what I was talking about, as he grunted with disinterest whenever I would come skipping along.

He and his cotton-crew buddies tolerated me because I was the preacher's kid. So, they'd stop all their cussing and conniving when I'd hang around, which wasn't for very long since I lacked the ability to generate much response to my chattering.

I'd give it my best shot because I was Daddy's floating PR man and had a responsibility to keep up good relations. Mr. Crabtree kept his distance from other people and was always a bit of a mystery to me.

Even in church, he would sit stiff and stolid with a stone-faced indifference to the shenanigans of religion. Every Sunday service found him sitting on the side of the sanctuary closest to the cotton gin.

Most folks said he was sleeping because he had spent so many hours running the cotton gin. So, it was tolerated. But I knew differently.

With his eyes closed in concentration and his head slightly tilted in the direction of the cotton gin, I figured he was staying in tune with the melody of the gin instead of the hymns of Zion.

While others were ecstatically caught up in the sounds of my father's preaching, Mr. Crabtree sat still and only moved once or twice in response to the changing rhythms of the cotton gin.

One day, one of my buddies discovered a litter of puppies under the wooden plank steps of Mr. Crabtree's office. An old stray dog had been forced to give birth in this most inhospitable of places. My buddies were excited. I was excited. And nothing ought to have been more exciting to anybody than the birth of six or seven new pups.

The pups would need to stay quiet and comfortable on the soft dirt floor under the steps until they could be handed out to all who wanted one. We had it all planned out: "For everyone, a pup, and for every pup, a home."

How's that old saying go? "When a newborn comes, share the good news." Since I was the local PR man, I saw it as my duty to spread the good news, even with Mr. Grumpy. I couldn't wait to tell him about the pups.

It was the perfect conversation piece to break the daily ice.

Old Man Crabtree listened as I told him excitedly about his good fortune. Mumbling and grunting, he poured out his usual boring dose of complacency. And so, I skipped away merrily to share the good news with others.

Later that day, one of my friends came to tell me that the pups were missing. "Where could they have gone?" I wondered. This was a great mystery. By George, this was prime-time stuff right off Lassie's television show!

Now, all you alphabetized generations probably don't know about the heroic dog Lassie and how she was always saving somebody from something. But every Baby Boomer knows that the mystic cult of Lassie often served as the fulcrum of our existence! Yet, here I was, caught in the middle of my own Hollywood production, and I couldn't imagine what had happened to those precious pups. Would Lassie come to the rescue?

Nope, I would have to stand in for Lassie and track down those pups.

"How could they just get up and walk away? They were too little." I knew that sometimes mama dogs would move their babies to better accommodations, but there was no evidence of this.

We found the mama dog moping around the office just like we were. My buddies and I organized a massive search of which even Lassie would have been proud, but we came up empty-handed as well as empty-hearted.

A few days after our search had become exhausted, grim and gruesome stories began to emerge from my community scouts that Mr. Crabtree had taken the pups over to Heartbreakers Bridge down in the Little Hatchie River Bottoms, tied them up in a cotton sack full of bricks, and tossed them over.

Could this be true? I refused to believe he could have done such a thing.

My heart cracked as I accused myself of being an accessory to the crime. I had told him where the puppies were. If I hadn't told him, he might have never known, and they might still be alive. I made myself sick and decided to go home, get in bed, and totally accept my sickness. I deserved it.

By the next day, my anger had fomented into an unbearable force. That's what I think now. At the time, I wanted to tie Mr. Crabtree up in a cotton sack and throw him over Heartbreaker's Bridge.

The old man was too foreboding and mysterious for me to publicly approach him and accuse him of killing the pups. And though he never mentioned it and the pups were never found, I came to believe that, indeed, he had committed this most heinous crime.

I don't recall ever attempting to talk to him again. I can remember going to church and glaring across the aisle at Mr. Crabtree's slightly cocked head and thinking, "How can this dog killer dare to worship in the house of the living God?"

I'd watch him closely on those Sunday mornings after the cotton gin murders. And every Sunday, a biblical wickedness wound his eyes tightly shut right in the middle of Daddy's most fervent appeals. I suppose being all snug inside himself made it easy for him to hide from God's wrath.

I didn't believe he could hide from God. Maybe he didn't really listen to Daddy's sermons, but on occasion, I did. Finally, I determined that, try as he might, he would not succeed in hiding from the benevolent god of murdered puppies.

More importantly for the vengeful-oriented, I knew he couldn't hide from me, and so I made darn sure he would never be able to hide from me.

Forever after, I made it my saintly obligation, in honor of the slain puppies, to drive him nuts and talk his head off with the "little boy speak" he so fervently despised.

For the next two years, until we moved away to the faraway place of Henderson, Kentucky, I made it my full-time job to ask him questions about every conceivable, obnoxious, infuriating, and abstruse thing under the sun.

"Vengeance is mine; I will repay," say the little boys everywhere.

WHATEVER HAPPENED TO
THE LITTLE RED HEN?

One day, when my daughter, Chelsea, was about three years old, she came over to me and positioned herself comfortably in my (much to my chagrin and mostly because of my weakness for chocolate) very adequate lap.

I could tell she had settled down for some sort of father-daughter encounter. She set her favorite bear, the same one I had placed in her crib the day she was born, carefully beside her. There was, after all, plenty of room on Daddy's very ample lap. (Well, I do work on it from decade to decade!)

She had come for a reading. A *Little Golden Book* was tucked neatly under her arm. I can't imagine why she loves books so much. Maybe it's because she has to use a machete to hack her way through my library every time she tries to find me.

"So, you want me to read you a book?" I asked perfunctorily, knowing full well that there was no escape. This was not a request, but an appointment. It had been appointed unto *"me"* once upon a time (meaning now) to read.

Tots are a trusting bunch. They can't read; they obviously have no idea what reading entails, nor do they, at this point in their lives, really want to know how to read. Then why do they make such a fuss about reading a book?

They might look at the pictures as you turn the pages, but the greater nourishment that comes from reading to tots comes from the touching, the holding, the cuddling, and the soft whispery tones of our specially designed 'tot-reading-voice.'

What does all that interactive, high-quality father-daughter time spell?

T-R-U-S-T.

H-O-P-E.

F-A-I-T-H.

There! You really can spell love in different ways. And this spelling of "love" is used especially for building relationships.

Loving, gentle, and cuddling time spent with a toddler is time spent reading from the real book of life loudly, clearly, and richly. Parents and children become the book, and all that jumbled word stuff in the middle that makes sense to us but appears as nonsense to them is erased.

The written words are replaced with the living words of a parent's smiling face and caressing hands, their pliant kisses, and their softly spoken *babyese*. (I first heard about the word *babyese*, meaning baby talk, when I was in college, and I have preferred it ever since.)

In return, the toddlers read back to their parents a pure and innocent love, expressed with high-pitched giggles of hope, and affirmed with nuzzling noses of contentment.

One day they will learn to read, but for now reading is to be lived in the cherished moments and in the remembered places of the heart. Reading at such a tender age is for growing and for loving—for believing and trusting.

"So, what book are we going to love today, Chelsea?"

She pulled the book out of its hiding place and shoved it within two micrometers of my face. For toddlers, things must have proximity to validate their authenticity.

"Red Cheekieen," she sang sweetly to me. Sure enough, right on the cover was a big, red chicken.

"Why, it's the story about the little red hen." My response was not directed at Chelsea, and I hadn't used the singsong harmony of my toddler style reading voice. I was riding a tidal wave of ancient and seldom-used memories.

"What ever happened to the Little Red Hen?" I thought. Glassy-eyed and stone-faced, I stared out across the room, lost in that all-too-familiar sea of yesteryear, until Chelsea's firm hand smacked me back to reality.

"Daddy, read me," she pleaded. Hail to all—LET THE READING FEAST BEGIN! We cuddled! She giggled. I stroked the long curls of her baby-soft, blond hair, and she buried her head tenderly into my chest.

When it was over, the banner over us was love—snow-white, unblemished love. And we snoozed for a while, full of the living words from the book of life.

But what was it about that storybook chicken that caused my brain to let loose a torrent of tranquilizing memories?

Once upon a time, when I was a little boy, I had a book about this very same little red hen. Mama read it to me so many times that the binding became ragged and threadbare. I hadn't seen that little book in almost 35 years—so long ago. And yet, it was once my favorite—a required reading before every nightly prayer.

What ever happened to *my* Little Red Hen? I grew up, and she moved away into the frozen storage places of my memories. What was so special about that book? Was it the story line?

The Little Red Hen was such a meticulous little chicken. She kept her house tidy and neat, and everything had its place. She busied herself mending and ironing her clothes and growing and cooking her own food. Everything had its purpose.

But one day, old Reddy Fox caught her, tied her up in a sack, and started out for home to feed her to his babies.

The journey was long and tiring, so Reddy Fox sat down to rest.

And while he rested, little Miss Orderly remembered her sewing scissors tucked away in her apron, right where they belonged.

Hooray for the Little Red Hen! She snipped her way out and surreptitiously placed a rock into old Reddy's sack, adroitly sewing up the escape hatch without detection.

She skipped home to safety, and the little, baby *reddies* got hard-boiled basalt for dinner.

Cute story! But why had I wanted this story to be read to me over and over again? There isn't anything in this story that can compare to the sophisticated stories, cartoons, and video games of today's culture.

It's just a tale of a little red chicken who wanted to live happily in her quaint home. She got kidnapped, but by marshaling her wit and her brawn, freedom was reclaimed. What's the big deal?

As I thought about it, I couldn't separate the images of the little red hen from the images of my sweet, young mama. The house from my childhood served as a complement to each vision of the hen's house.

ORDER...
PURPOSE...
SAFETY...
HAPPINESS...
LOVE.

I know you've got the point by now, but I like to splash around in the strength of this memory. Of course, I remember the book's illustrations, but I don't remember the written words. I remember the living words of our mutual love.

The book is one of the cornerstones of my life, providing structure to my character, substance to my faith, and a foundation for my sense of home and family.

It was a living book. My mother and I created a living bond that cradled and nurtured an emerging, growing story of how togetherness, loyalty, joy, and peace make life rich and complete. I would sit on her lap or snuggle up beside her on my bed and listen as she would exhibit to me repeatedly the living words of love, hope, and destiny. And the love of all the ages poured through her like fresh oil from sacred vessels.

Well, this shouldn't sound unbelievable. We become living books with our children because the magnitude of mutual love is like a super magnet, drawing us together, binding us together, and reading us as one. It makes sense.

Spoken words had an ancient and powerful effect on us humans long before the first written language was developed. Humans were being molded into communities that eventually became nation states not because of written words but because of loving, living words established at a much higher plane of human intimacy and interaction. How long has this been going on, you ask?

Since long, long ago, in the distant mists of time when ancient mothers and fathers whispered tales of love and hope and tenderness into yearning ears of innocence.

Chelsea, ME, and Grandbabies Jack and Emma Naylor, the children of Ryan and Rachael Naylor. This photo was taken at Chelsea's high school graduation dinner.

THE TENTACLES OF EXPERIENCE
OR WHERE CODY GOES TO PLAY

O nce, when my son Cody was about four years old, we had returned from shopping and entered the house through the garage. It was about five swift steps to the little brown door in the back of the garage that led one step up into the kitchen.

Wintertime's frigid blasts had made us all learn to move with the speed of the blowing wind when going back and forth between the garage and the house.

Like a lot of four-year-olds, Cody would often just freeze in front of people when he was supposed to be hurrying. Mysteriously, it seemed like crazy glue would get stuck on the bottom of his shoes every time he tried to walk in front of somebody.

"Walk faster or get out of the way" has always been a commonly heard phrase around our house.

While racing to the little brown door that day, I realized something was missing. Why hadn't I given my "walk faster, or get out of the way" speech yet?

I thought, "Why not? Where's Cody? It's too cold out here. Why isn't he hurrying to get in the house?"

Without turning to see what he was up to, I found myself mumbling over my shoulder another Cody-worn phrase I often used, "Hurry up and come on."

Cody's muffled reply was undeniable proof that he was lost somewhere in the jungle that lives inside our garage.

If your garage is like ours, it's a place where you can squeeze the car in only on special occasions. The rest of the year, it's an uninhabitable space for automobiles, a source of frustration for adults who hope to find whatever it is they lost last Christmas, and an adventurous playground for the imaginations of little boys like Cody.

The junk in our garage takes on a life of its own, constantly shifting and changing as more things are added. In the dark of night, it starts to change into new paths and twisted structures, and each morning, the tentacles of its configured imminence boggle the mind.

"Where are you, Cody?" I asked, squinting into the twisted mass of things once shaped like household goods that you could have found in picturesque relief being advertised in those days in what we called a department store catalog. Nowadays, everyone finds it at the tip of their nose by staring into their smartphones with bent necks.

These once-upon-a-time beauties from the advertising world now lurked in my garage, which looked like an impenetrable swamp of household junk.

Glittering bent edges and ghostly reflections created a

horrifying scene from the hellish graveyard of *Household Americanus*. "Lord, have mercy!" I remember shouting, "I've got to clean this place out again."

Cody moved lithely through the lifeless tentacles of inanimate monsters with the abandon of a fighter pilot engaged in battle. He always knew the paths through this jungle, no matter that they changed every day.

Adventurous paths called out to Cody every day, and he had a solemn duty to run through them with the electrifying energy that fired the channels of learning within his brain.

Cody was very good at making, updating, and using his neural maps for these kinds of tricky problems. He kept millions of them stored deep within the cracks and crevices of his memory. His memory was like a songbird.

His songbird memory was like that of the male Swamp sparrow, which neuroscientists believe retrieves bits and pieces of a song stored over two months earlier. When he needs to add it to his song, the Swamp Sparrow calls forth the tune that will bring resonance to his newest creation.

Every melody is different.

Every melody is a part of the past.

As a growing boy, Cody, as well, reached far into the storage areas of experience and took what he needed, making trailblazing look just as easy as when he used to slide with sock feet on Daddy's freshly waxed floors.

Every new experience Cody encountered caused a veritable thunderclap within his skull. The vast universe of his brain would reverberate with atomic activity every time he went freewheeling through the trails of experience.

When we experience something, the neurons in our brains are electrically stimulated, especially in the area called the hippocampus. (This sounds like a definition for wild hippopotamuses running loose on college campuses, but it's Latin for "water horse," which the hippocampus in your brain is supposed to look like, and, yes, I know this is a run-on sentence.)

Contrary to what most people think, this process continues after the formative years, even after Cody's. Indeed, it's a never-ending alternative to any life open to interactive experiences. Synaptic fires keep burning long past the dynamo years of our youth.

Now that explains why the ancient Hebrew prophet Jeremiah said he got fire in his bones when he was an old man. But there's no excuse for the rest of us. We can all slide on waxed floors forever, Cody-style!

Furthermore, synaptic formations within the brain are literally addicted to new experiences. Your brain can become addicted to drugs, but it is more addicted to having new experiences! But here's the catch: Unless we take the initiative to feed it with these new experiences it so desperately desires, growth will never happen.

Basically, that's why some people flip hamburgers their entire lives and others build spacecraft. I'll have to save that idea for another story, some other time. Don't worry, I promise.

But let's get technical for just a couple of paragraphs. Oh, come on, just for three paragraphs. I'll even count them. I promise it won't hurt you, and the new experience might cause you to grow some new brain cells, keeping you off the hamburger line. Okay, okay, if you don't want to, skip down three paragraphs because the ending to this story is something you don't want to miss.

1. Polyribosomal aggregates (PRA) are in charge of making proteins inside cells, which shows that new synapses are being made.

2. This synthesis is sort of like the churning and swirling that happens on the inside of an old-fashioned ice cream machine, making it possible for the milk, eggs, and vanilla to turn into the smooth white stuff that fills our cones. Something must set the process into motion in order for it to work. The ice cream machine needs the input of ingredients and the impact of human intervention.

3. Synaptic development in our brains begins with the hand crank of experience turned by the outside world. According to the famous neuroscientist William T. Greenough, "synapses form in response to experience from which information is to be stored."

(I think my reader will appreciate a little academic validation, proving that I didn't just make all this up. Thank you, Dr. Greenough!)

"What did all this have to do with Cody's ability to trailblaze through the junk in our garage?" you reasonably ask.

Cody's brain pulsed with fiery synaptic formations as it looked for storage data in the junkyard jungle, which was full of the moving tentacles of our household appliances. His mind would go into high gear when he read new arrangements and saw new possibilities in old things that had been thrown away.

The dynamism of his young mind demanded that every hole be explored, every chair be crawled under, every rope be pulled, every bucket be dumped, every stack of magazines be leveled, every discarded appliance be dismembered, and every wormlike trail be blazed.

His innate impulse was to just do it. To heck with all that social etiquette junk that always tried to make him grow up and know better than to be so destructive, er, I mean creative. He didn't know all of that yet, but one day he would.

It was the actual experience that propelled him forward like a force of nature. He lived for the experience. Our brains always hunger for experiences, and experiences make the brain a gluttonous pig.

That's why Cody-types are always in our faces, shouting, "Give me, give me, give me." And "Can I, can I, can I?" That's their theme song. They haven't succumbed to the complacency of adulthood, which often teaches us that it's normal to fear new experiences.

It's because human beings don't start stagnating until around age fifteen or sixteen that little boys and girls generally make us neurotically nervous. Kids explode into growth because they are unafraid to try life with gusto.

For many years, Cody did the same with nature. Often, I would watch him as he played in the backyard. He would run backwards, sideways, and upside down, using his head and hands any way he could contort them.

He would crawl under the porch like a lion, into his den, and slither back out again like a python. He could scream like the living dead one second and then sing with angelic innocence the next.

He devised new methods for throwing rocks: underhanded, over-handed, and with a flip of his wrist. He used both hands and no hands, or from out of his belly button, or flung random objects from his forehead with the forward snap of his neck.

Not only did he sit in the swing, he stood in the swing, stood on top of the swing, swung from the top of the swing, and catapulted out of the swing at its highest angle. And, in doing so, he forced me to watch him closely.

Before he would make his safe descent back down to earth, he would scrape the sky with the outstretched claws of the Hawk Man, which he had decided instantaneously to become in mid-air.

To search for new experiences was Cody's objective every day. It's what Cody did best. Experience is a banquet for the hungry synaptic formations within young brains. It's merely a process of consolidation.

Consolidation for adaptation.

The young brain has more synapses than the aging brain. It's not because we're losing the battle; it's because we are consolidating the fruits of our victories. Synaptic formations are precipitated only with the advent of new experiences. New experiences mean new brain cells! That's simple, right?

But they don't add to it; rather, they add on by consolidating with other, more primitive synapses in the same area, making them superior in value.

Aha! Experiences build upon one another, creating a more adaptable and successful human brain.

So why didn't Cody want to come in from the icy-cold garage on that wintry day eons ago? Brain-training notwithstanding, I didn't really want to wait for Cody to wade through all that junk in the garage.

Magically, thankfully, I remember the words of that day.

"It's cold out here, Cody," I whined.

"Wait, Daddy, I'm almost through." His words bounced from the junk pile with electro-magnificent voltage.

I could hear the commotion in his brain: "FIRE ONE, FIRE TWO, FIRE THREE! Store it! Keep it! Encode it!"

The tentacles of that heap of discarded garage junk, important only to yesterday, were fueling the growth of my little Cody-man.

"Okay, I'll let you take the circuitous route, because the road less traveled is always filled with the new and is the obvious road to learning," I mused to myself.

The road of experience is a never-ending road throughout everyone's life. Allowing the subscription to your experiences to expire is what causes life to get boring. Don't let life get boring because that will mean you aren't thinking, and if you aren't thinking, you aren't experiencing, and if you aren't experiencing, then you're dying.

We stop growing when we stop exposing ourselves to the challenges of everyday life. New experiences await all of us every day, no matter how old we are.

To satisfy the explosiveness of Cody's mind that day, I put down my packages and turned around, walking backward into the tentacled hole of household "used-to-bes." With full-throated adolescence, I started screaming like the living dead as I chased after Cody. He pushed me into positions and places I had long since given up on.

"Hey, Cody! Wait a minute, what's popping in my head?"

"Don't stop, Daddy; please don't; just come on and get me."

Ah, experiences built with love are unforgettable. Here is where memories bring back the images that ignite our tears.

Cody's Jeep. He got it for his 5th birthday while living in Princeton, New Jersey, just down the street from the house of Einstein's ghost! In this photo, JOSHUA helps provide instruction.

LIGHTING ARISTOTLE'S LANTERN

I strolled along the beach today looking for seashells and, instead, found memories. A sand dollar lay cracked and bleached on the shore. There are more than seven hundred different kinds of sea urchins in the sand dollar family. Before we began raping the oceans to placate our exotic tastes, there were far more than seven hundred.

This little sand dollar looked like it was trapped in a mess of small shells and tangled seaweed. It looked helpless. I picked it up to brush it clean.

While gently caressing its spiny white bumps, I tingled with the idea that maybe the bumps were not bumps at all but a kind of sea braille. Perhaps what I held was not a shell but a story.

"What's that?" my little boy Cody asked.

"It's a sea cookie," I answered, knowing such an answer would spark a thousand questions from a four-year-old.

"A cookie? Can we eat it?" Cody pleaded with his very best droopy-eyed, frowny face.

This boy can eat a cookie at any time, even in the dead of night. But this was a strange looking cookie, and it didn't smell anything like Grandma's fat, moist chocolate chip cookies. Daddy had said it was a cookie, though. Cody's question was more of an appeal to reason than a plea for something sweet to eat.

"No, we don't eat it. We call it a sea cookie because it's round and fat like a nice big cookie," the teaching-parent in me lectured smoothly and slyly.

"It's also called a sand dollar," I baited.

"Who would we sell it to?" I asked as I cradled it gently in his hands.

"Who would we?" Cody thought aloud, stroking the chalky plates that covered the shell.

"A DOLLAR? Can we spend it?" he begged, falling into the trap of my classroom by the sea.

"No, we can't spend it, but it's still very valuable," I said.

"Wow," Cody beamed, his eyes fully lit in that knowledge-consumption mode, "Can we sell it?"

Cody wanted to learn everything he could about this mysterious creature from the sea. When we got home, we found beautiful pictures of sand dollars and other sea urchins in several of the *Little Golden Books* that he keeps by his bed. Suddenly, these became his favorites.

We made it a father-and-son project to research this wondrous new discovery at the Fort Myers Beach library, where we lived at the time. We hoped for a more sophisticated level of information in a multimedia style. Learning together about these urchins of the sea was time well spent.

Sand dollars and sea cookies are scavengers that survive by scouring the ocean bottoms and eating almost anything they can find.

Society has its own little urchins that live on the streets of poverty-swollen ghettos, subsisting on anything they can find. Cody wasn't too interested in that part. But he'll care about it one day.

We learned that the reason for their culinary versatility is found in the gift that nature has given them. I suppose Mother Nature figured it was a good idea to give these little creatures an edge against the ocean's big bullies.

What they wound up with was a complex chewing apparatus made of five ribbon-shaped teeth, sort of like the incisors of a rat. While wildly gnashing his teeth unnervingly and making the most awful face, Cody conjured up a quick image of an ocean-stalking-ratfish.

Sea urchins have been scavenging around most successfully for quite a while, gnawing, rooting, and slicing. You know, like rats! Well, er, maybe in the minds of little boys. In reality, of course, they share nothing in common with rats.

A poet must have had pity on the little creatures in deciding what to name their ravenous mouth of scissors. Marine biologists refer to it as Aristotle's Lantern.

We couldn't figure out why their teeth (or masticatory apparatus, for you biologists) went by such a catchy name.

The great surrealist painter Salvador Dali devised a method for using Aristotle's Lantern as "the eyeglass of the painter." He would use the dried shell's skeleton as a creative window, through which he would peer for hours while finishing a perfect painting.

He went even further to acclaim that in using Aristotle's Lantern, one can see the "entire universe...a kind of cosmogonic and pentagonal flower... the very skeleton of heaven."

I don't really care to know why this little aperture in the sea urchin's body is called by such a curious name because Cody and I came up with our own explanation.

But before we did, Cody learned a little bit about Aristotle, the ancient Greek philosopher. Nothing boring. Just a little bit.

Cody learned that Aristotle was a great teacher and that great teachers become great because they ask questions of their students. They ask and ask and ask and ask. They take a mountain and ask all about it until its mystery is no bigger than a molehill.

A great teacher brings light to things that appear dark before us.

When we returned home, Cody went and found the old railroad lantern we have sitting in our living room and brought it to me.

"Can we light the lantern, pleeeease?" (He begs really well when he buys extra vowels.)

We turned out the lights, lit the wick, and saw how the lantern brought light to the room. Everything that hid from us when we turned out the lights reappeared under the glow of the old copper lantern.

Cody didn't understand in great depth all we learned today, but he had fun. He did learn, however, that things that hide from us could be found if we searched for them and kept searching until we found them. He did learn that things we don't understand can be explained.

Great teachers shed light on the darkness of our ignorance by inspiring us with their questions.

I learned just as much as Cody did today, if not more. The sea urchin's mouth is like Aristotle's lantern in that it goes about the ocean floor searching for everything that is salvageable. It chews and grinds, consuming every conceivable ounce of nutrition from the ocean's smorgasbord.

Aristotle once walked the vast Lycean gymnasium, peripatetically teaching the students of ancient Greece. They scavenged for knowledge by walking, asking, remembering, and learning.

Experience is the food that fuels our minds. We walk the corridors of yesterday, answering today's questions. Often, however, we are guilty of carelessly tossing away the things of yesterday.

Today's experience is tomorrow's memory, and its value is no less now than it was then. I don't want to forget the wonderful time we had today, or the day before that, or any day.

All the days of our lives are like lanterns of knowledge.

Memories are like lights, helping us to see our way through the present and inspiring us to expect the future. We feed upon them, and our hearts are filled with the wellspring of knowledge they provide. An important fellow once said, "Let your lights shine."

Cody helped me put the lantern back in the living room.

"Let's put the little sea urchin here too," he whispered with a breath of sudden insight.

"Well, aren't you a smart boy?" I crooned proudly.

Placed side by side in an inauspicious spot in our living room, the Light and the Seeker nobly stand. They're good reminders for us to keep seeing and keep searching every day!

PINE TREES AND BASEBALL

D ale and Patsy Hawkins, over in Paducah, Kentucky, used to be my spare set of parents. I rooted down there a lot on lazy afternoons, goofing around with their oldest son, Steve.

It was a matter of cultural choice to hang out at the Hawkins' little city-farm during the rudderless days of the late sixties and early seventies.

I call it a city-farm because it was a little bit of heaven smack dab in the middle of suburbia. A dash of this and a smidgen of that, and Dale had created a seven-acre homestead that sprawled out mockingly amongst the pip-squeaky subdivision plots everybody else had.

Dale wasn't rich. He was just smart. He had accomplished the American dream of owning a piece of Mother Earth long before subdivisions surrounded his paradise. Double rows of stately *Pinus ponderosa*, scraping the heavens, a few chickens, even fewer cows, a strawberry patch (which I always volunteered to help pick, eating most of what I picked), and seven rich acres made this a heaven on earth.

Assembled like columned ranks, the pines stretched tall, elegant, and mystic. They helped make a darn good baseball stadium, too. A home run had to clear their spiraling peaks. "Eat your heart out, Harry Carey, wherever you are," cry the baby boomers, and "whoever Harry Carey is," moan the millennials.

This tree-lined, cordoned-off cow pasture made for one of the best fields of dreams any young adolescent could hope for. It doesn't take much imagination to figure out why I spent much of my youth on the "Pinederosa." That's right, it was Pinederosa, not Ponderosa. Dale had this inscribed on a small wooden sign that hung from the light post in the front yard.

He always used to announce that when Steve and his younger son Darren (who used to make me sick when I'd catch him walking around eating cold, raw potatoes, but he was several years younger than me and didn't know any better) were ready to go to college, he'd cut them down and trade them for the cash needed to pay for the boys' education. (Well, it's a long sentence and could be fixed, but then that wouldn't be me.)

Fifty-five years later, Steve and Darren are grown and successful, the pines are still standing, and Dale was still "farming" until he was almost 90. Sometimes I tried to imagine what that beautiful oasis would have looked like, all denuded and exposed. I never liked what I pictured, and I suppose Dale didn't either.

I'm glad he didn't take the chain saw to those summer shades, because when I return to base and take a melancholy cruise past my old Kentucky home away from home, my mind flushes swiftly and sweetly with a veritable banquet of precious memories.

A sparkle of my Grandpa Hughes comes popping out of me every now and then, and I suppose I'd be sounding a lot like him if I were to say, "Give me a nickel for every ball batted and every ball pitched, and I'd be a rich man." But it's true.

I spent a lot of time swinging, throwing, running, and learning on the Pinederosa. Surely, they must have wanted to run me off sometimes. But they never said anything. And over the years, we developed a love for one another that only became stronger with every recollection.

I didn't know it then, but every moment spent at the Pinederosa was a golden coin saved in the treasure chest of my memory. I was getting rich and didn't even realize it.

Those Pinederosa scents of yesterday started resurfacing quite a bit when my son Joshua turned eleven years old and got all caught up with playing Major League Little League.

Oh yes, there is such a thing, too. Where could such a thing exist, you ask? That's a fair question that deserves a confusing answer. The answer revolves around the time we lived in the capital of New Jersey —Princeton! Oh, no, Princeton's not the capital of New Jersey, but it's much more interesting than the real capital because the unimaginable always has a way of coming to life in this little barony known in some circles as the research center of the universe. And that's where Joshua temporarily became convinced that he was headed for the real Major Leagues one day.

Joshua and I enjoyed walking around the city streets of Princeton and occasionally bumping into Einstein's ghost, who also enjoyed a good daily vigil. He was always looking for an answer to how the universe might be unified, which scared people there into breaking the arrow of pragmatism with illogical experiments, apparitions, and all kinds of strange concoctions. (That's a little inside joke there between me and Einstein and purposely filled with multiple multi-syllabic words.)

If you can't follow the logic, I'll be happy to explain. In the *known* universe, eleven-year-olds play Little League ball, right? What do you do with all the kids that can't play worth a flip without hurting anybody's feelings? Princeton parents appealed to the god of the "WOKE" for an enlightening solution.

They chopped up Little League into two categories. You get the idea, I bet. The best players were chosen to play Major League Little

League, and the not-so-good players were chosen to play Minor League Little League. Or was it the other way around? Well, whichever way you say it, it was a jolly mess—this often-murky cesspool of egoism and narcissism found in a most vicious league.

These little souls' future existence depended upon their parents' internal hard drives, which enabled them to learn more about how to be pricks than how to get to the Major Leagues of anything.

Wait! What? That just gushed out, and I have no idea what it means. Me...rambling. But the point is, they devised a plan to accommodate all the kids' skills as well as their sensitive feelings.

It sure would have been great if they'd had that arrangement when I was growing up. I was never a good ballplayer. The camaraderie was more important to me than being on a real team.

Does that sound like something a jealous kid might say? Well, when I remember things from my youth, I get inundated with all those nasty juvenile attitudes.

If the adults in my day had had the progressive mentality of making room for everyone, no matter how bad their ball playing was, I might have been good enough to play on one of the Minor League Little League teams.

As it was, I could only play in the cow field, surrounded by the shady pines on their way to the sawmill of collegiate ambitions.

To prepare for his Little League placement, Joshua wore a smart-looking uniform and had to have expensive, name-brand cleated shoes to go with it. He was also skilled in making old Dad feel guilty if I didn't give him twenty dollars a week to "buy" batting practice down at the neighborhood Wham-Slam-Got-Your-Kid-Addicted-Fun-Center.

His glove had been crafted from one of the finest cows that ever lived (which would have never happened in my day because our cows had soulful names like Daisy and Greg), and his bat was molded from super-strong, unpronounceable, multisyllabic metals that Superman brought with him from the planet Krypton. All of this made him a better ballplayer than I ever was.

He did have a lot of fun, and I didn't mean to hassle him, as he says, with a bunch of patronizing dribbles about "when I was a boy." BUT WHEN I WAS A BOY, playing ball down at the old Pinederosa there was a lot more to it than just making a run for the local pennant.

Baseball was life, love, friends, and family. It was filled with all that good stuff that goes into making memories rich and durable. Baseball was the wisest investment of my childhood years—building lasting relationships, learning mutual trust, and seeding the future.

Maybe Dale and Patsy never realized what a wonderful school of life they were running back in those days. And maybe they just thought I was making a pest of myself. I'm sure that on more than one occasion I made a nuisance of myself. But it is the nature of southerners' good graces to never say so.

What else are young adolescents supposed to do? Where else could a suburban kid go and find such wide-open spaces for playing baseball, picking berries, feeding cows, and teasing chickens?

I close my eyes and conjure up a forgotten, unglorified Little League field of yesteryear. A timeless field sheltered by misty blue skies, eloquently framed by a swaying wooden fortress, stood sentinel to the passing of innocence.

Memory's nostrils flared full of the pungent-smelling pine sap that made the trees all sticky and gooey, as well as the ubiquitous cow manure that taught me to look before I stepped.

Those unbearable, interminable summer days seemed like they would drag on forever sometimes, frustrating me with the thought that life was unfairly passing me by. What I wouldn't give to linger in the shade of yesterday's Pinederosa—just one more long, hot summer day.

"Pancake philosophy" is a rigid teacher, but true. The things we do when we're young get flipped over when we become older, and we find ourselves doing the exact opposite. And some of the things we wind up doing as adults turn out to be things we just tolerated as kids.

Intolerable? Unbearable? No, sir, not to me. Let me batter up to the plate of time. How about just five minutes? Those days were long, and now I long for those days.

To close my eyes and remember is to open my heart and be filled.

"Hey Dale, you pitch. I'll bat." PLAY BALL!

Joshua Naylor, out on a bigger playing field in Southeast Asia

AN ADDENDUM OF SADNESS

P eople normally don't like to read something sad after having read something that just made them smile. However, it would be remiss of me not to provide you with an addendum to the previous story.

A few years ago, I returned to visit Dale and Patsy at the Pinederosa after an absence of several decades. It was wonderful to see them and to take in the sweeping beauty of those towering sentinels once again, which by this time looked more like redwoods than the pine trees of my youth.

Dale looked good for someone who was 90+ years old, and he seemed healthy, if only a bit slower. It was a wonderful reunion, and I vowed that I would visit more often.

A few months later, I sent his son Steve a rough draft of the story, "Pine Trees and Baseball." His memories provoked by this story moved him to tears, and he vowed that he couldn't wait until he could read it aloud to the team at the Pinederosa.

Two months after that, Steve informed me that Dale had stage 4 stomach cancer. Anyone who knows anything about stomach cancer knows that stage 4 in 90-year-olds is a death sentence.

And so, I wrote Steve this letter:

"All of this about your dad is so painful for me. Selfishly, it brings back my memories from losing Mama last year, but it deepens my reflections on my childhood, making these feelings harder to bear. And then I think about what you all must be going through, and I know it is nothing in comparison to what I might feel. I know how physically draining it is to maintain your vigil, as well as how difficult it is to refuel before the next exchange.

Yes, your love for your father will see you through. And I know that you believe that God never places upon us more than we can endure, but the battle is nonetheless not without wounds of courage and scars from praying.

The battle for our loved ones is, as you say, "what it is." It is a battle. God is the great general, but the war is fought on a battlefield littered with the detritus of our efforts. In the end, we will all be winners.

Sometimes I wonder why the devil even tries to fight this battle against God's children when he knows that defeat is always his promised, bitter dish.

You all know we are keeping you in our thoughts and in our hearts. Tell Dale one more time that I love him dearly."

About two months after this, Dale died on September 27. Hardly could I have ever dreamed that only three years later, my father would pass away. They were both ancient men.

Throughout my narratives, you will read that they were linked in friendship and fellowship for half a century—Dale, 91, and my dad, almost 96 when they passed. They both suffered in ways unimaginable to me from cancer and bodily failures that compounded their passing into an irreverent ugliness, if not for the beauty of their lives.

I have much more to say about the memories of death and dying in another chapter. For now, I can tell you that Steve was eventually able to read my story "Pine Trees and Baseball" to Dale and Patsy in the twilight of their lives and that it thrilled them with great emotion.

But the story's creation and sharing had taken place in such a short period of time. From May to July, it moved from my heart to the listening hearts of others. I was happy to learn Dale was able to listen to my precious memories of his special place.

When Steve called to tell me about the funeral, he asked if I would be willing to read my story at the funeral service. Hesitantly, I agreed to read it, but secretly, I worried that it might prove impossible for me to do it without breaking down.

At the time of the funeral, I lived about a three-hour car ride away (that is, if I were driving 80 mph). I had planned to leave very early to be there on time.

The funeral service was to take place at Oaklawn Baptist Church, Paducah, Kentucky, where my father had pastored for 10 years in the sixties and seventies and another five years in the eighties and nineties.

My father no longer lived near Paducah, nor was he able to travel. I wasn't sure I would be able to travel. There would be great amounts of emotion spilling out at this service. It would not be like the bleak funerals seen in the movies.

This was going to be a funeral with memories shared, attended by hundreds and hundreds of people, noticeably marked by the flag-draped casket honoring this Purple Heart veteran of the Korean Conflict. Obviously, the service would be emotional beyond any service I had attended since I was a young man.

Finally, I became convinced I could not travel there, and I could not read this story before these people who loved him so much—who loved my father so much—who loved me so much.

So, I called Steve and gave him an excuse as to why I couldn't make it, and he accepted my excuse and then asked me if it would be alright if he read aloud the story, "Pine Trees and Baseball," before the church.

Later, I learned that as Steve read this lengthy story before several hundred people, there was hardly a dry eye in the church. Memories are life-changing and powerful devices that provide solace to our hearts and inspiration to our hopes and dreams.

They drive us forward with their narratives of the inspirational, but they also sadden our hearts when we stack them all up side-by-side and realize the depth of their soul-wrenching natures.

Memories are wonderful stories, full of happiness but ultimately shadowed by sadness.

Dale and Jack passed from the living world on the same day—September 27th.

Great grandfather, Jack Naylor, and Grandfather, Jeffrey Naylor, with Liam son of Evan and Yelka

FOR TOMORROW'S TEARS

My wife is a very sensitive person. She, like many people, lets the little things bother her too much. Oh, and the big things? Well, they just gobble her up sometimes. Because of her acute sensitivities, she often worries herself sick. I realize that's a difficult phrase to define.

When I was a little boy, I heard my mother and grandmother speak of people who were sick with "the worries." They weren't familiar with all the psychological terms that go into creating "the worries," but they recognized the symptoms.

My wife's worries have resulted in high blood pressure and, unfortunately, the medication that goes along with it. This makes her life vulnerable to the emotions of the moment.

The "worries" affect me a little differently than they do my wife. Foolishly, I allow them to build up deep within me. I know nobody else does this, but I do.

They reach a point of critical mass and then simply explode. The explosion usually ends with me taking a forced march around the neighborhood, kicking imaginary dogs, and mumbling vulgar things to myself about how ugly the neighbor's yard looks.

This really does make me feel better, and by the time I get home, things are great, and I'm ready to start my life again. Of course, all that really means is that I'm ready to start cooking up the next batch of psychological traumas.

You and I both know that the nature of the beast, that is our culture, demands more of us than most of us have to give. That's really all there is to this modern dilemma of the psyche.

We have too much on our minds, too much owed to others, and not enough time for ourselves. Most of our problems are self-inflicted because we don't know how to (or won't) draw those proverbial lines of deference.

Like a full pot of water set on the hottest burner on the stove, the struggle of the soul piles up and piles up, oozing outward to the edge of our sanity.

There's just not enough space in the engine rooms of our psyche to handle it all. We let it accumulate, we let it heat up to overflow, and then we wonder why it all explodes in our faces.

What makes all this even more horrible is that it usually blows up when we need to be at our best. Such blow-ups typically happen right in the middle of *the* company presentation, when the boss is over for dinner, or at the mortgage closing.

You know what I mean. It's like your kid burping at the table or something worse when you've finally invited the minister home for dinner.

My wife takes a different, more realistic approach to dealing with her "I - can't - stand - it - anymore - please - move - aside - while - I - die" moments.

She finds a nice spot, or if it's really critical, the spot where she's standing at the time will do fine. She crumples down to the floor like a rag doll and starts crying buckets. I'm talking about real, old-fashioned, gone-with-the-wind-but-I-will-rebuild-Tara sobbing. (Tara—the house Scarlet had burned out from under her by those "Darn" Yankees.)

Everything and everybody stops. This is a cry that comes from deep within the soul. The intensity of our mommy's tears makes the whole family want to cry.

Our arms get stiff and long, dangling at our sides like lost circus monkeys with widely gaping mouths and chins pinned to our chests. We stare at her. There sits our precious rag doll of a mommy.

She's the one who cleans our two-week-old dirty clothes, does our overdue homework, wipes our snotty, sick noses, works a real, full-time job, monitors our greasy consciences, and pushes us out into the world to confront the frightening stuff of reality.

Behold! She sits listless in a pool of ugh! in the middle of the floor.

No one can make her stop crying. Once she starts, she must finish. So, we mull around the room, shifting our feet and murmuring unintelligibly like good little circus monkeys, waiting for the tide to turn.

There we are—mulling, shifting, and helpless. We race around the room like emotional bumper cars, rolling our eyes at each other and accruing guilt at an alarming rate.

Enter Cody the Healer:

At three years of age, Cody was often both the cause and cure of household anxieties. During the course of one of these Cody-induced trauma-dramas, the little man gave us some pointers on how to deal with emotional crises.

Cody didn't feel constrained by the restrictions of his three years and four months of age. He believed he was much older, maybe ten. Cody's precious sister, Chelsea, was fourteen months old, and the tenderness of her age had inspired a personal motivation within him to guide, nurture, teach, and lead her down the well-worn PATHS OF DESTRUCTION.

It would be an understatement to say that they quickly and sometimes mysteriously came together to form a strong and formidable coalition.

What's really scary is that I know there are probably millions of such combinations in homes all across America. It gives me a Burl

Ives kind of shudder to think about it. (When I was a kid, Burl Ives was the portly guy who narrated the animated television story of Rudolph the Red-Nosed Reindeer year after year after year, until I shivered every time I heard him speak!)

Still, once Cody put together the coalition, they would stand like pillars of fire in front of a pharaoh (or behind Moses, depending on how you feel).

This coalition had and still can control and end any situation on any given day, at any given time, in any given place. Please note that the word "any" is neutral and does not exclude anything, so CHAOS could really happen in any situation.

In other words, their cherubic efforts were enough to make their mother fall to the floor, Raggedy Ann style.

A universal trait of a preschooler is creativity. If you think the methodologies for the destruction and devastation of a beautiful room have been exhausted, then, obviously, you have not lived with a three-year-old. You know the old saying, "Everything has its place?" Well.....

A three-year-old would say "no" to this dictum. "Keep an eye on this," Cody would say, "because everything that has a place has a new place. A place where I can drag it, kick it, break it, throw it, stomp it, chew it, rip it, stuff it, hide it, or... make it look like my sister did it."

As a result, a beautiful place, at least in the eyes of unimaginative adults, is transformed. It becomes a new place. Malleable in the hands of a creative mind, its transformation makes it a place where blood pressures rise like air balloons and heart palpitations beat like war drums.

Once upon a time, my wife entered such a transformed room.

I heard a shriek as shrill as that of a Nebraska Sandhill Crane. I never knew how to describe my wife's shrieks until we had a chance to live in Nebraska for a couple of years.

"I'm coming, Scarlet, er, I mean honey," I yelled.

Cody and his sister can come up with clever ways to cause chaos, but when their mother cries, they can be just as sorry and repentant.

As their older brothers and I entered the room, we were faced with the sounds of prolific weeping and sniffling. Mommy was crying, the maniacal three-year-old was crying, and his bamboozled sister was crying. They were all victims of their own emotions.

My wife, as you remember, must process her emotions completely before she can return to normal. The little ones usually turn to me for reassurance in these situations. And once they can see Daddy's calm, they stop their flow of tears as quickly as the turn of a faucet handle. Kids can do that. They can cry for hours before getting a shot at the doctor's office, but they start jumping around like happy beans the second it's over and done with.

After we'd all crowded into the room, the army of circus monkeys began shuffling and circling about their mother, the Rag Doll, as if on cue. Sackcloth and ashes would come in handy during these trying times.

We had gotten about halfway through the ceremonies of placation when Cody ran out of the room with that "quantum leap" look on his face. Pensively, I watched him sprint past me but dutifully returned to my somber mode.

Tiptoeing back into the room, he was carrying a wet and, unfortunately for his mommy, cold cloth from Siberia. He put the noble ice rag on her forehead with all the care and kindness of Mother Teresa.

"It's okay now," he said. "Isn't that better? You stop crying now?!"

He asked with a cute whine that, all in one breath, curled into the deflection of a terse declaration, leaving no room for doubt that the crisis had been "Cody-resolved."

Even though his mother was still clinging to the last, fading syllables of her lament, Cody promptly removed the cloth. He folded the cloth ceremonially and hung it over the open door of the antique Queen Anne dresser.

Turning to his mother with one outstretched arm, he gestured to the hanging cloth with the other. It is a picture framed in the memory of my heart. He looked like Michelangelo's Adam in the Sistine Chapel, with his arm outstretched to touch the hand of God.

"Cody, leave it right here for mommy, for tomorrow's tears," he said softly.

Whoa! Cody the warrior was gone "out to lunch." Cody the Destroyer could not be found. We stood in the presence of Cody the Great, Cody the Soother of Souls, and Cody the Liberator.

He poured oil on the troubled waters, and they abated.

Cody understands the concept of an emotional crisis. His mommy has cried before, and he figures by now that he'll see her cry again. He doesn't mean to make his mommy cry, and he is genuinely sad when she does. If he can't prevent the cause (called Cody's growing pains), then at least he can help with the cure.

Cody's philosophy for his mommy will always be, "Keep a wet cloth handy, mommy, for tomorrow's tears." Maybe none of us really intend to make ourselves sick with "the worries" or purposely over-load ourselves so that we live at sanity's edge.

We're all a little sad—read: miserable—because we put ourselves last while putting everyone else first.

Life is a rainbow with many colors, and each color has many shades. Some of the colors cast shades of crisis. Hasn't someone ever told you there'd be those kinds of days when your equilibrium would be thrown into static disarray?

Okay, maybe they didn't say it like that. But maybe they said something like, "There are going to be good days and bad days. You can't run from them or hide from them. The best any of us can do is face them."

Wet cloths won't assuage our bad days, but they might make us feel better. More than anything, we'll always be prepared **for tomorrow's tears.**

Cody Naylor

BETRAYED

I was about ten years old when I figured out that my mama couldn't catch me anymore. Effective discipline in my family was measured by my parents' ability to grab a hold of me and "jerk a knot in me."

It was always a mystery to me how my parents thought it was scientifically possible to grab me and pull me around, first one way and then another, leaving me in a triangular knot.

I'm sure they really didn't want me to suddenly knot up into a twisted Euclidean mutant. Asking them what it meant was a sure way to make them mad. "Oh, now you do want to get it, Mr. Smart Aleck," they'd warn. I never knew who he was, either.

I did understand that when Mama came running towards me, saying, "I'm going to jerk a knot in you, Mr. Smart Aleck," that I was in for it. I think it was all in the same category as being called a "knot-head." Being called a "knot-head" was, incidentally, a precursor to being jerked into a knot.

Left alone with Mama, I was potentially in danger of becoming the proverbial knot-boy. I know I exasperated her mightily because my kids exasperate me, adding veracity to the old saying, "What goes around, comes around." Or is it "What comes around, goes around?" I'm not sure how that goes. But if it comes around and you're standing in its way, you'll be sorry!

To say that I tethered Mama's emotions to the edge of my insane antics would be an understatement. But, in my mind, everything always evened out in this game of emotions. I pushed her closer and closer to a mental breakdown, and she kept me afraid of becoming the knotted son.

The year I turned ten, this threat began to lose its effect when I discovered that if I could get just a little head start, I could come out on top in any battle. After declaring that I was going to be turned into the knotted son—Geppetto style—the chase would begin. Suddenly, one day, I realized I had become old enough to outrun Mama, and for the first time in my life, she couldn't catch me. It was the turning point in the universal war for control that every parent and child must wage.

Mama never worked outside the home, making the two of us the primary combatants in this family conflict. That Daddy was not on the battlefield for most of the day was to my good fortune, because it would be quite a few years before I could cleverly avoid his grasp.

She eventually became a lot calmer in her older years, but in the distant days of my childhood, Mama was a ready slave to the pendulous emotions of her heart. She would get so mad at me that her body seemed to transmogrify before my very eyes. "Who was this woman?" the fears of my innocence would ask.

It was important to learn how not to get caught. When the attack came, it came ferociously. Her eyes bulged out like the cartoon characters that were still quite real to me. Simultaneously, her pupils rolled upward, hiding deep within her sockets. A Halloween cat couldn't have hunched its back as fiercely as Mama could. In the light, her werewolf-sized nails glittered brightly. Or so it all seemed to a ten-year-old.

Her favorite torture trick was to pinch, as she would announce maniacally, "a blue streak" in me. To add intensity to these special effects, she would part her snarling lips and grit her pearly teeth. I'm happy to report that I got through childhood without any blue streaks on my body.

From her mouth would pour a torrent of unbelievable condemnations. Like a seasoned ventriloquist, her gritted teeth remained in the battle kill position, unmoved. But I never heard Mama pronounce a vulgar syllable. And it wasn't because she was a minister's wife. Just the thought of such a probability was beyond her understanding. But, boy, was she creative in what she did have to say.

When she had used up her stockpile of the most popular condemnations, she would make up words with the ease of Shakespeare. They were words no one had ever heard before but whose meanings no one questioned. One time she ran through her make-believe dictionary until we all thought she couldn't possibly come up with another creation. But she did. Unpredictably, she yelled out, "*Blukey!*" And the naked absurdity of it made us all fall down laughing. We would hear this word often for the best part of a decade without ever knowing what it meant. To be sure, it meant for us to be cautious, whatever we were doing.

To have evolved to the point of successfully avoiding Mama's grasp was a revolutionary accomplishment. Mama never did much harm, but the special effects were cardiac.

Once I had cultivated the art of avoidance, I shuddered to think of ever again having to suffer the humiliation of getting caught. As my victories began to pile up, I became more and more fearful of slipping up. Once freedom had been tasted, nothing less would do.

I knew Mama could never hold a grudge. After she'd worn herself out trying to catch me, she'd have to lay down and rest. A little shut-eye, and she was back to normal, forgiving and forgetting.

She was not like Daddy, who would schedule spanking appointments to be held only in the intimidating enclosure of the bathroom. There's nothing worse than spending the whole day knowing you have a 7:30 p.m. paddle appointment in the hall bathroom.

I believe Mama was truly aware that her emotions could run wild at times and preferred the moments of timeout on her bed. Severe infractions would be turned over to my father.

She didn't play that wild card very often because once Daddy got involved, the battle took on an unfair advantage, with me always coming out the loser. Aside from that, she would generally concede defeat and chuckle out a firm warning, "Allllrighty, Mister, you just better watch out next time."

I loved my sweet mama then, as I did throughout our lives together. I still love her, even though she left this world years ago. I miss her mightily.

She never maintained a constant level of irritability on purpose, and the changes in how she felt often bothered me. Nowadays, I am sure she could be diagnosed with something to cure all the hell I put her through. The little boy's genetics of adventure, however, are predestined for chaos. This emotional game of "tag," initiated by my shenanigans, was merely an exhibition of adolescent survival instincts.

Not getting caught was a cardinal rule in maintaining the species of my boyhood. Remaining free from her grasp didn't mean I didn't care about her. I worried for her with tearful agony whenever she'd get sick or hurt. The truth is, I would panic. After all, she did take care of me all day, all week, all month, all year, anytime, anywhere, and everywhere. I had a valid interest in keeping her off the edge of the cliff.

She'd cut her finger in the kitchen, and I'd be afraid she was going to bleed to death. She'd cry like a baby after turning her ankle while chasing me, melting my defiant spirit, and causing me to cry as well. We fought and loved and wept and laughed together.

Sometimes I wish we could turn back the pages and do it all over again. I miss all those yesterdays.

Just to run... one more time, through that old house with its windows full of fans.

Just to squeal... one more time, like a springtime boy.

Just to hear... one more time, my mama's clear, young voice.

Just to feel... one more time, my thumping heart in wild escape.

Just to remember... one more time, the surge of my emotions, soft and pure.

One day I was playing in the kitchen while Mama was cooking at the oven range. A flash of fire and smoke caused her to jump and scream. I thought she was on fire. I just knew the house was going to burn to the ground.

"Come on, Mama," I screamed as I ran out the back door, "let's get out of here."

I didn't, and I couldn't look back. I ran around to the front of the house and kept thinking, "Where is she?" My eyes were glued to the house, expecting flames to burst through the roof momentarily.

I was moping around in the front yard, crying, and whimpering the death song that went something like, "My sweet mama is going to burn alive trying to put out that fire."

I waited and waited, but nothing happened. Finally, I reached down inside myself and pulled out enough courage to go back into the inferno. Slowly, I peeked in the doorway.

No fire.

No mess.

No charred mama?

The kitchen was tidy and straight, and I saw my mama dancing through the back of the house, softly singing one of her little happy songs like "Tweedly, Tweedly Doo" or "Jimmy Crack Corn."

At first, I was confused. I was thrilled that my mama was safe, and then I was angry that she had left me standing in the front yard without telling me that the fire was out, and she wasn't burned to a crisp after all. There she was cleaning the house and singing little happy songs, while I was out in the yard wailing a funeral dirge. How could she?

Mama could sing the prettiest little songs. Many were songs I had never heard anywhere else. I think she made them up the same way she made up her own words of condemnation.

Perhaps it was the feisty determinism of her creative spirit that caused her to face life with such unusual spontaneity. Great catharsis! Even better therapy. If you can't think of a word, make one up. If you don't know a song to sing, sing from the heart.

In the morning years of her life, she was a sweet, passionate woman who loved her chaotic children with uncompromising Christian devotion.

Never was I sentimental enough, however, to let my guard down all the way, because if I pushed the right button, "Jimmy Crack Corn" would spontaneously ignite into "Jimmy Crack the Whip."

Her life on the emotional edge had clearly made her touchy. I don't think I would have ever gotten caught and spanked again by Mama if my sister hadn't betrayed me. My sister was three years my senior. We got along, but we each had our own worlds of existence. Hers was the nineteenth century world of books. I should have known I couldn't trust someone who tried to emulate the world of Laura Engels.

But I did. And I should have known that given the chance she would betray me one day, somehow. And eventually, she did.

She turned the tables on me one day after I had provoked Mama a bit too much. I don't know whether it was the spanking I got from Mama or the feeling of betrayal from my sister that shocked me more.

How she could have done such a thing confused me more than anything I had ever encountered in my entire life. Despite how much I felt defeated, betrayed, and demoralized at the time, it became one of those growing-up experiences that helped prepare me for the real world.

How she could have turned on me that day is a mystery and would be a mystery to any kid who has learned to bond with their siblings as they daily confront the power of adults. It's sort of a thing kids do to keep balance in the home. It's not a modern thing to say, "I got your back, you got mine." And so, I felt we had an agreement to stand together in case of emergencies.

I especially don't know how she could have turned against me when she had recently waged a far greater battle against Mama than I ever had and WOULD ever have. Her war with Mama had become public knowledge on a trip to Grandma's.

We had made the thirty-mile journey to my grandma's house for our regular, boring weekly visit. The trip there seemed like something out of a Currier and Ives painting. Joyfully, we rode "over the hills and through the woods to grandma's house." Seemed like, but it wasn't.

The battle began in the car and escalated with every turn in the road. By the time we had reached Grandma's driveway, it had reached critical mass. Mama's emotions had been somewhat controlled by the strictures presented by the compact space of the car. But the car was stopped now, and the driveway became the battlefield.

Daddy had tried to stay neutral for the most part. He despised their fighting with a biblical zeal. That means, he tried to distance himself with the reserve of Moses and remain in his preacherly role of a non-combatant. Plus, he also feared Mama's wrath.

They squared off against each other like territorial wolves. Grandma appeared on the porch in her welcoming mode, smiling sweetly from ear to ear. Except for the front yard dog fight, it could have been an AT&T Thanksgiving commercial. I felt bad for Grandma that day.

As Grandma stepped off the porch with outstretched hands, my sister stretched out hers and slapped Mama's face with the force of a nineteenth century suffragette. Turning quickly on her heels, my sister ran like the wind and was halfway down the lower back forty before Mama could wipe the surprise off her cheeks.

Grandma froze in her tracks, Daddy's jaw struck the ground, Mama started crying like a baby, and I didn't stop saying "WOW" for about fifteen minutes. I suppose I truly realized for the first time that my sister was, indeed, waging her own war against Mama, which I knew nothing about.

So, let's go back to my fateful day running from Mama. Maybe you can understand why I was confused when my sister turned against me and joined forces with Mama to ensure my capture. Previously, in our wars with Mama, I imagined that my sister and I were sort of like the 18th century Americans and French fighting against the British. She had always been my ally. Unexpectedly, she became my Benedict Arnold.

At first, this appeared to be a happy fight, especially when I knew that Mama could no longer catch me. On this day, she had once again fallen over the emotional cliff and started chasing me with unusual zeal. It was raining outside, so the battlefield was confined solely within the house. But the mid-section of our house was constructed like a racetrack right out of Indianapolis, and I was confident that I could stay enough lengths ahead of Mama until she wore out.

Between the kitchen and the dining room was a swinging door. My sister had been watching this chariot race for about ten minutes when she slyly positioned herself near the dining room doorway.

I thought she wanted to be closer to the fray, and so I waved to her with a big, toothy grin as I passed through. I even thought she might be jealous and want to join in on the fun. Who knows? Maybe she would. I'd be back through in about ten seconds."Just wait a few secs, sister."

In ten seconds, my revolution ended.

I slammed into the swinging door with a thud. It budged a little but stood firmly shut. I tried again. It wouldn't open. I couldn't understand why it wouldn't open. It had no lock; how could this door not open? I needed this door to open!

It never entered my mind that my sister could be holding it shut from the other side. It was too late. I turned to check my rear flank in a split second, only to see Mama charging into me with the full force of the United States Army Cavalry.

As she stood victoriously over me, relishing her opponent's

capture, my sister peeked through the swinging door with the guilt of Judas written all over her face. I felt thoroughly defeated.

That day, I learned something that all siblings learn about one another as they grow up: everything is fair in love and war.

More importantly, we both had our own wars with Mama, but we both loved her with scorched hearts locked in truth with keys unique and secret.

Daddy Mama me and Vicki at my FIRST BIRTHDAY

REVISITING THE KITCHEN FIRE STORY
—THE SCIENCE TO UNDERSTANDING MEMORIES

Sometimes memories can be misleading as to actual events. It's especially common to find that another individual's recollections of the same experience might differ quite drastically from one's own. Does this happen without reason, or is there some explanation as to why people remember different things about a shared experience?

It does not happen without reason because when we encode memories, we do so specifically within the framework of our own brains. How one person processes and encodes those memories sometimes leads to establishing a long-term memory that is quite different from another person's.

When I was a small boy, I was Mama's baby. Being brought up in a home where I was the baby of the family makes it easy to understand how I might have had a closer relationship with my mother than most kids. Most kids in my neighborhood were part of large families. I chose to never leave my mama's side as much as possible. I am sure there is more than one event from my childhood where my mother and I might remember events differently, but the one great experience that is forever established in my long-term memory is the Great Kitchen Fire.

At the time, our house was far from most other homes, which were scattered far and wide throughout the countryside. It sat on top of a high hill, overlooking a large forest of pine trees. On this early morning, my mother was cooking with a large, iron frying pan in the kitchen.

The stove had been prepared long before I woke. As soon as I woke up, I ran to see Mama cooking my breakfast bacon in the pan over the fire. The smell of Mama's cooking always motivated me to move quickly from the bed to sit down at our tiny table. So, the memory is strong of admirably watching my mother prepare the food that day.

Suddenly, the fire seemed to leap out of the pan and attack the walls around the kitchen. Mama took action to try and contain the flames as they appeared to reach across the floor and strike me at my table. I jumped up and ran out of the back door of the house, crying for Mama to join me. I wanted her to hurry up before she burned to death.

As I ran out, it looked to me like Mama was fighting the flames from engulfing her dress. I ran around to the front of the house, crying and screaming for Mama. I waited and waited for a very long time for her to come out. She didn't appear. Not only that, but there was no smoke coming out of the house, no leaping flames, and no screaming cries from my sweet mama. Nothing!

Finally, I gathered the courage to run around to the back door and peek inside. There was Mama, sitting at the table, eating her bacon, eggs, and toast as she was humming the little tune she always hummed when she was happy.

When I entered the kitchen, there was no evidence of a fire, smoke, or destroyed walls, dishes, or tables. Everything seemed to be in perfect order. My mother thought I was silly when I asked how she could still be alive and where all the fire had gone.

We shared this experience with much laughter for many years.

But here is what my mother remembered about this event:

The grease in the pan splattered against her wooden spoon and sparked a little flash fire that was contained completely in the pan. As I was running outside for my life, she was throwing a kitchen towel over the pan, smothering its supply of oxygen. It didn't even burn the bacon. She wondered if I had just gone off to play and had no idea that I was sweating for my life out in the front yard.

For the rest of her life, I loved to tease her that while I was paralyzed with terror at the thought that my mother had burned alive, she was calmly sipping her coffee and singing melodies, eating her breakfast.

How could we remember this event so differently? A lot of it certainly has to do with how a child perceives, encodes, stores, and organizes events that are traumatic and life-threatening and what an adult would do with the same information minus the feelings of fear and anxiety. It didn't take more than a few seconds for this event to move from the experience to short term memory to long term memory storage.

The sounds, sights, and smells of this event became significant conduits for storage in my long-term memory for me, whereas they barely registered for my mother. She had almost forgotten about this event when I brought it up for the first time after I became an adult.

The only reason I think she does remember some of the details is because it has affected me so profoundly. As a child, I used elaborative processing over the years, which allowed the story to become "revised" and embellished with more and more horrifying details. Certainly, bits and pieces of it took on the character of a false memory. It is much easier to accept my mother's account, which makes no mention of fire leaping up walls and across floors.

This aspect of the memory no doubt prospered over the years in my mind by going through several revisions. It wasn't so much that my mother's misplacement of details was an encoding failure as it was the fault of my child's mind for this continuous, on-going revision.

My hippocampus, the workhorse of the brain, was working in overdrive. (Or if it helps you to remember that word better, you can call it the work-hippopotamus of the brain...FYI, hippo means horse in Greek.)

Anyway, the hippopotamus in my brain was building neural superhighways to secure this memory within my long-term memory —certainly because of the intense emotion that I had experienced.

Perhaps some of the things I thought happened, happened. Perhaps my mother cannot remember them because she never attributed much significance to the event, and over the years, through the process of disuse, she could have forgotten. Disuse could have led to the fading of memory traces.

One reason she remembers a few details of something insignificant to her is possibly due to her occasional use of just enough retrieval cues to keep the basic story in her long-term memory banks. And the only reason she would have done so is because she remembered, to some degree, how the event affected me.

She may have lost details because she allowed the interference of new memories to take precedence over less significant older memories. I know, there's a lot to unpack in this paragraph. Go back over it and read it slowly so it can sink into your brain. Then take a deep pause and get ready for the next paragraph!

Whereas, for me, the memory's significance has never faded. Nothing will ever interfere with the memory that I have established over the six decades since that happened. I would dare to guess that this was what social scientists refer to as a "flashbulb memory" because it was so intense and almost life-threatening.

The entire experience pops in my mind like the blinding flash of a lightbulb. Or perhaps I should call it my "flashfire" memory. Indeed, while it is a most intense and long-lasting memory, through the years it may have developed a thick layer of fiction over fact.

IN CONCLUSION, what I genuinely think about all this is something that I believe I can state in one long sentence. It's kind of dense, so hold on to your seats...First, I'll take a deep breath. Now here it is:

I think the simple key to understanding why we remember things differently sometimes has to do with how we respond to the event, how the chemicals within our brain guide us to label an experience as significant or insignificant, and how consolidation occurs to include or exclude the memory or to diminish or enhance its importance via revision.

The memory-place in our brains is a fairy tale kind of place where small fires that leap on walls and floors never really leave the pan.

And that's a fact of science you can take to the kitchen, folks!

THE SCOOP ABOUT POOP

"DADDY...DADDY...DADDY...," Cody Man's words gushed forth with the same speed he used for the "ath-ta-ta-ta-ta-ta-ta-ta" sounds of the G.I. Joe master-blaster gun. The title **"Cody Man"** got pinned on him one day and proved to be contagious with everybody.

"WHAT...WHAT...WHAT?" I mimicked back at him without getting up. We used to do a lot of shouting in our house. After six kids, I learned not to go running every time they wanted something.

Kids have an instinctive ability to "Pavlov-tize" their homes, conditioning parents to run salivating every time one of them screams for something. It happens. All the way from potty training days through prom night.

So, I just shouted back to Cody. I didn't know which room he was in, nor was I convinced, due to the nuclear-powered thrust of his voice, that I wanted to know.

He ran into my study and crashed against my legs. Looking up at me with a curiously cheesy grin, I knew a Cody-Fantastic kind of thing was happening (read that, toddler egocentricity). "What is it?" I asked, knowing I might be getting sucked in.

Giggling and gyrating to the tune of the jumping bean dance, it was obvious that he was Mutant-Ninja-Turtle-happy beyond explanation. He spun around and ran out of the room, squealing, "Mommy, Mommy, Mommy!" I was hooked. So, I went running dutifully behind the trail of screams until he found his mother.

Slamming into her legs as well, he nuzzled his snotty face clean against his mommy's pants. This business taken care of, he grabbed both our hands and jubilantly pulled us toward his little potty-chair in the bathroom.

"Lookie, lookie. Cody poo-poo, Cody poo-poo." He started hopping up and down like he was stuck on a pogo stick. Our "Cody Man" was flapping his arms and squeaking like Debbie Sue Carter used to when I'd put worms down her dress back in first grade.

"What a good boy you are," his mother correctly crooned.

One of the older kids had come to investigate, thinking they were missing out on something, and heaven help all our souls if they were to miss out on something.

There we all stood, softly oohing and awing, sounding like a bunch of fat pigeons.

Holding our noses, we gathered around the little potty and took part in one of the most important toddler rites of passage. The ceremony called for us to focus, meditatively, upon four little round objects clumped at the bottom of Cody's deluxe Fisher-Price toilet seat. I had thought they only made toys.

Cody gleamed with joy and seemed to stand outside the circle, as if he were the ringmaster for this show, saying, "Gather around everybody and see what the amazing Cody has done. What do you think of that?"

At the time, Chelsea was a little less than two years younger than Cody. And the puppy... Well, the puppy was a little less than three months old. For a couple of years prior to this event, there had been a lot of hoopla displayed around little potties and strategically placed newspapers. Our house was filled with a lot of jubilant shouting about pee-pee and poo-poo.

Our friends, who had neither kids nor puppies, didn't know quite what to make of us when, during a nice, calm dinner, everybody jumped up from the table and started screaming, flapping, and oohing. They would smile graciously at our shenanigans in a patronizing sort of way, and I know they were probably thinking, "So, that's what happens to you when you have kids." Well, that was certainly one part of it.

Such things were a lot more complex than they could ever imagine. It involved rituals and transformations that no one fully appreciated until they swam in the same pond.

Often, the insanity of potty training was laced with unexpected details. For instance, little boys eventually must learn how to stand up when they pee-pee, whereas little girls stay seated, learning how to tilt their bodies just right so their legs don't get drenched.

In addition, little girls must cultivate twice as many skills for properly managing that cumbersome and frustrating roll of toilet paper.

On the other hand, totally different antics surrounded the puppy's efforts. The kids and the puppy received high praise in their quest for an independent bladder.

But when Heidi, the puppy, would make a boo-boo and poo-poo in the wrong place, the "dogologists" taught us to cover the soiled area with coarse black pepper and shout, "No, puppy, no!" in a firm but fair voice.

Heidi the puppy would typically miss the newspaper by a few feet, necessitating the creation of a minefield of Kroger's finest black pepper to encircle the pre-selected newspaper zone.

The kids enjoyed seeing us try every night, in vain, to teach our dog how to use the bathroom properly. They liked getting all over Heidi about her poor potty habits. Toddlers love the opportunity to wield a little authority without getting into trouble for it. It wasn't often they got to shout "no" and get away with it.

On the day of Cody's revelation many years ago, I should have seen the writing on the wall in advance, but I didn't.

Not too many days after having watched this curious ritual, I walked in on Chelsea in the bathroom. She was sprinkling pepper on the floor around the little potty as well as the big one. She looked at me with that 'look-what-I-figured-out-aren't-you-proud-of-me' face and firmly shouted "NO, NO," followed by a reprimanding stomp of her foot.

Suddenly, I realized that she had taken one of those giant leaps of logic and decided that it wouldn't hurt to have a little bit of insurance in this unpredictable business of potty training, and while she was at it, the rest of us might as well have some too.

There were sure to be a lot of days ahead of us when a little bit of poop would be treated with shouts of joy in the land of the Naylors, but the lessons learned for Cody and Chelsea that week, and really for all of us, were fundamental ones.

They learned that what makes a family grow strong, healthy, and wise requires an unlimited supply of mutual love, praise, and support...and Chelsea might have added that it wouldn't hurt to spice things up with just *a little bit of pepper.*

MY GRANDFATHER FOREVER

My grandfather, George Thomas Hughes, was born during a time when the world was producing the Franklin Roosevelts as well as the Hitlers of history. When I knew him, he had already witnessed the feats of both the Wright brothers and Neil Armstrong.

It is difficult for me to wrap my head around the fact that it is the year 2023 and I'm relatively still a young man, right? But my grandfather was born in 1887. Indeed, he was a man of the nineteenth century.

The top of his head was thickly cropped with snow-white hair, enhanced by a wrinkled forehead ringed with sunburn. Taller than most of his contemporaries, he stood about six feet tall, slightly stooped. He was already an old man when I knew him, but he still carried himself with a prominent stance.

As I write this, it has been 52 years to the month since he died. It seems like an eternity. It seems like yesterday. I haven't seen him, heard him, spoken to him, or held him in more than five decades. Yet his presence is constant, pervasive, and abiding.

I walk through a crowded room filled with the sounds and smells of scores of people. Suddenly, I sense something that reminds me of my grandfather. Someone is wearing that cheap, watery hair tonic. I can't remember the name of it, but I can visualize the archaic glass bottle with its spiral tin top.

I'm in a different room at a different time. I hear a voice that pulls at my emotions. I hear it. I've heard it before. It is sweet and old-fashioned, generous and slow. It is soft yet authoritative. It's his voice, alright.

I know he's not there. Yet, for a moment, someone spoke a word or a phrase that resonated with the sounds of my grandfather's voice.

In these moments, I like to be imaginative. My grandfather was a devoutly Christian man. He believed with great conviction that one day he would sit in heaven as part of a mystic cloud of saintly witnesses and watch over this mortal race.

What an inspiring thought! Noble grandfathers are watching out for wayward grandsons! I visualize him as being a part of that great chamber in heaven, glancing earthward and spotting his loving grandson, and for a moment, he uses some power only saints can muster to transcend the boundaries of eternity.

Just for a moment, a fleeting moment, in a crowded room, he speaks through the mouth of some mortal and waits anxiously for my reaction.

I hear it! It has a sweet, generous, rasping southern drawl. "Hey, babe, I love you."

My sunny grandfather called all his loved ones "babe." Well, I know that such a thing does not happen, but those are the words I want to hear. I long to hear them.

What I hear are unintelligible familiarities. They're just a few muffled sounds, but behind the sounds, I sense the love my grandfather expressed. And once again, more than five decades after he left, I feel warm, safe, and precious as I bathe in the melody of my grandfather's voice.

Wait...there's more!

Once or twice, I've seen him standing across the street. Oddly, it's always at sunset when the glare of the sun, the dust in the atmosphere, or the reflections from glass windows and metal siding cast a spell upon my vision. Whatever the illusion, it appeared to be him.

No, I did not go running over to him. That's a fantasy bordering on insanity. There's an explanation for my hallucinations. Some lucky fella had the fortunate opportunity to look a little like my grandfather. It's the influence of the dust, the reflecting metal, and that misty haze at sunset that makes him seem so real to me.

No, I do not go running over to him. The gods of memory have been kind enough to couple the forces of nature with the powers of the heart to create an image of my grandfather, who "was."

And because he is the grandfather of the "was" and never again can be the grandfather of the "is," that is precisely why I cannot go running to him.

When these things happen, I just raise my hand and wave. He might wave back, or he might not. That part of the vision really doesn't matter. What matters is redeeming the memory, stealing the past, and feeling the strength of his presence just one more time.

The "was" of fifty years ago can become the "is" of those very special but passing moments. What matters is transcending five decades and realizing that the past is the present.

Emotions, so pungent and passionate from that time long ago, can flood my mind, my thoughts, and my heart and cleanse my soul. What matters is that, even after 52 years to the month, I can wave to this freak act of nature, this hallucination of the heart.

I can wave and mumble to myself and to my spirit, "Grandfather, I love you and I still love you."

So, if you happen to be walking in a crowded room or along a crowded street and, in the shadows of a drooping sunset, you see your grandfather, who was or still is, don't let the moment pass you by.

Smile.

Wave.

Tell him how much you love him. Oh, the magic **it** will work?

Grandpa Hughes, George Thomas Hughes, the sweetest man. After the house fire, I lost almost all of my photos of Grandpa. Mama had given most of hers away to relatives, etc. I think there are only 4 photos with Grandpa in them. In this photo, he is so young, about 21 or 22.

A TIME TO MAKE A DIFFERENCE

In the night...a long time ago...

It's 3:00 a.m. It's that time of night. The house is boiling, and I cannot sleep.

A million thoughts from yesterday's events lay like a rock on my mind. Mixed with this are the feverish ideas about what should and is likely to happen today.

The heat circles above my head, making me dizzy with sleeplessness. And the spiraling flux of dreams began, and dreams aborted frustrate me. So, I got up.

The flat heat and the drapery darkness shrouded in emptiness creepily coil themselves around the aspirations of my ideals, and I am suffocated by a pervading sense of vanity.

The Old Testament preacher in the book of Ecclesiastes said it a long time before I did. He said it. He felt it. And after a thousand sleepless, dreamless nights, he cried out in anger to the Great Creator of the whole show, "Vanity of vanities, all is vanity."

Out of his frustration, he asked, "What value is there to our labor?" or in modern slang, "Why am I working here? Why am I doing this? Does it really matter? Am I making a difference?"

Difference! Difference! Difference! It's a tough word, and it sinks like molten lead into the bottom of my conscience.

The house is still hot, and the weight of all my introspection has only served to escalate my frustration to a higher plane of somnolence.

In the distance, through the opaque boundaries of the shadowed night, I hear whispering down the staircase—a faint weeping of mumbled fears taking flight on the wings of tears.

I carefully listened to its consistency. The casual familiarity of it all piques my interest. I know who it is, and I know that the sounds are probably there every night, but sometimes the sanctuary of deep sleep becomes a merciful shelter from the notes of this melody.

The house is hot. I am so tired—tired of working one hundred hours a week. I search around for a cigarette, even though I quit smoking a long time ago. Just the thought of holding, lighting, inhaling, and exhaling gives me a vicarious bit of stamina.

Wedging my hand beneath the cushions of the couch, I feel the soft-papered body of wrapped tobacco. Cupping it gingerly, I pull my hand out slowly and straight. Unfolding fingers reveal the wayward Marlboro, and the memories of nicotine pump hard in my brain as my mouth tingles, wet and soft. Without striking a match, I enjoy the smoke from the first to the last make-believe puff and crumble the temptation to bits.

The temptation is gone, but the gentle cries are not. Behind the cries are the soft little mumbles that follow in refrain. So, I must do something.

It's something I've done many times before. There are not many variables in what can be done. I get up from the comfortable couch and tiptoe up the beckoning stairs.

At the top, I flip a switch that simultaneously turns on a ceiling fan and its decorative light, shaped like a drooping petunia. It makes shadows dance on the walls as it rotates, cutting through the awesome heat.

The door that leads me to the tempered cry is cracked open, and I slide through its space and back into the dark.

I turn around, tapping the door gently open. Light splinters the room's blackness with a triangular shape, giving subtle form to everything within.

Sitting hunched over on the edge of the bed is an elderly lady. Through her soft cries, she begs me to come and sit beside her.

Almost routinely, I move to her side and place her hand in mine. They are ancient and wrinkled, worn beyond even her years. Her hands are indicative of a harsh life.

A farming woman? A mother of many children? An unbending laborer? No! She never held a job or volunteered to work for others. She never married and would have never understood what it meant to conceive and bear children. She could no more have been a farmer than the farmer's seed could become the harvester.

On this night over three decades ago, she, along with five other ladies, lived with me, my wife, and our children in a teaching family home.

I wasn't there to help her construct grand theories that would bring about her cure. Why was I there? Oh, yeah, now I remember. It had something to do with why I couldn't sleep. Mine was a sleepless labor of love for the helpless.

But what value was there in this labor of mine? What good was I doing, really? "Emptiness, emptiness, all is emptiness." That is the quintessential translation of vanity.

To be filled with vanity is to be filled with emptiness. How can nothingness fill a void?

Ask any soul-searching insomniac, and they will tell you the answer.

On that lonely night, she leans her head against my shoulder while firmly grasping my hand. Kittenish cries become soft whimpers. The whimpering changes into a sweet hum. It has a real harmony to it.

It's not anything you might recognize. But out of this cry of despair, there grows a melodious humming. The tears in her eyes dry, and the tenseness of her fear dissipates. Her muscles relax as trustingly as she closes her eyes.

I stand up, providing support for her as I gently position her body between the sheets. As if in the hands of some great potter, suddenly and quietly, her body twists and turns into the security of the fetal position. Without opening her eyes, she snuggles her face into the pillow, signifying comfort and peace.

The little melody is still audible, but only faintly. I walked out of the room without having said a single word.

I didn't try to do a multi-step psychoanalysis on her or use the rhetorical logic of my rational world to give her advice.

I didn't try to talk away the dread of her night.

But I was there.

I did hold her hand, and I did become a shoulder for her tears. And despite all my doubts about personal validity and questioning the purpose of seeking the value of my innermost self, I did make a difference after all.

Indescribably, I flushed fully as I descended the stairs, feeling like a poet who had just finished a great sonnet. How can I make such a comparison if I've never been the poet who wrote such a sonnet, you might ask? Do I know how he felt? Maybe I do. Most likely, I can only guess.

Inspired by the *aria* of her despair, I became a silent poet of presence to augment the melody. Perhaps I cannot relate to the poet who writes the sonnet, but I bet we both finish our tasks with the same feeling.

It's the feeling of having made a difference.

Every season brings fresh opportunities. The season of modernity has brought with it a time to make a difference in the lives of others.

Difference!

Difference!

Difference!

Making a difference is the fulfillment of the emptiness that plagued noble old King Solomon.

I must make a difference for something greater than myself. There is a time in life when one must decide to make a difference in the lives of others. Making a difference needs to be prioritized and moved up to the major leagues of human conscience.

It's a way to fix the identity crisis that has been plaguing our culture for a long time. When refocusing on the needs of others can distract one from an identity crisis, egocentric petulance seems trite indeed.

The needs of others will keep track of time for those who give it.

They might need someone to come back every night and hold their hand in the same room of darkness. The commitment to difference must not submit to the constraints of time and effort.

Being an expert "people" person is irrelevant. The important thing is making a difference. The fact that one has to keep doing the same thing over and over merely heightens the permanence of one's commitment.

Making a difference is a holy act of reciprocity that mends forever the wounds of apathy and complacency.

That night, the bed felt guiltily good when I finally laid back down. My sweet wife felt wholesome and warm, and just lying beside her soothed my aching body and mind. Like my frail mockingbird upstairs, whose cries turned to melodies, my frustrations turned to peace and contentment.

At least for such moments, tomorrows are always another day, bringing...

New frustrations.

New challenges.

New opportunities for the commitment to difference.

On that night, long ago, my eyes became heavy, the room became dark, and the house became hot as I fell asleep.

LOST

"Okay, so everyone knows what to do if a stranger comes up to you and looks at you, talks to you, or tries to touch you, right?" I demanded it of my kids during a brainwashing session once upon a time.

"Yeah, we scream and holler for help, and we run away as fast as we can!" they answered in bored unison.

I remember proudly responding, "That's right! And what do we do if someone we know tries to do things to us that make us feel uncomfortable?"

"We scream and holler for help and run away as fast as we can," they giggled and yelled out as they ran away from their father, the catatonic taskmaster.

This conversation with my children might have seemed like the rantings of an overly paranoid parent to some folks. And perhaps I have placed an unduly harsh indictment against our society.

Images of violence, however, are an intrusive reality in American life. Newspaper headlines paint an unsettling portrait of a nation caught up in a fierce war against maniacal predators who steal our children in the innocence of their play.

The constant stream of news stories about horrible kidnappings only makes the atmosphere of fear worse and chokes our idea of freedom.

These circumstances have suffocated American morale and forced us to consider everyone a threatening suspect, potentially dangerous, and treacherous.

Once-reliable historical role models are no longer thought to be blameless in this scary game of human relationships.

We brainwash our children to expect the worst and inculcate in them survival techniques that only serve to alienate them from the great majority of people they meet.

Parents and teachers all over the country work together to change the way a generation of schoolchildren think, which gives innocent people a disturbing paranoia.

Sometimes I used to feel guilty about teaching a spirit of distrust to my children, and often it would bother me deeply. I remember when Chelsea was still a babbling baby in her crib, and I considered the possibility of restructuring my brainwashing curriculum.

The uneasy guilt of my wholesale condemnation of society had begun to taste bitter to my highfalutin, ideological taste buds. Perhaps I was unfairly instilling exaggerated fears in the malleable minds of my children.

Then two things happened. Like a farmer reluctantly putting an old mule out of his misery, I loaded the gun of family preservation and once again put the idea of innocent trust out of its misery.

The first thing that happened involved the disappearance of a little twelve-year-old girl not far from where we lived. She was found the next morning with a single bullet wound to the back of her head. I don't have to tell you that the parental juices of protectionism kicked in out of instinct when I heard that.

I suppose it could be paranoia, but wouldn't it be awesome if the things we do as parents to ensure the survival of our children were genetically programmed wisdom?

I mean, after all, if they found the fat gene, who's to say they won't find the "Parental Protection" gene?

The second thing that happened involved an oath I made once to never tell anyone what I'm about to tell you. It's one of those swearing episodes you make out of frustration and embarrassment, hoping no one ever finds you out.

It's not that terrible, but it stacks incriminating evidence against my ability to parent. No parent likes to have the office of parenthood scrutinized by long noses that have no business being there in the first place.

I reasoned that if I gave in to a moment of weakness and recognized my fault on this subject, I would be accused of poor parenting. That's why I kept my mouth shut.

Now that it has happened four times, I feel I have a civic duty to confess my sins and admit my guilt. Here it is: I have lost three of my six children a total of four times. (And that's a mathematical tongue twister in and of itself.)

They were four of the worst episodes of my life.

Four times of indescribable fear.

Four tidal waves of inundating terror.

Four merciless drenchings by the wild, debilitating palpitations of that famous 'fight or flight' thing.

Four...okay, that's enough; you get the point.

—FIRST, A SHORT FLASHBACK TO THE FIFTIES—

My mother says I got lost once. I was lost for three minutes. Losing a child should always be measured in minutes so that panic ratios can be worked out.

While standing at a crosswalk waiting for the light to change, I slipped down the crowded street of a real town in the USA. (Read that, Jackson, Tennessee.) Screaming and running, my mother turned up her radar and sought me out. She found me.

I don't remember any of the special gut-wrenching she experienced that day, but Evan and I both experienced enough nausea at Disney World to make up for it.

—RESUME NOW FOR LOST IN DISNEY WORLD—

The first time was in the Magic Kingdom. We were seven hundred miles from home, and all wrapped up in the degenerative experience of the family vacation. It was the last day of our little trip, and we were putting the icing on the holiday cake by visiting the world of Walt Disney.

We had practiced and practiced our what-to-do-if-someone-does-such-and-such scenarios, and everyone knew what to do if they got lost.

No problem.

I had the best brainwashed bunch in all the land of make-believe.

We plunged into the land of Snow White, Cinderella, and Tom Sawyer. "But remember," I said, "it's also the land of pirates and shipwrecked mates." We all laughed as I murmured something fretfully about trying to relax.

The day went great until it grew dark. The fabled "Parade of Lights" at the end of the day held people, long since deceased, glued to Main Street, USA.

We watched the storybook procession, dutifully oohing and awing along with everyone else. With a final triumphal appearance by Mickey Mouse, our misery was over.

Now came the time to begin the lengthy, three-part search for the automobile, which was parked near Pluto, which was roughly as far from the sun as the ninth planet. (Well, it used to be the ninth planet, until it wasn't.)

The crowd choked itself along that tiny representation of Anytown, America. First, we would have to stand in line again to board the sleek white monorail. Next would be the line for the tram that would orbit us around Pluto's parking lot six times before stopping. Finally, we would trek to find our lonely car crammed in with a million others.

"Let's get out of here," we all mumbled.

One minute we were all there, and the next minute one was missing. Like great waves from the ocean sweeping us along, we couldn't control our movement within the human *tsunami*. (That's the way the Japanese say, "tidal wave of death.")

Pushed forward by the billowing mass of flesh, hundreds, if not thousands, of people separated us from where we had been just seconds before. And nowhere, and I mean nowhere with a capital NO, in any direction, could I see my second-born.

Not hesitating a moment to begin my panic, I screamed with blood curdling authenticity, "EVAN, EVAN, EVAN, EVAN, EVAN." That's all I could say, over and over again.

Running in circles, I tried to retrace my steps but was staggered by the swelling crowds of people. I was climbing against a vertical slope.

The sea of people continued to move, push, and laugh. Why were they laughing? The torrent of this swaying, moving mass of people had washed away my young seven-year-old. No one stopped to help.

Couldn't they sense my panic? My despair? My urgency? There were so many children. And so many parents. Couldn't they tell by the strains of my voice that my child was lost?

Why didn't someone and everyone run up to me and empathetically say, "You've lost your child; what can we do? Don't cry! We're all parents here; we'll find him."

But no one did. And as I surveyed the crowd, I noticed there were OTHER people here—people without children. I hadn't seen THESE people before. They weren't riding in the boats in "It's a Small, Small World." Who were all these peeeeeople?

Suddenly, they all looked like serial killers and child molesters. MURDERERS ALL! Whirling around and around, I became dizzy with a ravaging fear.

All my planning.

All my indoctrination.

All the careful brainwashing was for nothing.

My child was gone, gone forever. I stared into the crowd like a midnight deer stalled before the blinding lights of an oncoming, driverless Tesla (an overused analogy, I admit, but I panic when I write about panic).

It was the most helpless feeling I had ever experienced. My poor little boy was lost in the dark.

So, so far from home.

Into the midst of so many people.

How could he ever be found?

An eternity of time had passed.

Nope! TEN MINUTES. Evan was lost for only ten minutes.

Now, that doesn't seem very long, unless you've lost your child. Old man time plays a dastardly trick on those who suffer from heart pounders like these. Elsewhere in the universe, the clock moves only ten small clicks.

When a parent is sick with the thought that their child might be gone, time moves into a dimension where nothing happens. It doesn't go back to normal until the fear is gone.

Every time I had a moment of doubt, time paused mockingly in front of me, dragging out the ungodly dilemma.

"Wait a minute," I thought. "Evan isn't lost. I'm the one who's lost in this crowd. He'd know what to do. He wouldn't walk up to just anybody and admit his predicament: 'Hello, I'm a little boy, and I'm lost.' He wouldn't say that to just anybody. Why, that would be tantamount to alerting the predatory snapdragons." (Look it up, it's more than a simple flower.)

No, they'd have to be wearing the right uniform and act like they knew a little about something. He is, after all, my son, regardless of how old he is. And he's sure not stupid—at least, please God, not today. No, not with all the propaganda his old man has stuffed into his head.

A good dose of composure was what I needed to stop acting like the donkey with his tail pinned to the wall.

"Stop being a blind mule and loosen yourself from this crowd," I ordered myself. Besides, the crowd by now was starting to annoy me in a Yosemite Sam sort of way. (Come on, you remember Looney Tunes, right?)

What would I do? What would you do?

There was a real-life Goofy character leaning against a poor little maple tree close by. He looked trustworthy. I'll run over and ask, "Just where are the real authorities around here?"

I mean, everybody couldn't be a fantasy character, even in Disney World. There had to be real people here that Evan could find and turn himself into for safekeeping.

I burst through the *madding* crowd. (Please, I'm trying to provide some education here. You know, *Far from the Madding Crowd*, by Thomas Hardy?) Now my search had purpose and direction. Goofy had disappeared in the meantime, swept up into the human torrent, I feared.

But wait, there in the distance was Alvin the Chipmunk-looking thing. He'd know what to do.

"I need to find the security department. I need help quickly," I trumpeted into his elephantine ear.

Now, I'm not usually one for fate or coincidence. Too much reality has wrecked my life for such nonsense. Generally, if unusual things combine to produce a happy ending, most folks attribute it to good luck. Whatever you want to call it, it was weird.

I mean, it was a "surreal" intervention.

I swear to all the idols in Hollywood, I'm not lying to you. Alvin looked at me and mumbled through his big plastic mouth, "Did you lose a little boy named Evan?" My mouth fell wide open, and a chill ran up my back that would've made any televangelist gyrate every which way but loose.

"Where is he?" is all that I could say.

And now, allow me to apply some parallel academic contemplation free of charge.

Since that hairy day (I know, hairy is such a disgusting word, right?) I've learned that famous quantum physicists, like F. David Peat, have put scientific teeth into the enigma of coincidence.

They call it *synchronicity*.

In a layman's nutshell, this means that events of coincidence will happen in life. They'll happen all right, but only if they have meaning. Well, you can believe that this Disney World nightmare had the full measure of meaning for me.

How is it possible that two lost people (because, believe me, I was just as lost as Evan) could find one another against such insurmountable odds? We were lost in a sea of Disney creatures, as well as an army of quasi-real Disney slaves. And what about all the patrons like us? How is it that Evan and I could turn to the same person for help? I don't really know how, but we did.

Why not Mickey Mouse, Goofy, Donald Duck, or the college student who runs the gift shop?

Why was it a chipmunk? A chipmunk!

I've tried to figure out the comparative psychological meaning of all of this as it relates to me and Evan and that kinetic energy stuff flowing through our lifeblood, but I just can't do it.

Maybe I'm just not smart enough.

Sometimes it's just a chipmunk!

Or maybe this father and son have a bond of synchronicity that lends validity to this bizarre branch of quantum physics.

Or it could have been just good old fashioned, earth shaking, mountain moving, hair-raising Providence. And I do mean with a capital P. Physics merely modernizes it. If there is a God who works in mysterious ways, who says He can't use chipmunks? As well as, I suppose, physicists.

Evan was sitting on a bench in Disney's Main Street mock-up of a nineteenth century police precinct. It was a place for lost children.

We embraced. We cried. We cried some more. There was no

scolding. No one could have been to blame. It just happened, and now that I had my little baby back in my arms, nothing else in the universe mattered.

I was so thankful that Disney had a place for lost children. But it wasn't really a place for lost children. It was a place for parents to find hope.

My search had seemed hopeless, and right then and there, I vowed before heaven and earth to never let this happen again. Besides, I didn't think my heart could take it.

But it did happen again. Three more times—

Each time it happened; I made the same declaration: "I just have too many kids."

I know what you're thinking. How could I let such a terrible thing happen so many times? I must be a miserable parent. You're thinking that, right?

—A MOMENTARY FLASHBACK TO THE FIFTIES—

My mother says I got lost once. I was lost for three minutes. Losing children should always be **quantified** in minutes so that parallel panic ratios can be calculated.

While standing at a crosswalk waiting for the light to change, I slipped down the crowded street of a real town in the USA. (Read that, Jackson, Tennessee.) Screaming and running, my mother turned up her radar and sought me out. She found me.

I don't remember any of the special gut-wrenching she experienced that day, but Evan and I both experienced enough nausea at Disney World to make up for it.

—BACK TO FUTURE: LOST IN PRINCETON—(Before college age)

Joshua got lost when he was eight. He wandered down a serpentine creek bed that lay behind our house. Joshua holds the record for being lost the longest, at 192 minutes.

At the time, there seemed to be something less frightening about this fiasco, knowing that he was somewhere in the neighborhood. In hindsight, after spending the last twenty years watching murder documentaries on Netflix, I feel like I know a lot about how neighbors can sometimes kidnap kids.

Well, the hunt for him was the kind that carried more anger than fear. Had we not just moved to the area, I would have been less concerned.

Unfamiliar surroundings, I believe, elevate the status of our fears.

My first barrier was that picturesque "Home and Garden" creek behind our house. I began by trying to walk on the bank. It became too difficult, and I abandoned my efforts to stay dry. I plunged into the middle of the creek, more fearful of toxins than life forms. After all, it was in New Jersey.

I splashed about with greater determination than anyone has ever splashed about in a New Jersey creek, I suppose, and I lived to tell about it. suppose. A mile and a half I splashed forward, and a mile and a half I splashed back.

I was defeated momentarily and decided to return to home base for refueling. I dragged myself through the garage, heaving from exhaustion, not knowing what I would do next.

I leaned against the large Lifestyler Electronic Ergometer, one of those horrible physical fitness walk-you-to-death machines, to unlace my muddy shoes. I might have to start exercising on that apparatus one day. Right then, it seemed to mock me with every wheeze I made.

AND THEN I SAW his muddy little shoes, his muddy little pants, his muddy little shirt, and his muddy little socks (read that part with a whiny, sarcastic voice). A puddle of oozing goo surrounded them as they lay crumpled up by the back door.

Where, oh where, is my muddy boy now? He was soaking in the tub, hiding beneath white bubbles. My wife said to leave him alone.

Oh yeah! Why not bring him a candy cigar and a glass of cool, bubbly soda pop?

He had become disoriented two miles down the snake-like creek due to the dares of his deceitful compatriots—eight-year-olds all! Since they were seasoned veterans of the terrain, they left the security of the creek bed and ventured off into the woods.

Joshua had been told to stay within the confines of the creek's banks, and he would never get lost. Afraid of being lost in what seemed to him to be the wilderness of the forested moon Endor, he scrambled after his friends only to lose them in the thickets.

He walked along the street calmly and resolutely, knowing that he would somehow find his way home. Knowing better than to talk to strangers, he knew he'd have to talk to somebody.

The flashing images of kidnappers that had been placed there by his paranoid father gave him a headache smack dab in the middle of his muddy little conscience.

Yet, finally, he decided that if the people who lived in these homes were in our very own neighborhood, then they really weren't strangers but friends. Talk about leaps of insight!

Gathering up the full complement of courage that an eight-year-old can muster, he marched to the front door of a friendly-looking house and emphatically pronounced, "Hi, my name is Joshua Naylor, and I'm lost." According to his kidnappers, er, I mean friendly neighbors, he then broke down in tears as if on cue.

The kind couple was on their way to a wedding, regaled in a sequin dress and tuxedo. They took him in, offering him a cold Coca-Cola to quench his thirsty despair.

Exhausted, compliant, defeated, teary-eyed, and loving, our little boy came home to us and was showered with all the love we could give. Then he was grounded for thirty days, lovingly, of course.

—ON BEING LOST TWICE—

—Round One—

Cody-Man (you should've known I'd get to Cody sooner or later) walked out the back door one day when he was supposed to be taking a nap. No one saw him. We had several friends over and were caught up in those things that friends get caught up in.

Our little forty-pound sweetheart was merely eighteen months old. Just by chance, we checked in on him not more than fifteen minutes after we had laid him down.

Cody had left behind an empty bottle, and we were able to calculate that based on the size of the bottle minus his sucking velocity (I mean, this isn't an exact science), he had probably been missing for about five minutes.

Eight of us bolted out every door in the house, screaming at the top of our lungs. Like a Disney World repeat, we acted like donkeys with our tails pinned to the yard, running around in a circle, bumping into each other, and finding nothing.

To the street, to the creek, and back to the street. Someone was commissioned to go back into the house and check all three floors. Racing back to the creek, I jumped dramatically from the bank into about two inches of water. He wasn't there.

But the creek led to the lake. All around our homes were these huge drainage pipes that led to the creek. And what about the neighbor's backyard pool? So many trees, so many bushes. The whole world appeared cluttered.

Despair, despair, panic, panic! Time locked its grip around my heart, and I froze in that all-too-familiar sea of hopelessness.

"HERE HE IS!" someone shouted. The clock started ticking again. The hunt had only taken six minutes. Cody had been gone for just a little more than ten minutes.

There he was, down the street, standing by the neighbor's pool, looking like Narcissus, admiring his image. CRINGE! Had we done all that running and searching in just six minutes? What prodigious strength!

I don't have to draw a picture of the reunion we had. We were separated for six minutes, and oh, how precious it was when we were "back in baby's arms." No wonder the first day of school is so difficult for parents. It's so hard to let go.

—*Round Two*—

Just when I thought it was safe to turn my back, almost a year later, I lost Cody again. This time, he was gone for a total of five minutes. We turned out onto the streets again.

Like idiots who can't keep the cat in the house, Cody had gotten loose again.

We ran, we huffed, we puffed, we screamed, we cried, and we cringed before the drainage pipe, the creekbed, and the swimming pool—all the usual suspects! Just when old man time was about to zap an eternal freeze on my mind and heart, I saw him playing in the back seat of one of my cars, safely parked in between two others.

Now, I don't approve of two-and-a-half-year-olds playing in automobiles, no matter how safely they're parked. But I'll take that over the neighbor's pool any day. I held him tight and once again vowed to never let this happen again.

As I carried him back into the house, I wouldn't let him down. Together, we hovered over Chelsea, his baby sister's crib. She was resting peacefully, impervious to the tumult around her.

For a second, her babydoll's ruby lips twitched. Or was she laughing at me? And then I thought, "I've got too many kids."

—**THE ALMOST LOST KID**—

ALWAYS PROTECT YOUR BABIES! On August 12, 2022, my life as a parent became level–SCARIEST! On the third day of school, Jenny, our 15-year-old daughter, was walking the two blocks to school, where she is a sophomore. Our subdivision is behind the school. No traffic, quiet living—walking less than 5 minutes to school.

Oozing out of the early morning darkness appeared a black SUV. Inside was a thirty-something young man, slumped down in his seat, alone. He pulled alongside her and started talking to her, then asked her where she was going. She kept walking. He slowly kept pace with her. He was saying something that she could not remember because she was so confused.

There was a little dog running around loose, as if it were lost. Jenny thought that was so odd because dogs must always be on a leash in our little universe of suburbia. To distract the man, she asked him, "Oh, is this your dog?" He immediately replied, "No, it's not mine. It's the neighbors (not which neighbor), and they have thousands of dogs...erected...I think they must eat their dogs like they do in China because they have so many."

Jenny did not let his cryptic words rattle her nerve, maintaining her steady walk.

He draped his thumb over the outside of his folded hand and motioned several times towards the backseat. She walked faster. He matched her speed. Finally, Jenny started crossing the road exactly behind the school, clearly visible, and he said, "Oh, I'm just messing with ya." He drove away.

Jenny didn't tell us about this until late that night. The next morning, at 7 a.m., when I made my police report, they assured me they had already arrested this man and he was still in jail. They couldn't tell me the specifics of his arrest, but I was guaranteed it was the same individual and that we should consider ourselves safe.

All I can say from this experience is: "ALWAYS PROTECT YOUR BABIES." As a parent, you are never too paranoid to stop teaching them about the dangers of our changing world. From now on, I will be walking and watching with Jenny. Do you think our children have matured enough and might no longer fall victim to every parent's worst nightmare? No matter their age, you must never think that.

Every image of every horror kidnapping documentary I have ever seen flashed before me all through that night. The more I tried to sleep, the angrier and more defensive I became, and when I learned about his arrest, I almost exploded with fear, but I was thankful that Providence was watching over her.

But I think God watches over all his children. So how does such evil happen to others? Because evil is strongest where evil lives, and love and perseverance aren't always strong enough. That is why it is important for parents to always be vigilant...vigilant...vigilant with their children.

Keep the night oil burning, even in the daylight!

Perhaps we can never do enough to protect them, but we must do all that we can to guarantee they stay safe and sound from the furies that dance in the shadows. Keep them safe, and don't lose your kids!

Evan Naylor, sixteen-years-old

RESURRECTION BUNNIES

Coming up with something new and zany for the Easter Bunny to pull off used to keep my kids guessing all year. It was a concern that even popped up in the middle of the summer when we were sizzling like strips of bacon on the beach.

This business of being the Easter Bunny was one of the longest jobs I was ever able to keep, the other being Santa—almost 40 years. Too bad I can't put it on my resume.

It would look pretty good on an application, especially that part where you get to tell all about your previous job responsibilities:

"Faithful and loyal to the task. Creative. Have taken initiative in beginning and executing multi-task projects. Never missed work in forty years. Good with eggs and chimneys."

Easter has always been a starting point for me. Spring cannot truly begin without the passing of Easter. The years they (the gods of calendar computation) mess up the holidays, causing Easter to end up near the tail end of April, inspire me to delay spring defiantly, philosophically speaking, of course.

My Baptist-preaching daddy loved and hated Easter. And we used to commiserate with him in his *angst*. He hated the hypocrisy that brought out all the "once a year" members. "Easter morning Christians," he called them.

Dressed in brand new clothes and sporting a newborn religious conviction, these backsliders would fill the church to overflowing.

The deacons would haul uncomfortable brown metal chairs from the recreation hall to place up and down the aisles so that the sinful masses might be appropriately accommodated.

Daddy despised the audacity and blatant pomposity of these once a year saints.

But he loved Resurrection Day and all it implied. For my daddy, Easter celebrates the risen Christ and the promises of renewal and empowerment, as well as His promise of a Second Coming. The Christ of Christianity did come again for Daddy. Every Easter.

It was evident in the enthralling delivery of his Easter sermons and in the sacred aura that surrounded him.

However (and this is a BIG however), Easter is also Bunny Day. And Daddy hated that part about this holy day too. He tolerated it, and over the years, he was swindled into supporting the baby chickens and rabbits, both real and chocolate, and candied egg rackets.

We'd always have the Super Giant Easter Egg Hunt out on the church lawn every Easter Sunday afternoon. He hated that too. But he had kids, and the old ladies at the church excelled at giant egg hunts. What else could he do?

So our family grew up loving and hating Easter. Along with our conscience-ridden father, we despised the annual hypocrites. And while Daddy would become enraptured by the thought of the resurrected and returning Christ, we'd wait anxiously for the magical coming of the Easter Bunny.

The Christ of Daddy's sermons did come to him every year, and so did our Easter Bunny. And the Easter Bunny has been faithful to arrive at our house and the house of my children every year for more than fifty years.

I will never forget Cody's first really wonderful year for expecting the Easter Bunny. I mean, as a baby, he wasn't old enough to know anything about the Easter Bunny. But after he turned three, he was old enough to start hungering for Easter Sunday way ahead of time. COUNTDOWN!

"How many days until the bunny comes?" he started asking in October.

His expectations had become so huge by spring that I knew the Easter Bunny would have to come up with something fantastic to maintain his credibility.

So, I bought two hundred of those cheap plastic eggs—the kind you get at Walmart that pop open in the middle and only cost a dollar for a bag of fifty empty ones. Every egg seemed to be a different color. I didn't know the rainbow of modern colors had become so crowded. They were bright, fluorescent, and oppressive to the eyes. I thought I'd go blind looking at the darn things before I finished my scheme.

I spent half the night before that Easter Sunday stuffing them with little jellybeans, candy eggs, and pennies. We prayed for a sunny day.

The dawn cooperated beautifully, and I, the Easter Bunny, went outside and scattered two hundred eggs across our yard like a farmer sowing seed. I was hoping the neighbors were still in bed.

Then I sneaked into the kids' bedrooms and took great pleasure in waking them up. They wake me up too early on the weekends, and being able to return the favor did my psyche good.

"The Easter Bunny has come and left stuff all over our yard," I shouted, like I was kind of put out with that crazy bunny for having the audacity to do such a thing.

"Where, where?" They scrambled around for shoes with their eyes still half-sleepy-shut.

Stumbling out the door, they focused slowly on the bits and pieces of colored eggs tucked away in nesting patches of weeds and grass. Then, heaven forbid, total chaos broke loose.

Cody and Joshua moved like fighter pilots that Strategic Air

Command had just called up. Swooping up their Easter baskets, they raced out the door and brooded over the yard, looking for the magical eggs laid by a rabbit.

Another Easter, another promise kept. The bunny had come again and left his bounty strewn across the lawns of those who had believed.

Once upon a time, I used to be a church pastor. A few years before Cody's special Easter, I was pastoring a small church in Indiana. I had spent a great deal of effort preparing my Easter sermon and had driven everyone around the house a little bit crazy talking about it. I remember feeling like everything had gone off without a hitch and my Easter oratory had been a smashing success.

The week after Easter, I heard Joshua in the backyard singing a little song he'd made up.

"One day...He's com-ing ba-ck. Com-ing ba-ck, oh, one day he's com-ing ba-ck."

I was so proud. He had finally understood the real meaning of Easter and was obviously singing about the Second Coming of Christ.

Or maybe not. I saw an opportunity to gloat a little about having helped him find this great spiritual truth, so I went out to ask him about his song.

"What are you singing, baby?" I asked proudly.

"Oh, I'm just singing 'bout some special things," he sang to me.

Thinking he was too embarrassed to talk about it, I left him to his sweet singing. As I opened the back door, I heard the precious song one more time, but this time there was an unexpected addition.

"Oh, one day he's coming back; yes, one day the Easter Bunny is coming back."

Well, I didn't feel like I had failed. After all, we can't expect kids to understand theological things like us adults, can we?

Through the years, I have learned one thing about Easter Sunday. Some of us learn to look for the resurrected Christ in our lives, and some of us learn to look for magical bunnies.

The older we become, the more the objects of our anticipation hopefully change, just as we ourselves hopefully change.

Young and old, all of us learn to anticipate the winds of hope that events like Easter and springtime bring. With its arrival, the renewal of our faith in one another and the world around us begins afresh.

Joshua Naylor all grown up

OF PIGS AND PROMISES

The banter in society is full of promises. We are barraged with the appeals of many that seek our patronage for their wares. Merchants, politicians, theologians, psychics, and charlatans competitively bargain for our attention with the bait of promises.

Car dealers guarantee us that their newest deal is the best in town and can't be beat. But really, their deal isn't much different from the dealer's across the street.

They'll try to convince you, though, that you can't believe the guy across the street because they may or may not stand by their product when your car goes, kaput! Four weeks and one day after you buy it.

At tax time, we hear promises from those who would do our taxes for us. Somehow, choosing the right agency to figure out our claims will make a tremendous difference in the amount of our refund. It seldom does.

Let's not forget the ubiquitous politicians with their broken promises of fixing the economy, creating new jobs, providing universal health care, balancing the federal budget, and making peace in all of heaven, earth, and even Pluto.

When has any of that ever happened?

The promises of others to heal our own inner weaknesses ring hollow with the sound of lechery. Am I lecturing? Oh, I'm sorry for making anyone think that they might be capable of finding the hidden secrets of their innermost selves all on their own.

Well, you can, you know? If you believe enough in yourself to search openly and honestly, no one else will find in you what isn't already there. You've just got to look deep enough and be willing to recognize and accept what you find.

The promises of suspect medical cures stink the worst. The nicotine patch was supposed to be the smoker's cure. They've decided now that it doesn't work too well, so the FDA approved it for the over-the-counter market, and you can find out for yourself.

Most smokers' therapists believe it's a matter of the mind, which responds little to gimmicks but mightily to the power of commitment. I suppose that because few people believe in it anymore, we shouldn't have to worry much about anybody buying it, right? Nope, somebody will.

One person's cure is another person's misery.

Old Mrs. Gander told me a few years before she died that her doctor had promised her total relief from a twenty-year-old sinus problem if she would submit to a series of operations. It had worked on others, and it would surely work on her.

Well, she agreed, and after five operations and forty thousand dollars, the over-the-counter antihistamines could still do a better job. What's good for the goose isn't necessarily good for the poor, suffering Mrs. Gander.

People make promises, no doubt with real and genuine intentions. Yet, for one reason or another, due to this thingamajig or that, they fall flat, often leaving our pocketbooks in the same condition.

So many promises go in default today that we are quick to say,

"Give it to me in writing first." But the courts are full of cases that deal with the broken promises of thousands of people.

Why is that? You guessed it. It's because we humans are not perfect (surprise), and it will always be our nature to make the best deals in life, whichever way seems easiest.

The bargaining chips of human nature are not infallible, and the best of promises will sometimes lie fallow upon the ruins of good intentions.

Yet, one of the greatest reasons for keeping memories fresh in our minds is that oftentimes they provide us with examples of the things we need most. One of the things we need today more than ever is the ability to keep our promises. The power of a promise comes to its fullest meaning for me when I remember **"The Case of the Raging Hairy Pigs."**

When I was about six years old, there was an old, retired schoolteacher who was a member of my father's church in Chesterfield, Tennessee. She was a seasoned old lady who had graduated from what my daddy used to call the 'school of hard knocks.'

Retirement had softened the mean streak in her, and I remember her as a firm but sweet woman. The kindness of her heart seemed to radiate through the deep wrinkles in her face. She spoke with a throaty, authoritative drawl that sounded just like what you might expect from an old-fashioned country schoolmarm.

She lived alone way back in the woods on an old pig farm. To my little eyes and my little mind, it appeared to be an eternity's distance from civilization. I always enjoyed going to Miss Ida's, whom I mistakenly referred to as Miss Idam.

As I recall, Miss Idam could make the juiciest red-eyed gravy and the thickest, softest homemade biscuits ever tasted by the *Homo sapiens* species. Of course, along with all that came the *pièce de résistance*—deeelicious country ham. She kept a drove of pigs, you know. And, oh yeah, she kept some mighty powerful promises, too.

Whenever she would invite us for dinner, she would warn me explicitly not to get too close to the pigs. She didn't raise the sweet little piggies of Charlotte's Web fame. She raised mean razorbacks. Hogs from hell, from which steel could be forged with the wiry stuff called hair on the spine of their backs.

As I can remember, there were one or two mean old mama pigs that were constantly dreaming of the day when some little chubby boy like me would fall over the fence into the muddy pit that was their world.

The endings to these horrific admonitions would always conclude with something like, "And they'll suck you up through the holes in their giant snouts." Miss Idam could tell a good story.

When we are small, anything with such vivid detail sounds convincing coming from almost anybody, especially when told with the rasping gutturals of Miss Idam's southern drawl.

Today's sensitive critics would label her a crooked old maniacal psychopath, but that was just Miss Idam's way of making sure I stayed far and safe away from danger.

Miss Idam must have had a strong sense of presence even for all the grown-ups in my world. Because when Daddy would go away on one of his two-week revivals, he'd send Mama, my sister, and me to Miss Idam's farm for safekeeping.

Her farm was so far back in the woods that we'd have to stop to open and close three pasture gates just to get to her house. Her two-story white frame house nestled serenely against the banks of a gurgling creek bed. Her farm was a living Christmas card.

The stream was brimming with freshwater catfish sporting prickly feline-like whiskers and dotted with steppingstone rocks made flat and smooth by rushing white rapids. Life down on Miss Idam's farm was fantastic for little boys who needed a place to run and play.

As bucolic a setting as it all appears in the storage centers of my brain, less appealing images also linger. They are images of ravenous packs of predatory pigs, instilled by the graphic depictions in Miss

Idam's tales. She would never let me forget the ferocious potential of boy-eating pigs, no matter how idyllic everything else appeared to be.

During one of those endless sleepovers at Miss Idams' house, I made a promise to myself to check out the dark, wooded pit where the monsters lived. A delicious meal full of cholesterol (no one cared back then) gave me new energy and the strength to face enemies I had been avoiding for a long time.

The "women folk" (that means everybody except me) were busy cleaning up the kitchen when I seized my opportunity to sneak away. I slinked off the back porch and dashed toward the forbidden and forbidding pigsty.

I had always seen the fence from a distance, but never the pigs. The pit covered several acres and reached far back into the deepest, darkest part of the bottomlands. The trees were as thick as the blades of grass in the yard that bordered the fence.

Smashing my face breathlessly against the wooden gate, the foreign earth beyond its cracks appeared pocked with giant hoof marks, odd and mysterious, like moon craters.

The mind of a small child really believes the most unbelievable parts of the scary stories that grown-ups tell. But there's something magical in a hair-raising tale that pulls, tugs, and taunts little boys and girls until they must find out for themselves just how true it all is.

"It couldn't be true," I rationalized, "pigs are so cute, like the one that goes to market and the one that stays home, and the one that cries 'wee, wee, wee' all the way home."

After completely convincing myself that there could be no harm in simply looking at these pigs, I decided to call for them. My "here, piggy, piggy, piggy" didn't quite get it, and so I prepared to climb over the fence to find them.

I scrambled over the fence only to discover that nothing had happened to me, and I was still in one piece.

"There's nothing to this after all," I thought.

Like a six-year-old should, I danced around in idle fascination, jabbing a stick into the air with adroit swordsmanship and kicking the clumps of moon dirt with disrespectful abandon. I seemed to be safe.

I peered into the impenetrable darkness of the distant pig forest. There was nothing but blackness, and since blackness represents nothing, there was nothing here to be afraid of. Aha! It had all been a charade. It's all just another lie from the world of grown-ups.

And then, suddenly, piercing the silence came the sounds that I had always imagined hell must sound like after Daddy finished preaching about it. Frozen in fear, I couldn't see anything, but the sounds echoed louder from the heart of the Black Forest.

The ground seemed to shake as the air thickened around me, and then I saw them.

These were huge, hairy monsters from a science fiction movie!

No, they were Miss Idam's pigs, as big as the backside of that rustic farmhouse that serenely nuzzled the creek bank, which was exactly where I wished I was at that moment.

It was a hoof race (they had hooves, I had feet), and I was the prize. Defrosting my fear, I turned to jump across the fence to safety. Mystically, the fence had moved further away from me, and when I finally reached it, I realized it had grown taller as well, making it impossible to scale.

Spinning around, I braced myself against the wiry mesh and began to cry with a breathless sort of whimpering. No one could possibly hear me, and thus, I would die just like the curious cat that Mama often read to me about.

Turning to clutch the fence and shouting once more for help, I could see through my tear clogged eyes the big frame of Miss Idam beating a pace slightly quicker than the hellish hooves behind me. "Come on, Miss Idam!" my heart sang.

But, as the fleeting seconds passed, my vivid imagination began to wonder, "Will she help me when she gets here? She warned me so many times to stay away, but I didn't listen. She may be running over to get a ringside seat to heckle out, 'I told you so, I told you they'd eat you up.'"

As I snapped out of the gruesome daydream, two heavy arms of steel swept me high and quickly over the fence. Miss Idam grabbed a large limb of Oak and hurled with Olympian agility over the fence, standing like a biblical Samson confronting the Philistines.

Dust enveloped the air, and I was blinded for a moment. The pigs had come to a furious halt when confronted with the fury of their master. Her voice boomed with supersonic velocity as she turned the tide of the raging, hairy horde. She had, after all, the power to make them into bacon. They disappeared into the darkness of the woods as fast as they had appeared, squealing all the way.

When it was over, I was afraid of the blessing-out I would get. Instead, she picked me up and showered me with hugs and kisses. I don't suppose I had ever given it a thought how she knew I was in danger.

My pathetic whimpering certainly was inaudible, but I'll never forget her words to me, "Miss Ida knew you'd be out here with these pigs, just like she told you not to, so I came running. You ought to know Miss Ida wouldn't ever let anything happen to you." Again, she embraced me and kissed me as tears streaked both our faces.

That night, as I lay in bed, I became afraid because the moon cast an unusual darkness across the room, and I realized that Daddy, my usual monster killer, was not in the house. The old cherry canopy bed with its thickly feathered mattresses sat high above the floor, and the fear of lurking creatures beneath it frightened me even more.

Overwhelmed with my uncertainties, I began to think once more of Miss Idam. I could feel the strength of her hands and how mightily they had rescued me. The promise of her presence permeated the room. Again, I felt her hugs and kisses as I sank deep beneath the thick quilts, thinking everything would be alright because Miss Idam would help me, just like before.

I drifted off to sleep, reciting the warm security of her words, "Miss Ida won't ever let anything happen to you, I promise."

The memory of my dear, sweet Miss Idam's promise has served me well for over six decades. The echo of her words still empowers me, despite her passing over fifty years ago. She can't really keep her promise anymore, and I don't delude myself with the thought of some supernatural intervention.

The memory of her promise, compounded with the precious promises of others in my life, enables me to face some of the question marks along life's journey.

Ultimately, none of us can expect to keep all our promises, nor can we expect the promises of others to last forever, no matter how well intentioned.

Oh, but promises remembered can serve as guideposts in the never-ending search for meaning, purpose, and direction in our lives.

How so?

Mirrored in the promises of humanity are the promises of the divine. Miss Idam's promise was merely a reflection of her faith in God and in humanity. And that's the kind of promise you can take to the bank!

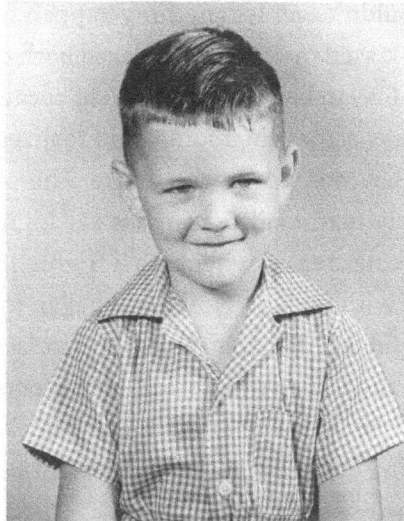

Six-year-old Jeffrey Naylor almost eaten by Miss Idam's Pigs!

WHEN IT SMELLS LIKE ANTS,
STOP THE CAR!!!

{*A disclaimer to this story: it absolutely does not apply to
***FIRE ANTS**...stories about those monsters from outer*
space appear in my second collection of memo-
ries....ouch!}

The windows were rolled down, and we were doing sixty-
five down the highway. Suddenly, the air stiffened with a
most familiar smell, and my nostrils exploded with the
scent of red ants. I put on the brakes and pulled over to the side of
the road. Bug-eyed, I looked at my wife and announced, "I smell
ants."

We hadn't been married for very long when we decided to take a
trip into the countryside for a few days, going nowhere in particular
but just wherever the road took us. I had pulled the car over on the
side of the old U.S. Highway 35 in Texas and stared with incredulous
eyes at my wife, like she was supposed to know what I was talking
about.

"What'd you say?" she asked in disbelief.

Oops! "Oh, didn't I tell you?" I whimpered innocently. "I can smell an ant hill from about fifty yards away."

She just glared at me with that annulment kind of look and asked, "What in Sam Hill are you talking about?" I don't know who he is, but in the south, anytime someone wants to really know what you're talking about, like within one second or less, they'll use the provincial phrase 'Sam Hill.'

The first half of my upbringing was in West Tennessee, where my kinfolk had lived since shortly after the Revolutionary War. During my early years, my father pastored rural churches. That means I was exposed to good old-fashioned country living just a few acres shy of life down on the proverbial farm.

In the 1950s, if you didn't have farm chores, there wasn't a whole lot for a kid to do living out in the Tennessee countryside. Well, I was the preacher's kid; I didn't have farm chores, and heaven help the cow or chicken that would have needed to depend on me for anything. So, I ambled around the pasture land that lay behind the church parsonage, looking for mischief.

Anthills dotted the landscape like a yard full of sweet gumballs. Today you can go to a newly retooled Toys R Us in Macy's (read the R backwards at your convenience) and buy compact little ant farm kits. Decades ago, two of my kids once created disasters with them.

I had scores of anthill farms stored away in the big gallon jars Mama rejected from her "canning" business. Yes, Mama used jars in her canning business. That's another story.

Anthill hunting was my number one job when I was a kid. I had them all: little ants, big ants, black ants, and red ants.

Sometimes I'd mix the colonies together and watch a full-scale war break out. Most of the time, I'd spend hours observing their faithful routine of getting and storing grub. They didn't have to travel far because I'd load them down with sugar every day. I was their Grubhub, sort of.

These were lucky ants, well fed. Why would they want to try and run away when there was no famine in the land? Yes, indeed, but often they did.

One morning I went to check on my jars, and the black ants were gone. Gently, I smacked the sides of the jar, thinking they might be hiding from the sun, but nothing happened.

Dumping the clods of dirt out onto the ground revealed an abandoned civilization. Weaving trails marked the clustered clods, but they were like deserted highways leading to ghost towns. They couldn't have gone far. And so, I took off, trying to find them.

I didn't realize it then, but I think I smelled them out. They were out of the yard and over the fence, headed towards the rich, thick soil near Mr. Crabtree's pond. What was out here that could beat the sugary hearth of my jars? It didn't figure.

A couple of hours later, I'd have them back in their jar, safe and sound. They'd stay a few days before taking off again. "What was their problem?" I wondered.

Smelling out ants took to me like bees took to Mama's gardenias. As the biblical apostle once said, "By the time I became a man and put away childish things, I could give an anteater a run for his money." Well, that's close enough...

Freedom!

The ants wanted freedom. They got tired of being creatures that got drunk on the unearned syrup sprinkled at their doorstep every day. Like the children of Israel who got tired of living off the rich, fertile soil of Egypt, they too went looking for a Promised Land of wide-open spaces of freedom.

I appreciate their unwavering tenacity now. I didn't care much for it as a kid. Respect for the freedom of ants is hard to cultivate, but I've learned a lot from these little creatures of the soil.

I've learned that all creatures deserve some level of consideration. The drive to be free and exist on self-determined terms is a common thread among all the creatures on planet Earth.

Collecting ants and cultivating ant farms isn't allowed in our house anymore. Catching a whiff of nearby colonies still makes me want to hunt them out, but only to see what they're up to and to admire the faithful movements of their laborers.

One day, when Cody was about four, I watched him raise his foot with the caution of a skilled hunter and hold it suspended above a little mound of dirt.

He was aiming to start Armageddon against an unnamed civilization of tiny red ants. I tackled him to the ground with one swift swoop.

"What are you doing?" I demanded to know incredulously.

"I'm going to stomp those ants," he said, as he struggled against my restraining arms.

"Oh, no, you don't," I said, jabbing my finger in his fat, round belly. "Those are good little ants, with mommy ants and daddy ants, and little baby ants just trying to eat dinner."

Cody mulled the preposterous idea around in his head. I thought he was going to bolt towards the ant hill in defiance. "Baby ants?" he asked sweetly.

"That's right. Baby ants. So, we can watch what they do, but don't hurt them, okay?" I asked, knowing my hook had worked.

"Okay, they can be Cody's baby ants," he giggled with delight, "and I'll watch after 'em." I fluffed up with the fatherly pride of victory.

At the age of four, Cody didn't understand all the socio-economic principles involved in treating other creatures with respect, but he did understand love and care.

That's what I want to teach my children more than anything.

I believed that if Cody could grow up knowing how to share that love and care for the red ants in our backyard, he'd have plenty for all the Earth's creatures in backyards everywhere. It was my dream that this would be just one of many wonderful things he would learn from this encounter with newly found friends.

Only time would tell what else he'd learn.

On that day, ten thousand summers ago, as I walked away, I turned to admire him quietly observing the little community of ants. Then, suddenly, he started to look a little strained and bug-eyed, and I swear I thought I saw him sniffing the air in a southerly direction.

WHERE'S GRANDDADDY BOB?

Memories, memories! Granddaddy Bob made us realize once just how precious an asset they are. It was Thanksgiving Day, and everyone had gathered at our house for the traditional feast.

It was the first time that the Kentucky side of the family had consented to come to a "young folks" house, and we were honored and excited about maintaining their high standards of good food and fellowship.

Thanksgiving has always been a hectic time for family gatherings. Everyone is expected to be present, and a great deal of the day is devoted to catching up on the effects of the family growth process.

So, the conversation is generally consumed by a lot of comments like, "My, look how you have grown?" or "Whose boy are you?" and "Doesn't' Aunt Dorothy look like she's aged ten years since last Thanksgiving?" (Out of earshot, of course.)

There are usually too many gourmet chefs in the kitchen, too many sports enthusiasts professing to know as much about football as they say they do, and too many kids running and screaming out of control. And during so much chaos, it's easy to lose track of every-one's whereabouts.

It wasn't until we were ready to cut the turkey and give the annual family blessing that someone asked, "Where's Granddaddy Bob?" Granddaddy Bob was the ranking patriarch on my wife's side of the family, and lately, he had begun to display some peculiar habits.

It seems that during the summer, Granddaddy Bob started wandering off to places he had no intention of going and found himself doing things for which there were no explanations. So, the festive mood shifted somber as everyone became anxious about the whereabouts of one lost granddaddy.

On occasion, I used to have tiny glimpses of my past that were so minute that I would have to call my mother and ask if such and such a thing might be true or just the inventions of my dreams. One day, a memory surfaced about my great-grandmother, which proved to be a reality and not an illusion.

It was a memory from a time when families cared for the dying at home. Even though these families would have appreciated the advantages of modern medicine, they would have found the modern hospital a forbidding place to live out their final days.

We may have come full circle in this battle for privacy and dignity in death. Today, many have chosen to fight for the right to die peacefully at home, far away from the intimidating and demoralizing contraptions of modern technology.

Millions of the elderly no longer have homes but only a cubicle in an assigned retirement center. The advances of medicine have contributed to a swelling elderly population whose only recourse for supported living comes in industrial settings.

Almost seventeen percent of American adults are over the age of 65, and according to the U.S. Census Bureau, this will almost double in the next fifty years. Fast-paced living by most working adults has created an ugly picture of neglect in the care of our aging mothers and fathers. It didn't used to be that way.

My great-grandmother died at home at the age of ninety-six, and no one could say that death had cheated her from enjoying the fruits of life because she had lived a long, full, and contented life.

In the last waning days before her death, my mother would often take our family to visit her in hopes that we might store away some precious memories. Moments with her might be the only real treasure that she could leave for us little ones. I was only a preschooler, and though I only have this one memory from my many encounters with my great-grandmother, it is from one of those special visits so carefully planned by my mother.

On a cold, drab Sunday, we went once more to visit this tiny, frail, white-haired lady, who lay bedridden in a special room cordoned off from the rest of the house. When we first arrived, I followed my mother quietly and solemnly into that special room and became overwhelmed by its stillness.

It seemed to be missing something that I found in other rooms. Even empty rooms were more enjoyable than my great-grandmother's room. It was a lonely room, filled with the rhythms of encroaching death. Of course, as a little boy, I didn't know that death was stealthily trespassing, but kids know without understanding the heaviness that weighs down such a place.

Cutting my way through the unfamiliar thick air, I approached the bed and became frightened seeing her stretched out straight and motionless, like an ancient sleeping beauty waiting for her release.

"Was she dead?" I wondered.

She stirred with a groan that sent me scurrying for protection behind the security of my mother's skirt.

"Who is that?" She asked cryptically, like the old, blind witch in Hansel and Gretel.

"It's Voncille, grandmother, and this is Bubbie," my mother said as she pulled me from behind her and shoved me closer to the bed.

The Hughes family loved to humiliate us kids with little, fat sounding names.

"Bubbie? Is that you, boy? I bet you're so big. Come here and let me feel how fat you are," she said. (She was right; I was).

But I didn't like the way it all seemed to be matching up with the Grimm Brothers' tale. She pinched me hard, and a pencil thin smile etched itself slowly across the plains and valleys of her face.

"I haven't seen you in years," she mumbled, falling gracefully back into the dreams that enabled her to cherish life a little longer.

Clinging delicately and tentatively, as it often is for the ancient ones.

After the grown-ups had gone out and got set up to visit together for an eternity in the living room, what was a little boy supposed to do in a house like this? It was too cold to go outside, and so I decided that my great-grandmother wasn't so scary after all and needed company.

I crept slowly back into the room and hovered silently around the headboard.

"Great-grandmother?" I whispered with all the impertinent insistence of a five-year-old. "Wake-up!"

It was like putting a coin in the hand-shaped slot of the talking genie at the county fair, as she roused herself mechanically in much the same manner as before asking. "Who is that?" she demanded.

Remembering my lines from the first rehearsal with Mama, I spoke up, "It's Bubbie, Voncille's boy."

"Bubbie! Voncille's boy? I bet you're so big. Come here and let me feel you," she said while groping the air.

I giggled, let her pinch me once more, and ran out of the room, tickled silly. Overwhelmed with a fiendish idea, I would wait just a few minutes to make sure no one was watching and go in for a second helping. I wanted to see if she would do the same thing again.

The novelty of such a game fueled my pudgy mischief.

I went for it. On cue, she responded as if it were our first encounter. Three more times, I raced in and out of the room. Wow, this was fun. I suppose I could have done this all afternoon, but fortunately for my great-grandmother's sake, I got caught.

Each time, my great-grandmother performed exactly as she had the time before, dutifully pinching me as if it were the very first time. It was flabbergasting as well as exciting to me that she could keep doing the same thing over and over. The oddity of it all intrigued me.

Just what was going on here, anyway?

Mother's pinch from behind had a different effect when she caught me. Everybody in this family loved to pinch. I was made to feel ashamed for teasing my great-grandmother, although I still didn't understand any of it.

I felt guilty for the same reasons all the other five-year-olds feel guilty. Simply getting caught was the extent of my guilt.

In my innocence, I didn't know anything about the disease of dementia that had wrecked the last few years of an otherwise marvelous life. Very little was known about her condition in those days. "Old age" was everyone's diagnosis.

Today we call it Alzheimer's disease, and it eats away the memories, gnaws relentlessly at the dignity, and tears away at the center of a person's humanity. Those who suffer from it are emptied of themselves and become like walking ghosts, casting unrecognizable shadows of who they once were.

They forget who they once were, where they are now, what to wear, what to eat, and how to use the bathroom. No longer do they recognize their families or how to love them, because they don't know them, nor can they process the memories adequately with which to formulate expressions of love. They seem lost to themselves and to those around them.

It is a disease that severely damages the brain as well as the hearts of their families. There was a time when no one knew what to call this disease. My great-aunt Flossie spent thirty years in a locked institution, until she was almost 100 years old. No one knew what to do with her.

"She isn't all there, anymore," concerned relatives whispered as they gestured to their heads, turning their forefingers in a clockwise circle of ridicule. A shameful gesture implying insanity.

Can you imagine suffering from Alzheimer's for twenty-five

years? Forgive us, Auntie.

"Here he is!" I shouted. Granddaddy Bob had bolted in the back door with that mischievous grin on his face, tilting his cigar up and out of the corner of his mouth.

"Where were you?" everybody shouted.

He laughed and reddened at all the fuss that had been made. Innocently, he had stepped out the front door for a stroll and walked around the edge of the house, but he couldn't find the front door again. He said he looked and looked for it, but it just wasn't there. For thirty minutes, he circled the house as if he had been placed in another dimension, which provided no clues on how to get back.

Granddaddy Bob didn't suffer as long as my tortured aunt. Nine months later, on a chilly, rain-soaked autumn day, he slipped away peacefully, unknowingly.

All these precious loved ones abandoned themselves long before their bodies were ready to go. They walked out of life's door and around the edge, never to find a way back.

A funny characteristic of my great-grandmother, Auntie Flossie, Granddaddy Bob, and most others who suffer from Alzheimer's is the loss of only recent memories. The inability to stay on top of new information causes a gradual shift away from coping with reality. Wouldn't it be wonderful if we could find out why their minds keep the facts of the past but disregard more recent information?

Neuroscientists have discovered that Alzheimer's is not just the predictable outcome of old age. Ten to fifteen percent of people over sixty-five symptomatically exhibit some level of senile dementia. Half of these are severe enough to be referred to as Senile Dementia Alzheimer's Type, or SDAT.

A loss of cells in the nucleus basalis, a region of the brain, can cause Alzheimer's, according to a team of researchers at Johns Hopkins University School of Medicine under the direction of Joseph T. Coyle.

The loss of these cells is thought to be the result of a lack of a neurotransmitter chemical called acetylcholine. This chemical is important in transferring newly accessed information to other areas of the brain that are responsible for storing specific types of memories.

Because of an acetylcholine deficiency in the *nucleus basalis*, the simple facts of daily life never find their way into the brain's vast areas of memory storage.

The memory of which door Granddaddy Bob came out of was never transferred to the proper storage area in his brain. The challenge before neuroscientists is how to make sure tomorrow's Granddaddy Bobs can keep processing enough acetylcholine. Emphasizing foods rich in choline, such as lecithin and egg yolks, as well as the promises of new drugs like Rivastigmine, Galantamine, and Donepezil, offer hope. Up until recently, these were the only three medications that the FDA had approved for restoring lost memories.

Perhaps the cure for this scourge of family memories is close at hand. In January 2023, the FDA reported several drugs were currently under consideration, and as of January 6, they had given emergency approval to a fourth drug—Lequembi. We can only hope that more and more cures will be proven beneficial.

Everyone loves to reflect on family memories, for they are enabling mirrors that help us see ourselves better. However, no one wants to live with the terrible memory of watching their loved one's mind fade away, leaving behind a decrepit body that only clings to life like a ghost.

Ghosts make no farewells or say good-bye. The family tales of failing minds, hopefully, will soon be a memory lost to humankind. Despite the cute shenanigans of little boys, there's nothing humorous about this disease. Nothing!

We are thankful for the new knowledge that is helping us to understand and cure this disease of our memories. It robs us of a thousand Thanksgivings and wounds our hearts as well.

MY FATHER'S VOICE

One of the many joys of fatherhood was watching all of my sons become men. With every birthday they celebrate, I become more aware of my own mortality. With the celebration of every birthday, the ancient process of generational replacement is casually but dramatically highlighted.

As their generation becomes the sunrise, mine becomes the sunset. As they become increasingly aware of life's vitality, I have begun to plan for its finality.

When I was a little boy, the mysteries of death kept me stymied. In my mind, the enveloping world served only as a gentle canopy, protecting the immortality of those who were closest to me. Never mind everyone else. Other people could die, maybe even distant relatives. But the link to my father seemed eternal.

The concept that my parents could or would die was benign to me. I assured my parents from time to time of their immortality. "You'll never die; you can't; it's not possible." I'd say this to them, reassuring myself.

They'd offer a patronizing smile and quietly redirect the conversation. Parents don't like to talk to their children about death, especially their own.

It's true, however, that parents die just like grandparents, distant relatives, and the rest of the world. Yet, I think it's a childhood ritual for those who are brought up in the security of their parents' love to feel compelled to proclaim their immortality.

My children are scattered across a span of thirty years. (Whew! Exactly.) When each in turn became old enough to put sentences together, they also asked themselves this question about parental mortality, marvelously concluding that parents will live forever.

When they were young, no argument could change their minds, and any talk about the topic had to be done with respect and dignity. As they got older, however, I was able to lighten the burden of this philosophical load with a little bit of humor, forcing them to realize the absurdity of their father being the eternal father.

When my third child, Joshua, was eight years old, we enjoyed taking long walks together through our neighborhood in Princeton, New Jersey, an area rich in American history. He was asking me serious questions that called for intense concentration on my part as a conscientious father.

You see, on this particularly sunny day, it wasn't one of those boring exercise walks. This was one of those strolls that was leisurely and easygoing and focused on the need to spend some time together. There were no boundaries to what we were talking about. The agenda was wide open, and he was shifting subjects almost as quickly as his feet.

I listened with all the fatherly care I could muster so that my answers would be right. Also, I was afraid I'd stick my foot in my mouth.

As he asked questions and I answered them, I detected something unusual kicking around in my soundtracks. I listened for it again. I couldn't hear it. I was trying too hard. Maybe it would pop up again if I didn't concentrate on it so hard. We moved along, and as I got caught up in my son's chatter, I forgot about it.

Naturally, when I wasn't thinking about it, that's precisely when I felt it ripple through my vocal cords again. Rich, tingling, subtle sounds—but very real. They sounded so funny to me as the crisp resonance of their tones soothed and caressed me.

I don't know why, but the gentle vibrations suddenly picked up speed and spread energy through my head and neck. The sound waves were followed by a strange crackling and tickling that made my throat constrict and my mind go blank. This happened in the blink of an eye, providing me with only the shadow of time to understand it all.

As my head flushed again with more blood, tuneful sounds poured forth, accompanied by a thousand memories riding piggyback. There were so many images, I couldn't process them fast enough. The more sounds there were, the more images there were.

Dizziness frightened me, and for a moment, I stumbled against the stubborn, unaiding asphalt. My inventive brain was like a universe suddenly alive with inconceivable creativity.

The cascades of images were from my past. The sounds were pealing forth select harmonies and recorded echoes, accumulated across the years—all with the richness of my father's voice.

Like buried treasure brought up from the darkened earth, my brain had unleashed the riches of their harmony for me to share. It was tender, but it made me feel lonely. I stood tall. I stood small.

The melody of my father's life force penetrated my emotions and rang forth in unison through vocalizations emerging from the swollen cords within my throat.

The sounds were like blissful songs: foreign but familiar, soft but strong. And I melted before the power of their immortal sounds. The sensations of these memories were complementary to an almost other-worldly experience.

This emotion triggered a mental image of a cozy fireplace in one of the older homes we once lived in. After spending hours looking for a Christmas tree, on the coldest day of the year, we would cuddle around the cozy little fire, rubbing our hands with zeal to speed the flow of blood throughout our chilled limbs.

My father and I used to spend many hours looking for our Christmas tree every year, and these sweet memories burned hot around my heart. The sounds of his voice within mine sparked the resurrection of images shelved far back in the deepest cells of my memory.

The moment enhanced a forgotten sense of security, and images of yesteryear evoked strong, enabling emotions that dressed my mind in the durable fabric of permanence.

"DAD!" My son jolted me back to reality by yelling, "You aren't listening."

Guilty! I was lost in the backrooms of my past.

My ears began to tune back into the sounds of Joshua's relentless chirping. (Yes, like little birds, children often only chirp.)

As we walked on, hand in hand, circling the block, I was seized by a pervasive presence, as if someone had reached down and taken hold of my other hand. It was three Naylors, not two, that circled the block that day—and every day since.

I have learned so much since that innocent day. Guess what? You may not understand this the way I do, but my father is, indeed, immortal. He will live forever, after all. The little nuances, the subtle tones, of his voice have come of age within my own voice.

On that day, I believed there was something much more wonderful to come. When the day of his death finally came, I felt his spirit join mine. My father's voice is my voice. My father's heart is my heart. My father's soul is my soul.

There is good news for all my sons and daughters.

They don't know it now and probably won't for a long time to come, but when they're about forty or fifty years old and take a leisurely stroll with one of their many, many children, without warning, a familiar sound will reach down and strike a nostalgic chord in their hearts.

Intrinsically, they will realize it is their father's voice, their grandfather's voice, and his father's voice before him. And whatever they say to their child, they can say this with assurance: "You will never walk alone."

On that special day, many, many years ago, mine and Joshua's walk came to an end. As we turned the bend toward our house, my son asked, "Daddy, you won't ever die, will you?"

This was Joshua's first experience with the great question of eternity. I had the impression that a higher power had set me up and that there was some sort of mystery at play. For the first time, I did not try to reason it all away. The entire experience left me numbed.

I looked tenderly into his little face and said, "No, son, I'm going to live forever."

Jack Naylor, Daddy the Minister. This formal church photo of him was taken in his late middle age.

UP, UP AND AWAY

"**O**h look, Chelps-pea, there's your balloon," Cody sadly said, with all the veracity of a Wile E. Coyote (You know, the guy who forever runs from the Road Runner on Looney Tunes cartoons.)

For Valentine's Day one year, I gave little Chelsea and "Cody Man" each a helium-filled, heart-shaped balloon. Identical in color and size, each balloon had an eighteen-inch ribbon dangling from where it had been tied off.

The kids had been playing with them for about fifteen minutes when Cody began to fuss at Chelsea.

I had gone into the kitchen for a glass of something, knowing I didn't dare let these two out of my sight any longer than it takes to blow out the candles on a triple-decker, cream-filled German chocolate birthday cake.

"What in the world are you two doing?" I demanded in my best fatherly voice. Cody had gotten the spiraling ribbons tangled up and taken both balloons for himself. Simple Cody-physics here. Because they were stuck together, they had mysteriously become one in some symbiotic sort of way.

It was possession by accident, and the international law of toddlerhood caused him to believe that they were now both his. CASE CLOSED.

Don't laugh.

I imagine Columbus claimed most of the New World for Isabella and Ferdinand under the same pretext. They all sort of stumbled into it, so they figured it must surely belong to them.

There was just as much at stake for both Columbus and Cody, to say the least.

I took the balloons from Cody, assuring him I would be able to separate the ribbons, and once again he and Chelsea would each have one balloon.

Untangling knotted balloon ribbons is much like untying a kid's shoestrings. That's right; it is an infuriating ordeal.

The level of exasperation is directly linked to the level of the *tyee's* ability. In this case, Cody is the *tyee*. (Since I made up this word, I'll elect to spell it tyee instead of the more phonetic—tieee.)

Cody is a very good *tyee*, if your definition of good is one who can place simple strands of material into an ultra-Gordian Knot, unfathomable even to their older brother Alexander the Little, (AKA Joshua Alexander Naylor.)

For the young folks who might come upon this strange talk of knots, you might ask, "What is the Gordian Knot?" Skip this paragraph if you aren't interested in a 2,300-year-old dead guy. Otherwise, pay attention!

Alexander the Great of ancient Greece woke up one day and decided to conquer the world. After arriving somewhere in modern-day Turkey, he heard about a gigantic knot that no one had ever been able to untie. The rumor was that whoever could figure it out would be able to conquer all of Asia. Since he was in the business of conquering the world, he decided to give it a shot.

Some old Roman dudes said he figured it out by removing the linchpin that held the rope in place. But the more popular version is that he just hacked it to pieces with his sword. The last version would play out much better in a 21st-century movie. Either way, he did conquer a lot of places after that.

Cody the Tyee had surpassed himself in his unusual display of making a "good" knot, totally frustrating his father in the process. Just as I finished separating the Siamese ribbons, one balloon slipped away, stopping only as one of the heart-shaped crests gently bumped against the ceiling.

Though the ribbon was still within my reach, by Cody's reckoning, it may as well have been on the moon. It floated out of his reach and was therefore irretrievable.

In the meantime, he had surreptitiously grabbed the other ribbon out of my hand and pointed with feigned sorrow at the balloon that was now orbiting the light fixture near the ceiling of the next galaxy over in the living room.

"Oh no, look, Chelps-pea, there's your balloon," he deceitfully commiserated.

I suppose we all get that Cody attitude about life from time to time. I know I do. In the end, it's bad business.

Maybe it sounds too old-fashioned to some and downright insulting to others. But if we're ever going to last on this planet long enough to make a difference, then we're going to have to help each other with this balloon-holding business. Not everybody's grip is as good as it should be, and we can all admit to losing it from time to embarrassing time.

It's not going to hurt one iota (read: not even a little bit) for everybody to keep a benevolent eye on one another. Who knows? Some of them might be people you care about.

They might be one of those mysterious chance people who, unbeknownst to the probability experts, for some reason or another mysteriously bump into your life and make a big splash of a difference.

It doesn't take much effort for me to be watchful and helpful to others. Things can always get tough for me, and even for the fellow next to me. And who knows when I might need a friendly hand?

When your balloons get all tangled up with somebody else's, don't get greedy; get acquainted. The world's got room and balloons enough for all of us.

Cody wore me out trying to get this point across. After I figured he had learned all he was going to about balloon sharing for one day, I gave up and went to Walmart, where I brought back a whole bag full of balloons.

Sure enough! There were plenty of balloons for all of us.

Alexander the Little, (AKA Joshua Alexander Naylor.) An accurate photo of Joshua when the little ones were fighting over balloons

JUST A LITTLE JAR OF PICKLES

Ready-to-eat food stored in a jar was invented by a French restaurateur, but an unusual appeal from Napoleon made its popularity universal. The little French maniac, trying to conquer Northern Italy, was having trouble feeding his troops. They had ravaged the countryside until the fields and the scavengers were exhausted.

In those distant days of war, no food meant no army. Once they got hungry enough, they'd go home. Napoleon sent out an appeal for someone to come up with a way to feed his troops for the glory of France. *Vive la France!*

And so, history took one of those unexpected turns that would change everything. This time, it changed how people eat. The restaurateur had been storing pre-cooked food in the thick glass bottles used in the Champagne industry. Stout and durable, they stood up to the rigors of being moved about without breaking or spoiling the contents.

This proved to be a godsend for Napoleon, but heaven help those who got in the way of the little general's armies.

Folks have always stored food away for future use. But pre-cooked? This was a new business. My family was already living in America when this newfangled idea took hold. These were frontier Naylors. They were hardy Brits who had made their home in Kentucky and Tennessee, arriving hot on the trail of Daniel Boone.

My great-grandmother, who was born just after the Civil War, passed down a recipe that she got from her grandmother for preparing and storing pre-cooked food in bottles and jars.

By the time I watched great-grandmother Naylor perform the art of this family tradition, they were calling it "canning." I never understood why they called putting food in jars "canning," but I suppose "jarring" just didn't sound right. (Well, actually I do know, but let's not ruin the story with too much history.)

My mother was an expert at "canning" food to be stored in jars, à la Napoleon style. She'd spend half the fall "canning" food that church members would bring from their garden harvests by the bushel. Slaving all day long in a hot, sultry kitchen, Mama was as good an artist at sealing up high-quality food as the Campbell Soup Company.

Now, don't you think it was properly and securely sealed by a simple twist of the lid! No! They'd have to make a popping sound to pass Mama's litmus test of acceptability. We might not eat some of that stuff until a year later, but it was just as good as the day she cooked it.

Even into her eighties, she'd "can" a few specialties to satiate the appetites of her children. As grown-ups, we always begged for the savory taste of memories her canned goods could resurrect.

She could preserve almost anything edible, but her *piece de résistance* was dill pickles. Claussen, Heinz, Valasic, Yeehaw, and anybody else, forget it. She outdid everyone. She could make them spicy, hot, or mild. She could make them tiny, large, or huge. She could out-New York New Yorkers.

I don't know what her secret was, but when she left us for Heaven's Kitchen, she took her secret recipe with her, and as far as I'm concerned, there just aren't any pickles on earth anymore.

Now, when she sealed the lids, they were sealed...*tout à fait!* (Touché Mr. Napolean.) Mama never had to worry about us kids getting into the pantry and stealing away with a jar of pickles because we couldn't possibly open one. She couldn't even open one. It took the mighty hands of Daddy to open one.

"Here, Daddy, p-l-e-a-s-e open this jar of pickles," I used to sing with salivating anticipation.

He'd tease us and play around with the jar before he'd open it. And then we'd sit around eating a pack of saltines, devouring a whole jar at once.

Now I know why I fight this salt war with my physician every year. Anyone who grows up eating salty pickles and salty crackers all the time is bound to have salt flowing naturally through their veins. It was almost a sacred rite.

"Please, doctor, don't make me give up my religion too." I'll try that line next time she tries to take away my salt!

Watching Daddy open pickle jars by the hundreds concretely cemented in my mind just how strong he was. (And I mean hundreds, because Mama would have shelves and shelves stacked and triple stacked with nothing but dill pickles.) It was a nice daily reminder to never vex Daddy the wrong way, but it also endeared him to me.

Kids love to believe their daddy is the strongest daddy in the world. Daddies like this are invincible, making the world for children bucolically secure.

Every time Daddy opened a jar of pickles, my world was confirmed to be safe and sound. It was a testimony to all that is good and wholesome about the solidarity and value of family.

I must have said, "Here, Daddy, please open this jar of pickles," a thousand times when I was growing up. And a thousand times, his strength demonstrated to me how strong his love was for our family.

A few months before his unexpected open-heart surgery in 1994, I had gone to visit him. His secret mystery of heart disease had yet to be revealed to us. That year, we lived a thousand miles away, and opportunities for visitation were rare and treasured events.

I was sitting in the den watching television with my rowdy kids when my father came in from the kitchen holding a jar of Mama's dill pickles.

"Here, son, please open this jar of pickles," he asked with a silly grin.

Comfortably leaning back in Daddy's favorite mahogany lounge chair, I just sat there laughing at him. I thought he was playing a joke on me.

"Here," he said, jabbing it into my hands, "open it."

I sat up and stared at him. "You *are* kidding, aren't you?"

"Hurry up, so we can eat!" he demanded as he walked back into the kitchen.

I flipped back through the pages of about forty years and followed behind him like a little child, hesitantly holding the jar of pickles.

"You mean you can't open this jar of pickles?" I moaned with disbelief.

"No," he said. He looked surprised that I was making the question so problematic.

"Well, if *you* can't open it, how do you expect *me* to open it?" I whined like I had just been asked to clean my room.

There was no answer. The room got heavy around me, and I realized he didn't have a clue as to what all this meant to me. I tightened my grip on the jar's top because I fully anticipated feeling ashamed of my failure.

Astonishingly, it popped open right away. My eyes glazed over the tips of the pickled cucumbers, and a chill ran up and down my back, giving me a smart case of goosebumps.

"I can't believe I opened this so easily," I mumbled to myself as

Mama snatched the open jar out of my hands and emptied it into a serving dish.

I didn't care too much for this feeling that was sticking sharply against the Adam's Apple in my throat. All afternoon, I struggled with the freezing, tingling feeling that hits hard when hard things hit my life.

Life had shifted. Daddy couldn't open the pickle jars anymore. My kids couldn't open them either. A rite of passage was taking place here.

I was now the family pickle opener.

With a single twist of the hand, I had become the family's symbol of strength.

"No, not me," I reasoned to myself. Nobody else was listening to my philosophical dilemma.

The next day, Mama asked me to open another jar while my No. 3 son, Joshua, was in the kitchen.

"Here, Dad, let me do it," he begged.

Wicked laughter erupted from my entire body!

"You can't open this; it's too hard," I mocked as I handed it to him.

He grunted and groaned. The jar lid stood fast.

He ran hot water over it and used a wet cloth. The jar lid held.

Reluctantly, Joshua handed it back to me. "Whew," I thought to myself, "I narrowly defended my crown." I fastened my grip around the jar, and with the smooth agility of Mohammed Ali, my fingers turned the metal top. "Pop!" it sounded as it came unglued.

"Wow, Dad, how'd you do that?" Joshua asked with the amazement of Barney Fife talking to Hercules. I was still the family pickle opener—for a while anyway.

Just like my great greats handed down the recipe for "canning" pickles over the last two hundred years, my father handed down to me the standard of family strength that every parent eventually extends to the care of their children.

Inherent in the job of family standard bearer is the responsibility for maintaining the ideals of unity, love, security, and strength. I hadn't realized that so much depended on **just a little jar of pickles.**

Napoleon did. Now I do too.

The entire clan, minus Mama who had moved on from the living, and Finn who hasn't been born yet

FINALLY, A GIRL!

My first child was born in 1976. A bicentennial boy. What better way to celebrate the birth of American independence than to add another name to the roster of freedom? Three more sons followed the bicentennial boy. It wasn't until 1991, fifteen years later, that I finally realized a lifelong dream of mine.

On November 25th, smack dab in the middle of being turkey and dressing thankful, Chelsea Danielle was born just down the street from where Albert Einstein once strolled, and quantum leaped.

Little girls are immensely different from little boys. But they are the necessary ingredients for experiencing a proper balance in life. The real gusto challenge that they only hint at in beer commercials is raising a multi-gendered bunch of kids. Little girls put the pizzazz into the whole deal. They bring the dimensions of sugar and spice to life.

Instead of just trucks and cars, little league and toad frogs, everything hues up a little bit pink. I clarify this with the word "just," because nowadays girls play with anything they want to and can grow up to be anything they want to, including Supreme Court justices—believe me, I believe it!

Along with blue jeans and t-shirts come little silk ribbons, lacy pants, and black patent leather that emerge as necessary items in a male-dominated environment.

Of course, nowadays girls can dress any way they choose, and I like some of the creativity flowing through the female fashion world today. (Reference the recent movie *Barbie* to feel the power of PINK!)

In 1991, baby dolls and high-pitched giggles vie for prominence against G.I. Joe and the boisterous gutturals their commanders give. Such a little girl struggles vociferously against diverse circumstances to become the master of her fate. She may be outnumbered, but she exerts a force with which the boys cannot compete.

The force is called femininity.

It exudes its ambiance with a lingering permanence throughout the home. Whatever she wants, she only needs to get pretty in pink, pucker her lower lip, and go pleading through every room until she finds the right male to manipulate into granting her heart's desire.

And if by chance all the males refuse her contriving machinations, all she needs to do is run to her mama, crying "chauvinism" or something that sounds like it, looks like it, or smells like it. And woe be to those fellows who dare not cater to the always unopposable female sex.

I am no match, nor do I really try to be. Why? Because she was the baby girl I'd been looking for during all those "boy" years.

Please don't misinterpret my conception of women. I believe in the power of womanhood. I am pleased to say that one of the smartest and most influential women I have ever known raised me. In addition, my little Chelsea has grown up to become one of the most powerful and pervasive women I have ever known.

These pillars of influence are merely two of several other women who have impacted my life as deeply as craters on the moon. But it is the particulars of this memory from November 25, 1991, that have become so precious to me. I will never forget the moment of her discovery. After all, it was only on that beautiful November morning that I first discovered that finally, I had a girl!

Even though technology existed to predict the gender of our children long before they are born, in her case, we didn't know. We only knew, thankfully, that she appeared healthy with ten toes and ten fingers, which are the only things we should ever be truly concerned about.

All they could learn from the myriad of tests was that this baby was either a boy or a girl. Ha! Those are some pretty good odds for betting that line, right?

We were aware that she would require a cesarean delivery, following the precedent set by her older brothers. So, Chelsea had a scheduled appointment to be born exactly at 8:00 a.m. Alongside the obstetrician would be an oncologist. One would remove the baby, the other would cut out a worrisome ping-pong ball-sized tumor that had mysteriously appeared during the pregnancy.

First would come the baby, then the ping-pong ball. The baby turned out to be my beautiful Chelsea, and the ping-pong ball was determined to be non-threatening to her mama's life. Whew! Game over—CHO!

Because the delivery was concomitant with cancer surgery, I was not allowed to be in the delivery room. I waited anxiously by the thickly padded, forever swinging surgery room doors. Every time someone came out, I stood up. Every time someone went in, I stood up. Each time the swinging doors barely budged open, I began to sweat more and more profusely.

I made a nuisance of myself asking questions. No one could tell me anything. But I couldn't shut up, so I kept asking. You can easily place yourself in my shoes and understand the predicament of being trapped within the vice grip of fear and happiness simultaneously.

Of course, eventually, the obstetrician appeared before my blood-drenched eyes. In his arms, he cradled a brand-new Naylor, marked in white crusty ugh and mucky slime. Like a warrior fresh from the field of battle he stood grinning before me with bloody spots smeared on his gown and her blanket. "Mr. Naylor, you have a daughter, and your wife is doing great."

As he gently handed her off to my waiting embrace, I shouted, "Finally, a girl."

Mama VonCille and Chelsea Naylor at her High School graduation as Valedictorian

THE CHICKEN LADY

Once upon a time, I was the senior minister of a Southern Baptist church. It wasn't in a quaint little "holler" or tucked away on the pastoral slope of a rural hillside. Nope, I pastored a thriving suburban congregation in the state capitol of Kentucky, just a stone's throw from two large and cosmopolitan cities (well as cosmopolitan as any Kentucky city can be).

I had not pastored this burgeoning congregation for very long when, one day, as I was poised in meditation, the phone rang.

Ordinarily, I would not be in the office at this hour, and the secretary who normally answered the phone had already left for the day. There I sat, lost in the throes of a theological tune-up, as the phone rang somewhat emphatically to be answered.

"Hello," I said. There was no response.

I slipped into my Sunday morning voice, registering a more authoritarian "Hello?" Still, there was no response.

Having to revert to such vigor to deal with what was plainly turning out to be a prank call did not contribute to the atmosphere of my celestial contemplation.

Realizing that my moment of inner retrospection had been mercilessly blasphemed, I decided to slam the phone down (in a Moses kind of way). Suddenly, I heard a soft clucking. As I placed my ear closer to the phone, the sounds became unmistakable.

"Cluck. Cluck. Cluck!" These were the sounds of someone's barnyard. "Why am I listening to this?" I thought. So, again, I tried the communication approach—the basic concept behind phones.

"Hello? Who is this?" What's the joke, in other words?

"Cluck...Cluck...Cluck...Cluck...Cluck." Slow, deep, and rhythmic came the response. This fella was a real pro; he sounded like a genuine Colonel Sanders special.

I decided that the only thing I would be able to accomplish with this trickster would be to hang up the phone without being made a fool.

In seminary, I learned that pastors should never hang up on anyone. Their ears are supposed to be on 24-hour call for even the most miasmic of situations. Having tried every conceivable approach and utilizing every tone within the range of my *pastorality*, I hung up!

You have probably had a phone call like this, one that leaves you frustrated, perhaps angry, yet with just enough mystery to drive you crazy and ruin the rest of your day.

By the next day, I had decided to label the whole experience a prank. Calling it a prank absolved me of any pastoral culpability.

A week went by, and I was studying late in my office again. The phone rang! Without hesitation, I answered, "Hello."

"Cluck...Cluck...Cluck...Cluck...Cluck," came the response. I don't know why, but I laughed.

Out loud.

Over the phone.

It wasn't very pastor-like. I begged. I talked.

I sermonized. I counseled this faceless chicken on the phone.

I was determined to win this battle. It went on for half an hour with nothing but soft, gentle cluckings in response.

What else could I do? I hung up!

The next morning, I came to the office exceptionally early for a meditative makeup. As I nestled down with a good grip on my innermost self, the phone rang. That's right, it was a *fowl* call. (I'm sorry, I couldn't help it.)

"Cluck...Cluck...Cluck," came the sound once more.

Fortunately for me, and very timely, I might add, the church secretary arrived. Having thoroughly frightened her as she entered the office (not being a morning person, perhaps she had misidentified me as a most unholy ghost), I waved to her to take the phone and listen.

The bewildered expression on her face slowly began to be replaced with a grin that stretched from ear to secretarial ear. Suddenly, she burst into laughter and hung up. Realizing that I was about to qualify for some type of "gotcha," I waited patiently for her to finish her hee-haws.

"Okay, okay. Who is this chicken man?" I asked.

"Not a chicken man," she snickered. "It's the chicken lady."

It seems that there was this lady who was a bona fide member of our congregation. She had not attended in many years. Indeed, she was mentally unbalanced. She lived alone, harmless to herself and others. Her only companions and friends were the chickens who lived on her farm.

No one else had much time, only pity for the chicken lady. She refused, for whatever superstitious reasons, to talk over the phone. It wasn't clear just why she did it, but whenever she wanted the pastor to make a visit, she would dial the number for the office and let the chickens do the talking.

I knew that soon, very soon, I would need to go visit this "chicken lady."

I put it off for a day or two out of embarrassment over my phone counseling attempts with chickens. Finally, I went.

Her place was a little haven wedged in between the transitional zones of country and suburbia.

That place that has no name and no distinct future...

Halfway between yesterday and today...

As I drove down the neglected driveway onto her little farm, I became disoriented. It was like those dreams that come at the end of the night, jolting the mind with conflicting images of many bygone eras, all jammed up into one discombobulated tapestry.

The atmosphere looked and smelled like memories. There was an eeriness that gradually unfolded itself upon me as I reached her house. The timelessness of the place was blurry with motion.

Chickens were everywhere. Like the creatures in a Hitchcock thriller, they exerted their importance.

Cacophonous chickens!

By the dozens.

Running free and confidently.

Maybe I'm too confident.

I later heard many testimonials from neighboring suburbanites who admitted to having run over at least one of the chicken lady's chickens.

What imagery! Liberated chickens are loose in the subdivisions.

She was quite famous.

Uncomfortably, I walked up to the house, carefully watching my steps. The chickens sat comfortably, almost wisely, on the front porch swing, as if they were thinking, "Yeah, we've seen your kind around here before. We're not worried; you won't stay."

Bedraggled and incoherent, the chicken lady appeared and flung open the screen door, motioning for me to come in. She knew who I was before I could open my mouth.

Inside, chickens ruled the roost. They projected an ominous ownership of every room.

On the couch.

The chairs.

The tables.

In the hallway.

And quite inauspiciously—near the phone.

It was the quintessential display of disorder and, arguably, the weirdest visitation of my ministry.

As funny as it may seem, I don't remember much about the chicken lady. It is the picture of total disorder that I remember most. A yard and house full of chickens, ramrodded by an old lady slightly out of tune with the world around her.

During the one year that I was the chicken lady's pastor, the chickens only called a few times. I would go, stay a few moments, and attempt to talk to both her and her chickens.

There was not a lot I could do except go, be there, and listen. I let her know that even though I didn't understand her world, I would come and hold her hand and speak kind words to her chickens.

There's a chicken lady in all our lives. They stay in the shadows—the lonely, hidden places lost in time and space. They are slightly out of step with the norm of society, whatever that is.

Sometimes, they may do the most bizarre things to get our attention. They have the chickens call you and hope you won't hang up on them.

You may wonder what to do with people like this in your life. You don't need to do a whole lot or completely understand their world. Just be there sometimes. Pick up the phone and listen to their sounds. Talk to their lonely ears.

Years later, I received word that the chicken lady had died. Immediately, I thought about the chickens. Those precious chickens are dear only to one slightly tilted old lady, and I wonder if they ever learned to use the phone on their own.

I have run into some soul mates of the chicken lady over the years. In fact, when I first told this story to someone, I'd been living and working in a house full of such folks. I was often asked how I could ever get through to the developmentally disabled. How could I live with them? How did they know that I cared for them?

It's really very simple. All you need is some time, a little love, and, oh yeah, don't forget to hold their hands from time to time and speak kind words to their chickens.

NO RESORTS

It's been a few years, and I can't remember exactly where I was when I heard it, but I'll never forget the crescendo of panic in the announcer's voice. The car radio was turned up just enough so I wouldn't have to listen to silence.

As quickly as lightning zigzags back and forth from the center of a dark cloud, the muffled music is replaced by the murmuring of a newscaster. (A speaker I heard when I was a kid always used to say that zigzag lightning thing and I've always wanted to use it.)

Anyway, the reporter's frantic voice uttered something about cars and tragedy, and hogs.

"Hogs?" I asked myself.

Finding myself hooked, I cranked up the volume. He was into his story in full stride.

"It was a 400-pound hog...two people have been hurt...the ambulances are here...cars are backed up for miles on the interstate...twisted metal is everywhere." Hmmmm...What the heck was he talking about?

I'm listening to this story about a hog with tremendous concentration. Well, you would be too if the top story of the day was about a pig.

The despair in the announcer's voice was so convincing that I remember I caught myself wondering if this was what people felt like when hearing about the crash of the Hindenburg, the fall of Rome, or Kentucky losing a basketball game to Louisville! (I wasn't around for two of those events, but I've often thought emotions of chaos might be measured by these standards.)

I thought, "Should I really be getting emotionally concerned about this? I mean, after all, no one was dead. Or were they?"

The announcer's rasping intensity caused me to hover close to the steering wheel. "Authorities aren't certain what happened to the hog."

"Now just what is it that they mean when they say they don't know what happened to the hog?" I wondered.

The music returned abruptly, and I felt cheated. I wanted to know what was going on, and here I was stuck in my car, far from the action.

What a crazy thing! I couldn't get it out of my mind and soon found myself asking the oddest question:

"Do they mean they don't know what happened to the hog before the accident or after the accident?"

What's the real story here? What had happened in the life of the old hog that could lead to such a tragedy? To answer such questions, my imagination got busy.

And so, I imagined...

Had the hog gone berserk, and his family's life been ruined by low agricultural prices? Perhaps, in a suicidal break with reality, he had waddled to the nearest interstate and thought, "If the chicken can do it, so can I." And so, throwing caution to the winds of I-80, he crossed the road in desperation. (I remember I was in Omaha!)

Did the passengers of the first car recognize any sign of defeatism in his eyes as they swerved into the guardrail? By any chance, did they hear him say anything about worthlessness, loss of self-esteem, or lack of respect from others?

Car after car careened off the road in their attempt to dodge the fateful hog. The din of confusion was unbelievable.

Cries, screams, sirens, obscenities, consolation, and questions merged with broken glass, blood, and burning rubber.

Uncertainty filled the air, as the authorities really had no clue as to what had indeed happened to this hog.

Was there anyone to call who could shed light on this tragedy? Maybe they could talk to the farmer who owned him.

The farmer said: "He was a good hog...weighed 400 pounds...always cared for the piglets. Lately, I have heard a lot more squealing than usual. I wouldn't know why, though."

The farmer's wife chimed in: "Charlie was a good husband." Suddenly, the listening audience became attached to the victim because now we know his name. The loving way the farmer's wife pronounces it tenderizes our hearts. "He was good to the piglets; it just ain't fair."

The hog's wife hysterically rattled off critical details.

"He lost the top spot at the main pigsty downtown. After so many years of hard work, he became depressed. All he wanted to do was wallow in grief. He started drinking like a swill and grunted that we didn't love him anymore because he wasn't bringing home the bacon.

"But we told him that didn't matter to us and that he'd always be a blue ribbon in our hearts. Then, suddenly, the day before yesterday, he was gone—no word, no note—he just disappeared. I knew something like this would happen; it just ain't fair."

His schoolteacher: "I knew he'd turn out this way someday; he was so pigheaded about handling problems."

Why is it that schoolteachers always know how everyone turns out after they turn out that way?

His boss and fellow co-workers: "Yeah, he got laid off, but it happens everywhere nowadays. Charlie didn't seem like the kind of guy who would allow this to bring him down. He was good to the piglets. He was always happy, a real ham; it just doesn't figure."

No one seemed to know exactly what caused him to snap. The journalists began their speculations and continued to interview everyone who had ever met or even brushed up against the hairy hog.

They constructed a postmortem psychological profile. Their conclusion: "He was psychotic, distant, forbearing, self-centered, mysterious, inconsiderate, and despondent."

Gradually, a picture evolved, solicited and unsolicited, of a 400-pound enigma. The bottom line is that it was a waste. Furthermore, it was a senseless waste. (These types of tragedies characterize waste very specifically.)

So much damage, so much pain, and leaving behind so many broken hearts.

What really happened? No one knows for sure, but perhaps it all started when he lost his job. What followed is an all-too-common scenario for those whose luck has run amuck in the mud.

He became disgruntled at home, lost his sense of productivity, and no longer felt he could contribute anything to his family.

Despairingly, he turned to corn whiskey, and his personality darkened. The **pig**mentation of his skin grew pink due to his lack of nutrition, and no one knew the real Charlie anymore.

As he struggled to redeem himself, the lack of alternatives drove him into what is to us an incomprehensible dimension.

It was the dimension not of last resorts but of NO RESORTS. The semblance of normality does not exist in this dimension. It's a place of no return. The brink—no, not the brink, but the first step over the brink—of personal destruction. In this dimension, many enter, but few exit.

Here you find the terminated Charlies...

The lover who was rebuffed one too many times...

The embattled old man who no longer values life alongside his beloved but vegetating wife...

The lady whose cancer is so painful, only death can provide relief...

The laborer whose promotion was denied for the umpteenth time...

The shopkeeper who owes too much and owns too little...

You know these folks. They live next door, down the street, and across the room.

The dimension of no resorts is filled with thousands of Charlies. They are farmers, merchants, doctors, lawyers, ministers, postal workers, factory workers, housewives, and streetwalkers, male and female, young and old.

To them, life turns the card up empty, confronting them with no options except the concessions of defeat. They run, they hide, and then they explode.

Very often, they explode in public. Opening up for a moment so the rest of us can see a little bit of the hellish dimension into which they have entered.

Insanely, they spray their gunfire at their co-workers. Mercifully and lovingly, they kill their spouses and themselves. Fanatically, they lead faithful worshippers into sanctuaries of fire. Murderously, they plunge into a noonday cafeteria line. They sit off a main highway to OD in the company of silence.

Or, fatalistically, they cross the road, finalizing their solitude.

No one knows everything that's involved when people snap. Sure, we can make guesses and construct after-the-fact profiles. But human personality is so complex that there will never be a gauge that can totally measure or monitor the mind or the heart.

What good comes from psychoanalyzing those who have become crippled by the burdens of life unless we reflect introspectively?

We look inward in hopes that our look outward will have greater focus. And when we do it collectively, we look inwardly at society itself.

As we examine ourselves, both individually and corporately, we will need to search for the solutions that will forever bar the door to this dimension of no resorts.

It makes headlines when the citizens of No Resorts crack. Dumbfounded and long-faced, everyone goes around crying, "We are certain of what happened." Yet we know deep down in our hearts why most of it happens. The news should be that few are doing much to stop it.

It can be stopped when we restore purpose, hope, dignity, and self-worth as unalienable rights for all people.

"How do we do that?" you ask.

Oh no! Backup for a soul-searching second, please. It's not that easy. There are no quick fixes. There is no single formula for all that ails us. But to ask is a beginning.

The next morning, I couldn't wait to find out what happened to the old hog.

The radio announcer obliged with this more accurate explanation:

"They found the body of the 400-pound hog early this morning, 500 yards from the scene of yesterday's debacle. His mangled body lay wedged in between the side of Johnson's Warehouse and a large boulder at the mouth of Tyler Creek."

"Ooooh," I thought, "so, what the announcer really meant was that the authorities didn't know what happened to the hog after the accident."

What really happened?

Well, maybe he scampered across the highway in a blind spirit of fear, dodging cars and trucks and squealing all the way. He got hit and kept running. He got hit and ran again. He battled against the railing and repeatedly found himself thrown back into the traffic.

The effort was all too much for the old hog. He kept taking hits from things over which he had no control. The more he got hit, the more he got hurt.

Finally, he found himself wedged between a rock and a hard place, bleeding to death with no options. No one knew where the old hog was, and so he bled to death all alone at the mouth of Tyler Creek.

People aren't hogs, and no matter how rigidly we find ourselves wedged between the rocks and hard places of life, there are options.

What options? What can be done?

Those who are hurt can let others know they are hurt. There's nothing wrong with crying for help. Those who can help can look harder for those who need it.

The nooks and crannies, the rocks, and the hard places are very visible in our society.

Some can look out for, and some can cry out to, and together we'll close forever the door that leads to the dimension of no resorts.

GETTING STUCK

Cody got stuck in the attic one day. He'd never had the opportunity to go up into the attic before. It's above the garage and becomes the final resting place for the following things:

1. Things we can't pay anybody to haul off,

2. Things we think we'll need to use again one day, but never do,

3. Things we don't want anybody to know we own,

4. Things we can't sell at yard sales, but because we paid so much for them, we won't throw them away, and

5. Things we use once a year like plastic Santa Claus, Christmas trees, Easter baskets, hanging pumpkins, and creepy cardboard skeletons.

Cody used to always assume that it was a place filled with ghosts as well. And they are the materialistic ghosts that remind me and his mama of our rampant consumerism.

But to Cody, they were Casper-friendly kinds of ghosts. And on this day, having become a bit older, he accepted his mother's offer to go into the attic with her. After he'd been up there a while, he became hooked and wanted to make the place into a fort.

Thoroughly excited, he yelled for me to come take a look at what a big boy he had become in just a matter of a few minutes and a few rungs.

The pull-down ladder had needed fixing for a long time. We were reminded of that as it moaned and cracked a little bit more every time we used it. My two hundred and twenty pounds required an extra brace beneath it to guarantee that we both stayed on a vertical slope.

So, I acquiesced to Cody's plea to "come on up" and revel a while in his new-found freedom.

Freedom from attic ghosts and

Freedom from climbing tall, creaky ladders.

"Let's go, boy; it's time to get down from here," I said as I backed down the ladder.

He stared down at me, and I could tell he was getting dizzy looking at the distance between him and the garage floor.

"Wait, wait, wait a minute," he fretted, pointing his finger at me. He was serious. This was serious.

"No, come on. I'll carry you." I reached up and tried to take him under his arms.

He squealed like he does when he runs through the yard sprinkler on a hot summer day. But the happy squeal turned into a scream. I understood this kind of fear.

One of the many hats I have worn in my life was that of a chaplain in the United States Army Reserve from 1977 to 1989. While in college, I had gone through the Basic and Advanced Reserve Officer Training Corps, knowing I would switch later into the chaplaincy. You see, I didn't want people to have a chaplain who hadn't been through the same training they had. I considered my preparatory training to be good PR.

But, in training, they expected me to repel down the side of a small mountain, even though I was against war. How could they dare do such a thing? Anyway, I got stuck at the top, just a few feet over the edge. I wasn't stuck on anything except my own fears.

"Get down from there, Naylor," the drill instructor demanded.

"I can't," I whined as I looked down at the ground that twirled beneath me.

"Somebody go get the captain," the sergeant said after I had successfully held everybody at bay for about fifteen minutes.

"Get down from there, Naylor!" the captain authoritatively screamed.

"I can't," I repeated for the fiftieth time.

They threatened me with everything short of death and called me things I didn't even know existed. Climbing up the mountain was easy. I didn't care much for going straight down tied to a rope. We were supposed to be repelling, not falling to our deaths.

Chaplains really didn't need this skill. I mean, really?

Obviously, I got off that mountain. And when it was over, my fears were obliterated so mysteriously that I wanted to go again. They wouldn't let me.

"We want to eat sometime today, Naylor," the drill instructors mocked.

It's funny how, after serving more than a dozen years in the reserves, I was never called upon to repel down a mountainside.

"Let's just sit down and rest a while," Cody begged.

"Rest awhile? Okay, just for a minute," I agreed.

The attention span of six-year-olds can be measured in microseconds. Cody timidly turned around and backed down the ladder with his eyes focused upward. Like a cat stalking a blue bird, he guided his feet gingerly from the last rung down onto the concrete floor.

Then he jumped up and down, giggling like a contestant on The Price is Right.

"Let's go again, let's go again," he piped.

Incredulously, I just stared at him. I was having a fit of ROTC flashbacks.

SPRING WATER

We have a spring water cooler in our house. Get one. You'll be glad you did. Somebody can pay me for this endorsement if they'd like to. Once you get stuck on spring water, you won't care a drop about tap water ever again. Just don't pollute the environment by using plastic bottles.

Nutritionists are warning us about the value of good minerals nowadays. Initially, I didn't care for anybody telling me how bad tap water was and how I needed to be drinking purified spring water. I got over it. Now I'll go thirsty before I drink tap water. Well, maybe.

I wish I'd had this fetish in 1980. An Atlanta businessman had paid for a group of theology students from five seminaries to take an archaeological tour of the Middle East. Each seminary nominated five students. The Southern Baptist Theological Seminary chose me for some reason.

We were warned about drinking the local tap water in Jordan, but I got thirsty. We'd been traveling along the King's Highway all day, on the way to the Red Sea. It's a godforsaken, dusty, and winding stretch of road that leads from the great capital of Ammon down to the Gulf of Aqaba.

We stopped to eat lunch at an old Crusader castle that had become the local diner. My thirst was screaming, "Quench me, quench me!"

A modern-looking water fountain heard my screams and called to me, "Over here, over here, there's w-a-t-e-r."

Burp, burp, burp, followed by slurp, slurp, slurp. Three hours later, my stomach was groaning, "Why did you drink that water? Now I am going to have to make you miserable."

I have been to many countries with suspect water fountains, including Mexico, but I never had "the runs" like I did on the King's Highway. The road twisted every centimeter. And when it did, so did my guts. I became dehydrated and again begged for water.

"There's no water here; are you nuts? We're in the middle of the desert, and it's the twelfth century," a little voice in my head mocked. I think I had my first and only hallucination on this trip. It would be miles before we reached our hotel.

"Stop this bus!" I yelled. Several of us got out to revisit all the wonderful things we had eaten that day. It was some consolation that others had made the same stupid mistake.

"How far?" I pleaded like a begging Bedouin.

"Not far," was the patronizing answer.

We drove on for another thirty thousand miles before we came upon our oasis in the desert. "Aha, a nice cool room, some spring water, a nice soft bed, and hopefully a toilet," I dreamed.

"Okay, we're here, folks, but since we're late, the restaurant's closed, and we'll have to go straight to our rooms. And be sure not to drink the water," our professor shouted out like a tour guide to the underworld.

"What?" my gut bellowed. "No water. How will I live?"

It was after midnight when we got into our rooms, and both my roommate and I were dying men. We took turns in the toilet all night. As soon as I'd get through, I'd hear him scratching at the door.

And after he'd been in there for about thirty minutes, I'd crawl from the bed to the bathroom door and scratch the same code.

One time, when it was my roommate's turn, I went crawling down the balcony, scratching on everybody's window screen.

"Water, has a-n-y-b-o-d-y got water?"

I started promising people my inheritance for just a little water. The sick would moan back to me in a commiserating way, and the few who were not told me to try going back to bed. Right.

When I got back to my room, it was my turn for the bathroom. I suffered through the agony and climbed back into bed, thinking that, as weak as I was, I might be able to fall asleep and escape this nightmare.

At 3:00 a.m., a man began to pray through a Walmart bullhorn from high atop the local mosque. A donkey began to bray, not pray. And, between the two of them, they vied most boldly for God's attention until dawn.

I lay there half-awake and half-asleep and had surreal visions of spring water. I whispered the assurances of Psalms 104:10 over and over, "He sendeth the springs into the valleys, which run among the hills." But we were in the desert.

Death was the name of that hotel. It was the worst night of my life. As we boarded the bus the next day, we all wondered, "How could anything be worse? Nothing could compare to this night, right?"

Pulling away, we watched the maids take the sheets and towels from our rooms and merely shake them out over the balcony before putting them back into the rooms. How enterprising were these hoteliers, saving on wash money?"

I started getting sick all over again.

Three cheers for spring water, now and forever.

Grandbaby Finn, son of Joshua and Meaghan

GIMME THAT OLD TIME RELIGION

After the Korean War, Daddy had become a Southern Baptist minister for whom beer was anathema. While war might drive some folks to drink, it turned Daddy into a teetotaler.

While finishing up his preacher's degree at Union University in Jackson, Tennessee, our neighbors' rowdy weekend guests often tested Daddy's resolve to face the evils of beer-drinking.

Beer cans slung up under the car of a freshly ordained servant of God, who was beginning new beginnings, did not sit well with Daddy's temper.

Southern Baptists were fervently against the drinking industry and still are. Mostly. Well, that is on Sunday or any other time during church services.

Pastors stood completely against the idea. Deacons, laymen, and all others, on all other occasions? Well, I think that's still up for debate and depends on the nature of the occasion, who's there, who's not, and who'll tattle.

These particular beer cans under our car didn't belong to any Baptists, though. At least, not in Daddy's mind, they didn't. They must've been denominational "unknowns" tossing cans under his car. Obvious heathens.

Today, I realize they weren't heathens, but back then, I wasn't old enough to know much of anything except that whoever was doing it, it wasn't my mama, my sister, or me!

As it turns out, they were just some country and jazz songwriters trying to make their mark in something new in the music industry called *rock 'n' roll*. They were just people struggling along, writing songs, trying out tunes, and dreaming of making it big one day, which, with a song like "Blue Suede Shoes," I guess they did. (Elvis didn't write it; he only sang it.)

Top 40 notwithstanding, back then, they appeared to be heathens to conservative Baptists. Daddy didn't care who they were or how famous they might become, but I, on the other hand, must admit it brings a bit of a prideful smile to my face to know the likes of Carl Perkins and Elvis Presley were throwing beer cans under MY daddy's car. It's a myth that Elvis didn't drink. He simplified his drinking to a select few. And sometimes that included the beer cans that wound up under our car in the fifties!

The church folks out at Hatchie Bottoms, Tennessee, were not so rowdy but just as colorful. I don't remember his name, but there was a famous revival preacher who could stir up the locals like none other.

They were called revivalists, sort of like the televangelists of today. This guy didn't have the marvels of cinematic technology to help stage his crusade, but he did have his own peculiar technology of pizzazz. His preaching was what I call a *screaming-screeching-hollering-stomping* kind of preaching.

It wasn't a golden oratory like Daddy's preaching. Daddy's preaching was powerful but dignified.

This fellow would yell and shout at the top of his lungs while implementing a twisting gyration that would perk the interest of most anybody and make their eyebrows pop upwards. He would attempt to keep pertinent dramatics in step with scenes from his frenzied stories.

For effect, he'd run around in a circle, jump up and down, stomping his feet, or howl like the mythological hellhound, which I used to read about as a kid. His performance was gauged for whatever the story line needed.

He could get on his knees and tell a sob story about some little heathen repenting before God and weeping like Jimmy Swaggart, asking for forgiveness after sleeping in compromised company. Country revivalists would use drama (and, unfortunately, scary tactics) to get religion into people.

Every country church had to have at least two revivals every year. Revivals would last for two weeks, providing both morning and evening performances, er, I mean, services. It was good socializing and even better live drama. Back then, most people could only get one or two television stations if they even had a television.

People may find this sort of thing amusing today. But these folks enjoyed spending two weeks, both morning and night, listening to some raving would-have-been actors rant and roar and scare their mortal skins to death.

Boredom makes people tolerate the strangest things. It's funny, but it's not.

Though most of those same people wouldn't stand for such a thing today, they did then. They not only took it like a good dose of medicine but also allowed its strange theology to dictate a backward and condemnatory mentality to be fostered throughout the entire culture.

They did so to the point where good common folks were harassed into the fields of the heathen.

Daddy's preaching was the kind that brought folks into the fields of God's love. The flowers smell better in such a field. People much prefer a God of love to a God of unwavering condemnation.

All in all, revivals were the meat and potatoes of community socialization. The centerpiece was not the preaching but the potluck dinners that preceded every service. The banquet tables were covered with something that everybody else made; you could stuff yourself silly, and I did!

Elongated tables set up outside were decked with pecan pies, chocolate cakes, pumpkin this and that, rhubarb pies, custard delicacies, and a thousand other things, with scores in every category.

"Pecan pie? Whose did you have? You didn't have any of mine, pastor," twenty squatty-hatted ladies would pine.

So, everybody made everybody eat everybody's pecan pie, and everybody made everybody eat everybody's custard pie, and, well, there you'd go eating like a pig.

After that, everybody would go off to the revival services stuffed and satisfied, if not with a little upset stomach. With gurgling stomachs, they'd listen to the revivalist pound the misery of sin so sickeningly before them that it's a wonder all of them didn't become so convicted in their heartburn as to throw up all over the place.

What a mess that would have been! But you can count on it. There would have been somebody who would have found God's movement even in something like mass vomiting, discounting without exception that it could have been the movement of their gastrointestinal perturbations.

Most famous revivalists had a single, most popular sermon that they would preach at every revival. Whether or not it had been preached before to the host congregation was irrelevant.

They would announce at which service the famous sermon would be delivered, usually on Saturday night. Sort of like the Saturday Night Movie Special. They would advertise how many times the sermon had been delivered and how many souls had been saved.

Dr. R.G. Lee, the three-decade-long pastor of Bellevue Baptist Church in Memphis, Tennessee, delivered his famous sermon "Payday, Someday" over 1200 times before he died in 1978. Check it out; there are about 50 videos of it running all the time on YouTube.com.

But the revivalist in my story often delivered a sermon with the title "The Red Lights of Hell" and drew such a crowd that the service would have to be carried out of the building onto the hillside. Hundreds of chairs would surround a sizable platform, and even more people would sit on the grass further up the slope.

Out in the dark of night, the revivalist was surrealistically illuminated with only a few primitive, low-watt bulbs strung across tree branches and the stars in the heavens above.

The preacher wore a bright red suit with little, red, light bulbs wrapped around him like Christmas tree lights. His sermon was about the ten decisions in life that would lead one to Hell. (Only ten?)

With the introduction of each step, he'd manage to make one of those lights click on, and by the time he was finished, he would be all lit up.

Beaming in the starlight, the old fellow moved about like magic in his red suit and ten red lights, kind of like a real-life Santa Claus Christmas tree. The difference was that there were no ho-ho-hoes or joyous rejoicings.

This revivalist was a true blue "Hellfire and Brimstone" preacher. There wasn't supposed to be anything joyous to rejoice about while walking the ten steps to hell, and this guy made sure of that.

This sermon, as well as his other ones, was packed gruesomely with all the good old-fashioned best sellers of biblical horror. These images would do little to extract much emotion from today's blood-thirsty, Hollywood-indoctrinated public.

On a balmy Saturday night, sitting on a hard rock anchored on the slope of a Tennessee country hillside, his picture-graphs crushed down upon people with the full force of Lucifer and all the wolf hounds of hell.

What an effect these pictures of pain and suffering must have had on little kids who were safe and sound on grandma's lap! I'm thankful I was only five. I can't imagine why I don't remember so many of the hellish shenanigans of this 1950s Dante. Psychologically traumatized, maybe?

I heard others tell parts of this story a thousand times for twenty years, and often wondered why a man like that had such celebrity status. Compared to the elegance and intelligence of Daddy's oratory, I felt like it was a disgrace to call them both members of the same calling.

I used to daydream about this fella, preaching and stomping and shaking loose whatever godliness these good common folk had in them. He'd get to that point where he would switch on that tenth light, and a faulty wire would start smoldering, short-circuiting both the lights and the preacher.

I can remember envisioning him with his hair frizzed up, his body and face ablaze and smoking, as he ran, jumping and screaming, off the stage and across the rustic, country hillside. Amen! Hallelujah!

"*The Red Lights of Hell*" by that old revivalist and "*The Beer Can Melodies*" by Carl and Elvis make for some great memories. I admit some of them are only memories of stories that were told to me as a child, but since I was present in little boy form, I get to count them as real memories. They turn the crank of my soul, making me hunger for their taste.

I search for memories about the days when security could be defined with the word family and good fellowship could find expression through the sweet, innocent decency of well-meaning common folks.

Skip all the fancy talk about what kind of ideological conflict the present might have with the past. What's important is that the memories are there.

Wholesome.

Pure.

Sacred.

They are like wellsprings of fresh water, providing wisdom from a flowing brook. I drink from these waters from time to time, and they revive me long after the hectic, apathetic spouts of the 21st century have run dry.

Army Sgt. Jack Calvin Naylor in Mid 20s. Daddy served ten years in the military during WWII and the KOREAN WAR. Five years in each AND five years each in the Army and the Air Force!

THE MAN IN THE BOX

I t's a large box. Its address is a curb at the intersection of Seventeenth and Walnut Streets in Center City, Philadelphia. The ancient skyscrapers surrounding it are out of focus, dwarfing its presence.

The stream of people that move past it is noticeably unsettled. Cadence strides lose their momentum. Some folks lose their balance as they stretch uncomfortably to see without the appearance of staring.

It's a brown box. The texture is weathered, but there is no doubt that it has been firmly positioned, and only deliberate force will move it.

A shadowy figure mysteriously moves inside. It's a refrigerator box. Giant letters boldly dominate its side.

WHIRLPOOL.

The box is dry; yesterday it was wet.

❧

Few children can grow up without becoming fascinated by boxes. Back in my little boy days, I loved playing with boxes.

Our house was always full of old boxes, new boxes, little boxes, cigar boxes, hatboxes, and shoeboxes.

My favorite, however, was a big box. Precious collectibles found a special place in the little boxes of my childhood. It was, however, only in a big box that I could enter a world filled with fantasy.

I could turn it into a house, a fort, a castle, a store, a church, a train, or a spaceship. Like many things from childhood, it could be anything my imagination might decide.

Big boxes did not come along very often. When they did, my parents would not stand for the clutter they created. So, it was urgent business to begin as quickly as possible playing with these big boxes. After all, they might be gone tomorrow. While they were available, however, I was transformed.

Taking possession of a new box required a process of conditioning.

First, I would place the box in the best possible place. Then I would cut out the appropriate windows and doors. Crayons provided color and pizzazz. I would finally enter the magical doorway in a special way full of secret boyhood ceremonies, and that would begin a day of untold adventures.

My grown-up eyes just can't see how I could have spent the entire day captivated by a box. But I did. And my guess is that you did too.

I admit that the thought of playing in a box no longer holds me spellbound. Yet, it continues to hold my respect in some special way.

My father used to preach on Sundays about old Diogenes. You know the ancient Greek guy who went around with a light, ever searching for an honest man? The evangelical fervor stirred up by my father's depiction of Diogenes is one that lingers in my mind.

My father described Diogenes' home as a box standing like a citadel in the middle of a once golden but now egocentric culture. What imagery! A philosopher roams the streets, looking for honesty. But instead of finding the truth he seeks; he is hounded by skeptics while holding a light against the darkness of their despite and intimidation.

All of this pushes him home to sleep—in a box!

One of my best friends says his father used to put him in a box when he was misbehaving. It was an innocent thing, and he remembers it as humorous, lasting only a few seconds. But for me and his other friends, it's a chance to "get his goat." That's an idiom for, "Let's drive him batty." It's not a baby boomer saying or a southern saying; in fact, nobody really knows who said it first or why. The point is, if someone plans to get your goat, look out because your friends are about to have some fun at your expense.

So, nowadays, when my good friend starts acting a little nutty, we threaten to put him in a box. It's almost always only an innocent threat because the logistics of spontaneously pulling off something like that at the slip of the lips make it impossible, but sometimes we've been known to find a box nearby that at least fits on top of his head. We laugh a lot about it, but what if—what if every time we began to lose control, we could take a little "time out" in the safe haven of a box?

Secluding ourselves...

Meditating and praying until it was safe for us to face reality...

It might be good therapy.

I've discovered that hiding in the bathroom during those times when I absolutely must get away is a pretty good strategy. The bathroom seems to be a sacred place where no one bothers me. I'm sure it is because they would feel rudely intrusive if they did. Maybe.

I do remember one time I became comfortable and settled in our brand new, giant, ceramic claw-foot tub. I was going to break it in with a new book, but I barely got sudsy before a pack of kids were dancing at the door for relief.

It's nice to have a hiding place. A box would do fine.

On the flip side of that coin of thought, I could dribble philosophically about how we still live in step with a boxed-in world, both psychologically and physically. We certainly do if the definition of a box is a confined space with four sides, a top, and a bottom.

Thus, most of our houses are boxes. Most of the places we work are boxes. Most of the places we shop are boxes. And to continue the symbolism, most of our daily routines are boxes filled with self-inflicted demands. I know, I know. I'm over the edge. But it's true.

Maybe that's why we never recognize the truth when we see it; we're always pushing it over the edge, so we won't have to confront it. You know, out of sight, out of mind!

Not quite. In the matter of confronting the truth, out of mind is out of reality! (I'm glad I finally figured that out.)

Chelsea was about four years old when I first saw her setting up business in a computer box. When I told my wife, she confessed that she too used to play in boxes. All these years, and I never knew. In fact, according to the annals of her memories, she once had a palace of sorts built when her father brought home a new refrigerator, washer, and dryer. It was her mother who helped her construct a series of connecting boxes that would have aroused the envy of any child.

Joshua was about twelve years old when he heard this tale and believed with great conviction that his mother must have been the "luckiest person in the universe." I must admit that when I heard about this cardboard kingdom, I was both jealous and intimidated.

One day, my little girl Jenny crawled into an old, dirty box that was headed for the dump. Before I could stop her, she had already set up housekeeping. She had her purse, her bear, a napkin, a piece of apple (for sustenance), and a determined resistance to being evicted.

Like all toddlers do, she kicked and screamed when "Daddy the Demolisher" dragged her out and destroyed her home. She forgot about it within five minutes, but she found many more in the years that followed. Boxes are fun, and every kid knows that.

Or are they? There's someone who lives in a box on a thousand street corners. We read about it. Multimedia constantly projects images of it. Some of us see it.

Up close.

Everyday.

But few of us think about it.

I realize that no one wants to think about it, let alone be preached to about people living in boxes.

It's not fun to think about the inequities of a society that allows for palaces for some and cardboard boxes for others. Besides, box people are demented, disgusting, displaced drug addicts, aren't they? They don't have to live in boxes, do they?

If they really wanted to, couldn't they find a job doing something or live on welfare or in a shelter? An institution will scoop up the demented, won't they? Why should we have to think about this anyway? Somehow, the biblical writer Paul seems to have come up with the answer for this one:

"When I was a child, I spoke as a child; I understood as a child; but when I became an adult, I put away childish things."

Steam rises from the ventilators along the street. It is 10:22 p.m. when I walk past the man in the box—asleep, weary of the pace of his existence.

I stop to stare at the storefronts around me. They are crowded with decorative French furniture, exotic tapestries, porcelain vases, and a thousand other trinkets that the vanity of our culture imposes upon us.

Stores with multi-million-dollar inventories ominously mock the man in the box.

Suddenly, I see his face peering from a doorway that is just like the one I had cut out with my mother's fine sewing scissors 65 years ago. A cold chill runs up and down my body, exploding at the top of my head.

Why is he here? I don't want to look at him. I want to keep my boxes hidden within the memories of my childhood. He distorts that image and takes all the fun out of playing in boxes.

I don't want to put away childish things. The confrontation has left me frozen. Yet, I know that the reality of life has already mandated that I put away childish things.

"When I became an adult, I put away childish things."

What will I put in its place?

As I turn to walk away, I glance at the store window in front of me. High in the display hangs a huge red heart. A little angel perches on the crest. The reflection of oncoming headlights makes its metal eyes come to life. They center on the large, brown box.

The whole scene becomes surreal.

The huge, silky, red heart shadows his world.

The angel's enlivened, gleaming eyes keep watch.

With enlivened eyes and huge hearts, the world around us becomes more centered. More meaningful.

§

Half a block away, I stole one last peek. A shadowy figure moves mysteriously inside the large, brown box on the corner of Seventeenth and Walnut Streets, Center City, Philadelphia.

Jenny no longer plays in boxes but dances in fields of flowers!

FEEDING ON RUMORS,
MY GRANDFATHER'S WEAKNESS

An American artist landed in a Guatemalan jail back in the nineties. The little town of Escuimtla called out five hundred policemen to protect her from the lynch-minded crowds, but still, her safety was jeopardized. When the military came in with federal troops and armored vehicles to keep the area safe, order was restored.

A drug smuggler? A murderer? A pervert? What was her crime? Nope, none of the above. Locals believed she was stalking around for babies that could be stolen from loving mothers and taken to America to be put to death.

Why? At the time, the locals had been led to believe it was to stock a bank with infant parts needed for transplants by desperate Yankee patrons. The accusation smacks bitterly against all Americans.

Millions of Americans are hungry to adopt infants of all nationalities. My oldest son, Ryan, and his wife, Rachel, traveled the world looking for a baby to adopt after having had two naturally born children of their own. It took years of frustration, time, money, and love to fulfill their dream. Finally, they came home with twins—not babies, but loved all the same.

The American artist in that Central American tropical paradise had not been searching for babies on that fateful day. The newspaper reported that she was sipping a cool glass of pineapple juice in the little town square when officials spirited her off to jail in order to save her life. Locals had turned into vigilantes and were preparing to dispense justice at the end of a noose.

For decades, Americans have continued to adopt babies from practically every country in the world. Nowadays, U.S. citizens are prevented from adopting children from Guatemala. But in the 1990s, Guatemalan babies were adopted at a rate of ten a week. It was big business, but mostly good business.

The Guatemalans of yesteryear lived in overcrowded, poverty-stricken cities and couldn't understand why their neighbors to the north needed so many babies. Didn't Americans have enough babies of their own?

When the American artist arrived in the early 90s, there were whispers going around that there had to be another reason why a wealthy country like the United States needed tiny babies from unimportant Guatemala.

The rumor mill concluded that rich Americans needed baby parts. What else?

Idle American women sitting around drawing, making jewelry, and drinking pineapple juice were dead ringers for undercover body snatchers.

The emotions of rumor accused, judged, and condemned the American artist. Authorities got wind of the planned execution and intervened to save her life. But that didn't prevent the outraged citizens from storming the jail, fighting with five hundred riot police, and destroying ten vehicles.

Fears stoked by lies served as the fuel for their rage.

Wait, let's put that into the present tense:

Fear, stoked by lies, serves as the fuel for people's rage—even today! (Sound familiar?)

This isn't the fault of only developing cultures. Americans have a history rich with the blood of rumors. Rumors got us started in more than one war.

Politicians were so eager to rev up the engines of imperialism that when the battleship Maine blew up in Havana's harbor, a rumor that the Spaniards did it resulted in the Spanish American War.

In 1915, German U-boats sank the ocean liner Lusitania, and American officials cried murder. We lied. Americans had agreed not to transport munitions to England aboard passenger ships, but the Lusitania was full of the stuff.

We denied it to the Germans and our own people. But a tempered attitude had been sown that would make it more acceptable for Americans to enter the war later.

Don't even mention Vietnam's Gulf of Tonkin. (Millennials, Generation X, look it up!)

Americans dwell on rumors, crushing anything and anybody that gets tangled up in one. Some rumors turn out to be accurate accusations. Others don't. Either way, people get hurt or destroyed in the process. Never mind innocence until proven guilty. That's boring.

My grandfather was a gullible, trusting soul. I think I told you that once before. In the community where he thrived, there were a couple of old codgers who relished the opportunity to torment him.

Radio hadn't been around long enough for people to understand everything about it when he was a young man. Only country stores or social halls even had radios. Radios? I know, crazy, right?

My grandfather's only encounter with radios was the occasional broadcast he'd hear over a quick game of checkers down at Carter's Country Store near Brownsville, Tennessee.

These two old rats had decided in advance exactly what prank to play on Grandpa Hughes the next time he was scheduled to stop by, which was at least once a week.

The mid-day heat drove him out of the cotton fields and into the shelter of the store for a smidgen of news, a little cool soda pop, and a quiet rest from the hard work of the fields.

When they saw him coming up the steps, one of the old farts ran and hid behind the huge radio that stood up against the wall. The other was prepared to toss out the bait.

"Georgie." He never shucked his childhood nickname. Hughes' loved those fat sounding names.

"I sure am sorry to hear about your wife," said the first rat, feigning grief.

"What are you talking about?" Grandpa asked. "There's nothing wrong with my wife."

"It came across the radio just a while ago that she was dead," the Tennessee devil responded. My grandfather shook with credulous fear and called the man a liar.

"It's true. Here, I'll turn on the radio. Maybe they'll tell all about it again," the man affirmed as he walked over and turned the knobs knowingly. Grandpa Hughes didn't know much about tuning in to radio stations, and as far as he was concerned, the man was being kind in helping him find the truth.

Disguising his voice, his wretched partner immediately began his morbid pitch. "Birdie Hughes was found dead just an hour ago in the living room of her house. She leaves behind her loving husband and four helpless children," intoned the ostentatious schmuck.

Quicker than the sweat of guilt could bead the brows of their consciences, they turned the radio off, and my grandfather tore out of the store and headed toward home. His mind was tormented by images of lost love, motherless children, and forfeited happiness.

The demons' bellies rolled in laughter while my grandfather wept with the nausea of defeat.

I love my grandmother's given names. She was born Birdie Lucinda Trimble. Like the swan she was, Birdie was gracefully tending the home when my grandfather burst into the house to discover what a fool he had been.

A practical joke and a rumor from hell had wounded his spirit and were a bitter wake-up call to the viciousness of human nature. Others got wind of the rumor by the end of the week, and many had come by to offer condolences.

When I was a young man, I once flew halfway across the country at a moment's notice to help a friend who had made an urgent appeal for help. He was in Las Vegas, a victim of malicious chicanery. So, I traveled at the drop of a hat (I love those old idioms) and flew from Louisville, Kentucky, to Sin City, USA.

While I was gone, the rumor mill whirled with nuclear velocity. By the time I got home 72 hours later, I discovered that instead of rescuing a friend, I had gambled away more money than I had made in two years without even knowing it. No that's not true, but I just wanted to say it! However, it is true that somebody does, every day.

Those folks down in Guatemala couldn't get control of the propelling force of a rumor that almost ended in tragedy. People will probably always be interested in the shock value of twisted accusations and information that has been scripted and inflated with lies.

But as long as the human race rules the earth, there will continue to be rumors plotted against the innocent by conniving sensationalists and plenty of gullible Georgies to make them work.

Grandma Birdie Hughes and Aunt Flossie, namesake of Mama (Flossie VonCille)

PORTRAITS OF BEAUTY

When Chelsea was a little girl, if she broke something, it would immediately become ugly. She wouldn't have anything further to do with broken and ugly things. I don't mean to hold that against Chelsea. She was a little girl, and one day she would learn all about the meaning of true beauty. But her reaction was pretty much in line with human nature.

The broken, ruined, and distorted have a rough time fitting into the scheme of things. People seem to have little variance in calling things beautiful, especially the broken things of life.

Different things qualify as portraits of beauty in my life.

Back in the 1980s, I was employed as a chaplain for the Veterans Administration hospital system. I got along great with the veterans since I was also a young army officer serving as a reserve chaplain. We could talk about war and its gritty stuff.

Part of my duties was to counsel two 100-bed units. One unit was for the terminally ill, and the other was for old soldiers and elderly government employees who didn't have anywhere else to live.

I had received a lot of training in how to hold hands with the lonely and dying.

Even though that time has passed, the beautiful people I encountered there will remain etched in my mind forever. About half of my patients were old soldiers, and the other half were retired federal employees.

Old Mr. Go-Go was my favorite. I could visit with him all day, and he would laugh and nod along approvingly, but all he could say was "Go-Go." A massive stroke had damaged the left side of his brain, stripping him of all the tools of speech except for that one silly phrase. But why the words Go-Go?

In 1954, he had been one of the government's leaders in a program that was to promote the development of a more efficacious bureaucracy. How anyone could imagine such a possibility is beyond me.

The effort was tagged with a snappy slogan for promotional purposes: "Go-Go Government." He spent several years seeking the attainment of that goal. I guess he lived and breathed it like a lot of folks do with work. It dominated his life. But he had a cerebral hemorrhage, and all he could utter for the rest of his days was "Go-Go."

It's a sad exclamation point that mockingly marks the end of a life of dedicated service. He was bubbly-happy when I visited. With tender, yearning eyes, he painted colorful images of his life. Mr. Go-Go was the master of a two-word language. He was a beautiful old man that I will always find swinging on the front porch of my memories.

Yet, remembering the man who lived in a bucket often helps me shake free from the crust of selfish indifference that mats up on me now and then.

I was told he was the only person who had ever survived this type of surgery. The disease that infected him was so pervasive that the only way surgeons could save his life was to cut off all his body below his lungs.

Nurses propped him up in his little bucket every morning. He had a head and a chest. A man who once stood six feet tall had been reduced to no more than eighteen inches of flesh.

Despite the gentle promises of his physicians, he knew he couldn't live long. Full of bright greetings, he met me every day with encouraging words that still ring out louder in my mind with every passing year.

The smile etched across his dying face created within my mind a portrait of beauty that will last forever. Although his body had become misshapen and shrunken, his spirit radiated sublime elegance and stature.

Don't get me wrong. I'm not trying to play melodrama here and lead anybody to believe that my definition of beauty can only be found around hospital wards.

I was traveling through the Austrian Alps one summer when I came across a storybook park just off the main highway.

There, at the edge of a timeless meadow, stood a monument to the famous child heroine Heidi. It was a large, oval-shaped water fountain made of black basalt. At one end, an ancient sculpture of Heidi rose high above the pool, which rippled with droplets of water pouring from the tipped bucket in her hand.

Her sculpturesque arms stretched out stiff and straight, clutching the rim as her body leaned slightly over the edge. Her face focused downward, and her gaze seemed lost in the mirroring water.

Huge brown milking cows grazed a few feet away, free, and undaunted. The giant, clanging bells that swung around their necks deafened my ears.

And where was my camera so that I might capture this Alpine masterpiece? In a mad dash, I ran to the car, retrieved my camera, and nearly killed myself trying to get back before the cows moved.

While I was gone, time melted my vision. A little girl had appeared mysteriously at the pool's edge. She hovered in ignorant mockery of Heidi's statue, which was directly across from her. She mimicked the same characteristics. Leaning, gazing, and reflecting.

The noise of the cowbells created an ethereal atmosphere, and I was almost afraid to go closer. I didn't see any other people. It was just me, the cows, and the two Heidis. It was a portrait of beauty, rich with an enchanting luster normally found only in dreams. Where did this girl come from?

I needed more film. I hadn't expected to record such an entrancing scene. The car was only a few yards away, but far enough for her to slip away unnoticed before I could return. Most of those pictures were destroyed during processing. (Fate or coincidence?) Only one survives, and for decades I kept it locked away in a safety box. The other images are locked away safely in my memory.

Fast forward about 35 years. It's not the snow-capped Alps but the hell-fire jungle of the Philippine tropics. My wife Jeramie and I took our youngest daughter Jenny for a tour of the very first Catholic cathedral built in all Southeast Asia located in the country's second largest city, Cebu. It was near the place where the Spanish explorer Magellan met his fate at the hands of the native folks, who weren't too keen on entertaining his marauding band of sailors. Anyway, oh my, that's another story.

On this special day, my wife and I were attempting to keep up with six-year-old Jenny as she raced around touching things that I'm pretty sure could get us into serious trouble if we didn't bring our little whirlwind under control right away.

Behind the cathedral was a little garden, and in that garden was a well that had been made in colonial times and preserved with reverent hands over the centuries. I had been so focused on keeping Jenny from breaking precious artifacts that I had missed the transitional moment when she finally relaxed and bent down to watch the water in the little well.

I can't explain what happened next, but it is the pure truth from my heart to yours. I stopped frozen in the jungle heat. A primal, yet gentle caress embraced my mind, which then just as quickly released me with the sound of a great *swoosh*! Inexplicably, my mind was transported back across the decades to that Alpine fountain dedicated to Heidi.

In her place, I saw my Jenny, lost in lazy abandon, leaning drowsily on her elbows with palms to her cheeks. With sublime innocence she cast her eyes into the same mirroring waters of my past. Two angels coalesced.

At that instance, past and present merged into one glorious, sensational memory that overwhelmed me to sit and observe. I, the observer of two giant universes representing past and present, consumed me with the knowledge that our memories are sacrosanct to the very existence of the present. I felt drenched in humility.

But as quickly as I sat down to marvel about my newfound insights, I jumped up! "Where's my CAMERA?" I screamed.

Rushing over me was the same fear I had experienced many decades earlier. I was afraid that I was going to miss recording this most precious event.

Hold on! Nowadays, no one needs to worry about film! "There's a camera in your phone dummy," I screamed inside my brain. Aha! Snap. Done. Saved.

This time, there was no need for my camera to capture a mystery girl. It was my very own little Jenny who starred in this most heavenly scene. Jenny was my Heidi. Both photos are framed side by side in my office, forever.

I know another girl who is so beautiful that all the queens who ever sat upon all the thrones of all the kingdoms, would slip from their chairs to become her handmaidens. With golden skin and raven-soft hair, her voice melts hot into the mantle of my soul. What do you do with a girl like that? She is the absolute definition of beauty. She is my beloved, wed to me in purest charity so many years ago.

. . .

Like starfire, her eyes forever search deep into my heart.
Like rose petals, her cheeks feel so soft to my touch.
And when she looks my way so much,
It's not my fault that I always fall in love.

Beauty is her name, and beauty is her smile.
Beauty is her walk, and beauty is her touch.
Beauty is her voice, and beauty is her taste.

Maybe you have one of these Cleopatras in your house. Well, maybe Cleopatra isn't the greatest example to use here. History seems to verify the outward beauty of the mighty queen. However, I'm ineluctably led to believe that she was a veritable mess on the inside.

No, her portrait of beauty and those like her is false.

The truest portrait of beauty is that which is purest in love for those around them. How they appear outwardly is irrelevant to the cartography of their hearts.

Wife Jeramie and daughter Jenny

CANTILEVER OF TRUTH AT THE BOOT BARN

For the first time in thirty years, I decided to buy some cowboy boots. So, I went to "THE BOOT BARN," a store sublimely, if not pompously, named! A pleasant young lady was overly eager to help my wife and me as we walked through the store.

With just a twist of my head, I had an eerie sensation flood over me, causing me to think that I just might know her. Without delay, ''I asked her the obvious, "Don't I know you?" She answered with a big cheesy grin, "I don't know, do you think?" And then I realized she was teasing me, and I accused her quickly, "You're one of my former students!"

Her answer rushed over me so unexpectedly. It was a strange, unusual, and rarely felt feeling. "Yep!" she said with an accent befitting anyone working in a store filled to the rafters with cowboy boots. (Yeehaw!)

I answered back, "Did you learn anything in my class?" Almost without forethought, she blurted out, "Truth," and we all laughed at her expertly tallied response to her old ethics professor.

What a response, I thought! Many might have given vague

answers just to make the awkward conversation with their old professor go away.

This girl's abrupt and confident answer caused the hair to jump up, (not stand, but jump) on my neck. She had an answer!

She proceeded to inform my wife, Jeramie, that she was not a philosophy major but had a degree requirement that led her to my ethics class, and since she didn't really want to take the course, she hadn't paid much attention in the beginning. But take a breath; you guessed it, eventually it became her favorite class.

Tirelessly, she seemed to talk as fast as a runaway train. As her gushy burbling caused me to feel that she was taking things too far, I shied away from her compliments, saying, "It's not necessary to brown-nose," and we all laughed again (like people do in unusual and awkward situations).

As she busied herself half-heartedly back into a stack of boots, I asked her, "Can you please tell me seriously, all brown-nosing aside, did I teach anything worth knowing?"

As I spoke, she was hanging from one of those rolling cantilever ladders that employees must use to glide around the store, retrieving high-altitude items. While riding this twenty-foot-tall stick and yielding a wondrous smile, she candidly shouted, "TRUTH, I told you! You taught us the importance of truth."

"Okay, okay, compliment accepted!" Suddenly, I felt like Socrates, Plato, and Aristotle all rolled up in one giant burrito. (I attribute that phenomenon to the Mexican restaurant next door.)

"Wow," I thought to myself. "After a lifetime of teaching, someone had truly listened. Who knew it would be the girl adeptly riding the cantilever at the boot barn?"

COLLEGE: RESPONSIBILITY? OR GUILT?

The letter of a lifetime arrived unceremoniously one day. Ryan, my oldest child, had been waiting for it for several months. I had been waiting for it for almost eighteen years.

"Congratulations! You have been accepted for admission into the 1994 freshman class of Vanderbilt University."

It went on to relay that Ryan was one of only 1,400 students selected from a pool of three gazillion applicants. Well, Vanderbilt University in Nashville, Tennessee, isn't quite that difficult to get into, but almost.

Several other outstanding colleges accepted him. Vanderbilt was originally at the top of his list, but finally his allegiance to home forced him to select Centre College of Danville, Kentucky. (The Harvard of the Bluegrass state.)

I was proud that he was going to go where he wanted to go and just as proud that he'd been admitted to any academic institution. He did it the way all parents hope their kids can—by doing excellent work, "burning the midnight oil," and making the grades.

Maybe he didn't realize it at the time, but the big push towards higher education was partly my fault. I'd been that haunting parent who tries to push and pull the best out of their kids in the hopes they'll make something of themselves in life. But is it the embrace of responsibility to do well as much as the dread of guilt that makes kids strive to get into a good university?

Ryan has always been an achiever, but for many years of his life, he worked overtime trying to make his family proud of his schoolwork.

His overachiever streak kicked into overdrive when he was about ten. He had been getting into the Encyclopedia Britannica at night and working on getting from Volume A-Anstey to Volume Vietnam-Zworykin.

That was back in the days when information was contained in books! He had hoped he could knock that out in a couple of months.

"Whoa, boy, back off the Starbucks," I remember thinking.

"Why's he doing that?" His grandmother had asked with her nose curled up, like she thought he was nuts or something.

It made me take one of those introspective pauses.

"Was it my fault?" I wondered.

Ryan had either become overwhelmed by the weight of his own personal responsibility to learn or had felt excessive pressure from his parents to do so. I had never wanted him to feel like he had to study 24/7 just to please me. Had I become one of those crazy education fathers? Was it responsibility or guilt?

It could be guilt. Ryan was good at assuming where guilt didn't rightly belong. When he was about three years old, we were riding down a congested four-lane street in Louisville, Kentucky. He saw an old wreck of a car that somehow managed to catch up with us at every traffic light.

It would puff and huff right up beside us. It didn't matter if I had switched lanes since the last traffic light. Whichever lane I was in, the old wreck managed to get out of it and end up right beside us. It was as if we were playing a game of car chess. We'd go check. And it would go, checkmate.

Ryan was amazed by the old wreck and was driving everybody nuts talking about it. Every time it would meet up with us again, he'd start asking, "Who did that? Who did that?"

The first time I answered sweetly, "Well, I just don't know, baby."

By the tenth time, I was gritting my teeth and saying, "I said, I don't know, now sit still and be quiet, please!"

Have you ever noticed when we're yelling at the kids to be quiet, the word 'quiet' tends to get yelled out the loudest? Great lesson, dad.

The last time the old wreck had gotten close to us, I suppose Ryan had decided that the only way we were going to rid ourselves of this nuisance was for someone to take responsibility for this mess of a car.

As it chugged into the spot beside us, Ryan sighed and resignedly announced, "Ryan did that."

Guilt? Or responsibility? Whichever it was, Ryan felt like he should place the burden of this mechanical disaster on his own shoulders.

Maybe it was because he usually got blamed for anything that showed up broken around our house. "WHO BROKE THIS?" has always been the name of the daily quiz show around the Naylor home.

It was a tender moment for our hearts when Ryan innocently announced his guilt. He was a better "man" than I was at the same age.

One day, Grandma Hughes put me in charge of watching over a brood of little chicks until she finished working in the kitchen. She had brought them into the house in a box for me to play with in the mudroom. I started picking them up, gently nuzzling their cottony, soft feathers against my cheeks.

One by one, I took them out of the box and loved them a little before placing them down in front of me. I had planned on getting them all out and building a corral for them with my legs. Then we could get down to some serious playing.

They started wandering off, and I started dragging them back. I hadn't learned to count yet. Nobody had told me how important that counting thing was. I thought they were all there. But as I moved to sit down, I heard and felt a squish. Baby chickens don't hold up too well under forty pound three-year-olds.

Baby chicken guts were all over the bottom of my pants, but I couldn't see the bottom of my pants, so I assumed no one else could either. I scooped up the flattened chicken pieces and threw them outside. No one could possibly see them lying at the bottom of the back steps. Right?

Grandma soon came back and said, "Where's that other chicken?" When did she learn how to count?

"I don't know. I didn't do it," I answered unusually contritely.

"Do what?" she asked in her best Sherlock Holmes voice. Uh-oh! What's she doing, trying to trick me?

"What's *them* feathers doing on your backside?" The big bad wolf —er, I mean grandma—asked.

Caught. Caught. Caught. I started crying. And as I had been learning, tears came in real handy in turning the tide of grown-up emotions. I made a childhood career out of trying to escape prickly predicaments like this.

I didn't care much for the guilt thing and only learned how to accept responsibility for things after many hard lessons and even more burned bottoms.

Like her father, little Chelsea used to run from these kinds of burdens. Before she was twelve years old, she had become very skilled at it. If you wanted to know who to blame for any disaster in our house, all you needed to do was ask Chelsea. There was no mercy. Even if the fault could be blamed on her daddy or mommy, she wouldn't hesitate to boldly proclaim the indictment against whoever or whatever was closest.

Even when she was really, really little, she had gotten so good at redirecting responsibility that she could convincingly ascribe the occasional wet sheets on her bed to the monster that faithfully slept in her room. That scoundrel!

As I've morphed into an old man, I've begun to fight against assuming guilt that's rightfully mine. It's not something I'm proud of, but I think a lot of people fight the same battle. It's part of the drive of human nature called "denial." We like to deny things that are going to pull us down and make us feel crappy. Sometimes that can be okay, I suppose.

Ryan never needed me to apologize for being a little pushy about his education during the first eighteen years of his life or any years after. Oh, I'm sure I get a little obnoxious about it sometimes. Looking back, I think I did a pretty good job of knowing when to let up.

He went to a good school, was proud of his high marks, and was always anxious to do his best. He always worked hard, from kindergarten to the time he started working on a doctorate in German philosophy. He always went into his studies with a sincere desire to take responsibility for himself and make the most of every opportunity.

I don't think I should have worried myself sick with the guilt of an overbearing parent.

When he made "A's and Okays" (as my daddy often liked to say), I was happy to give him the praise of fatherly credit. When he didn't make perfect grades, I was still happy to give him fatherly praise for his efforts.

There should be no guilt for those who learn. I promised that I would love him all the same.

Four Generations, Jeffrey, Little Jack, Jack, and Ryan Naylor.

THE ART OF PERCEPTION

I love watching little kids play in the sand along the seashore. As adults, we sit back lazily in our beach chairs, smiling godlike at our younglings, knowing they are utterly fascinated by things that we consider old news. Our kids find the wonders in the sand fascinating, but us grown-ups find the mysteries in the ocean's depths much more fascinating.

The ocean is so deep that we can't begin to understand its true secrets. The advanced technologies of our times provide scientists with unprecedented tools for learning more about the world than we have ever dreamed possible.

Microorganisms are being discovered every day that seem infinite and immeasurable. Yet, new findings every day lead us deeper into nature's once limitless depths. There aren't enough trained specialists to keep abreast of the unceasing barrage of new information. And yet, it's information that's been there since the beginning of time, but we are just now finding it.

Recently, I watched a documentary about ongoing explorations in the icy Alaskan waters. The unenviable scientist scooped up a pail of water and explained that he held in his hands various organisms so challenging and imperceptible that few could have imagined them to exist even ten years ago.

Wow! Just when we thought we knew it all, there's a universe of life in every bucket of water that surrounds the "forget-me-not" state.

It's not just Alaska. Every section of the earth is full of the unfathomable. How can the unfathomable ever become fathomable? If there aren't enough scientists to do the research, how can the rest of us regular folk ever hope to fully appreciate and understand the riddles of Mother Earth?

The earth is rich with millions of known and unknown lifeforms, many of which were imperceptible before the invention of the electron microscope. Humans have been too busy climbing the food-chain ladder to stop and perceive just how deep the ocean really is.

How deep and rich is the Amazon jungle?

How thick is the universe of life there?

How high are the crevices on top of Mount Everest?

Sure, we are amazed at every new fantabulous discovery the specialists of nature tell us about. But only a few can travel down nature's yellow brick road of perception. The rest of us wait for the report but never cash in on the reality of what others find.

The specialists tell us about their findings, but it all seems so mind-boggling. Besides, most of us don't have the luxury of being explorers.

We've got to continue working so that we can keep climbing the food chain, the socio-economic chain, the political chain, or whatever it is we must keep doing every day of every year to keep up with the pack of the "fittest."

We just don't have the time to discover the undiscoverable things around us. We don't have time to stop and smell the roses, let alone see if there's another universe hidden in each petal. No, leave us alone. We've got to go to work. To heck with the "*peri-peri-hayling*" butterfly teetering on the brink of extinction in the Amazon.

And so, we can't climb the new chains of knowledge because we're too busy climbing the old ones.

Unfortunately, only a small number of people can learn new things and then incorporate them into their understanding and view of life on Earth.

There's some irony here. It creeps up on you.

The race to the top of the food chain has left humans with little time to contemplate the vastness of the ocean.

Don't reach out for the new, the different, or the unfathomable. Everybody should remain calm and cling to the security blankets of what is known. Steer clear of the unknown! It might change you or deepen your perceptions about the world around you.

Let me wax and wane a little bit here. It makes me feel good.

The secure chains of tradition bind us, which inhibits our ability to perceive the depth of things that have always been around us, including ourselves.

The oceans are deep. The jungles are thick. The mountains are majestic. The prairies are vast.

These are common descriptions of those parts of our environment that have always overwhelmed us with their mystique.

Deep—Thick—Vast—Limitless—Infinite—
Unfathomable—Incomprehensible.

The dictionary is full of hair-raising words like these. I encourage you to think about what scares the veritable insight out of you because the world is full of daunting and marvelous things. Just google it! These kinds of words appeal to the unknowable of the world around us, or at least we think they are unknowable.

When Cody-Man was little, I used to take him on long walks, which is something I recommend all fathers do with their kids. Often, without provocation, I would jump, scream, and run around in circles at something that wasn't there, just to try and get his blood pumping. It caused his heart to start pushing some extra thinking juices into his brain.

The innocence of his young age allowed me to play this trick quite a few times before he caught on to Daddy's mischievous ways. And I don't have a clue as to why my wife still falls for it, but she does!

Recently, someone posted a bunch of videos on multimedia showing several different scenes of two people casually moving about the room, doing their chores. Suddenly, one of them screams, jumps, and runs out of the room. In each case, the other person also screams, jumps, and runs out of the room—without a single clue as to what is going on.

The first thing I thought when I watched these videos was that somebody had stolen my gig. Even though I used to do this all the time decades ago with my kids, I know I won't get any credit for it. And that was before viral videos were even a seed in someone's brain.

But I won't make any money off the idea—a dollar and four decades too late! Grandpa Hughes used to say it when he'd missed out on something, "I'm a dollar and a day late." (This seems as good a spot as any to record that memory!)

Well, silly tricks of this kind are innocent fun. However, it turns out that there's a little bit of science to this phenomenon that's not too different from that old biological concept of "fight or flight."

Just in case there is still someone out there who hasn't heard of the term "flight or fight," I'll be happy to let loose the professor in me and explain. It's an automatic physiological reaction to something that is "perceived" to be frightening. "Perceived" is the key word in that definition. If we perceive danger, there are only two options available to us, and it's been that way ever since we were sleeping in caves with one eye open.

The sympathetic nervous system takes control—there is no choice—and activates a secret power we all have locked away inside of us. In command central, we are forced to RUN or FIGHT. Most of us run. In its own way, *fight or flight* is most definitely an ingenious use of the art of perception.

So, in this instance, most everyone takes flight and runs! If we are standing beside someone and they start going crazy, it seems to be human nature to respond in the same way. Human nature dictates that if we see someone running and screaming, we have a 50/50 chance of doing the same thing.

And so it happened that Cody-Man and I were once taking a walk. Without warning, I threw my arms straight and stiff into the air and started screaming, "The sky is high. The sky is high." He froze, with fear splattered all over his face.

For a second, he didn't have a clue what I was up to. Maybe his daddy really saw something up in the sky, but when he saw me laughing, he quickly realized this was just another one of Daddy's classrooms about Mother Nature. Slowly, his overwhelmed face broadened with that trusting smile of childhood, exciting him to jump and shout with agreement, "The sky is high."

He loved these kinds of adventures. Daddy was speaking his language. He understood this truth, simply put. For him, the measurement of the sky was settled. No questions. It was a total, absolute, and complete definition.

Then we would continue along the road hand in hand, each equally but differently content. We walked with our heads pointing skyward, lost in our own worlds, each happy with our own perceptions. And the joy of perceiving that simple truth brought us closer together in understanding our world as individuals and as father and son.

The older my kids got, the deeper our conversations became. After walking with Cody-Man that day, I might have decided to have a less simplistic conversation with my oldest son, Ryan, when he was a teenager. On a clear, starry night, I could step out onto the deck and say without emotion, "The universe is infinite."

Now he could respond in one of several teenage ways. The

patronizing way: "Sure, whatever you say, Dad." There would be no thrusting of arms, no faces of unquestionable belief. There would be only the type of faces that scream, "Is-there-anything-else-to-eat-around-here?"

Or he could look me straight in the eye with a focus on my soul and say, "Yes, Dad, *the universe is infinite*." And we could stand, gazing up at the vastness above us, arm-in-arm, each equally but differently content.

We could look at the stars and the unending darkness of the universe, and we could think of a thousand ways to describe how infinite the universe is. And the joy of perceiving that truth would bring us closer together.

Through our willingness to perceive the obvious and the not so obvious, we come to a greater understanding of our worlds as individuals and as father and son.

You must surely be thinking what darling children I have who perceive so profoundly. I try not to be prejudiced, but after all, I have worked overtime brainwashing them.

How does one become perceptive? It must be taught, dear grasshoppers. How does one teach such a thing? I'm glad I asked that question. After all, that is the point of this story, which began with those swimming microorganisms in Alaska's frigid waters.

Whether it's determining the existence of an unknown species or how high your father thinks the sky is, perception alone is not the ultimate goal.

It is the *depth* of perception that counts.

Developing one's perception so that its depth increases with age is an art form. You can't just go through life indifferently, tossing around the idea that you already know enough to get by.

There must be meat to your thoughts.

There must be substance to your faith.

There must be commitment to your values.

There must be hope for your aspirations.

There must be depth to your perceptions.

How does one perceive depth? Let's take the "depth of perception" litmus test.

When we say, "the sky is high" or "the universe is infinite," how are we supposed to define these beliefs?

If I think of them no differently as a forty-year-old than when I was ten, twenty, or thirty, then I have failed. Sorry. No buts. No excuses.

I know some folks must stay busy all the time to make a living.

I know they don't have time to keep abreast of the latest physics, chemistry, and mathematics that explain our universe.

I know they don't have spare weekends to go shuttle-cruising in the whatever-sphere. But I'm not referring to just academic perception.

The kind of perception that deepens with age deepens in response to how one reacts to the everyday experiences of life. Things like work, marriage, social events, civic duties, divorce, children, education, success, and failure are the old bump-and-grind stuff of life.

Through those crazy formative years, our parents or those in charge of our care must guide us. We, as parents, guide our children. But it's one of those reciprocal things.

This initial guidance is the basic training that prepares one to go solo. You know—making the most of it on your own—going for it.

How does one make any manageable sense out of one's life experiences? Before we dare ask such a question, we must do a reality check.

Here it is: Do we really make the most of every experience life gives us? How deep is your ocean?

I don't know the answer for you, but you must take the initiative and look deeply within.

You have the psychological skills to see your innermost self at its greatest depth. It's called perceiving with your guts, your heart, and your higher consciousness. Whatever you decide to call it, it's there. You've got to be bold enough to confront it.

Every day you go through life, something—yes, something—happens to you. Whether it's good or bad in your opinion at that emotionally charged moment is irrelevant.

But you must look, grasp, grab, and reach down inside of yourself. Use the experience to meet yourself at a deeper level than you ever have before.

Each day, you will grow in your perception of yourself. With each new experience, you jump higher into the sky. And with the jump will come a heightening of your perceptions and an expansion of your knowledge of what it means when you shout into the heavens, "The sky is high."

You could say that you are too busy or too involved in maintaining the survivalist instinct to do this.

You could go through life with your head stuck in an ostrich hole.

Never attempt to see the ocean's depth.

Never jump for the sky.

Never contemplate the awesome infinity of your neighborhood galaxy.

You could.

But you know you don't want to.

You won't be satisfied with a life that never attempts to become inwardly deepened.

Old *Soo-CRATES* said it right almost 2,400 years ago, "KNOW YOURSELF." When Daddy used to try to be funny (and he really had to work at it), he'd phonetically jam up the syllables of Socrates' name. It made him feel closer to us common creatures.

The older you get; the more valuable experiences get added to your account. The more experiences you have, the deeper your hunger to explore yourself.

The wellspring of knowledge releases itself to the surface of your day-to-day grind with new ideas and new avenues for enjoying life, new ways of loving, and new ways of developing your faith.

All those things combine to create and recreate the depth at which you can perceive the world in and around you. The more you can perceive and pragmatically apply things to your life, the more your personality will become enriched.

You will find yourself breaking away from the ranks of the bored and boring.

You will become a specialist of a very different kind. You will be able to perceive your own world at its greatest possible depth.

You will know the depth of your ocean, the vastness of your prairie, and the intuition of your soul.

This journey begins with oneself. You don't have to be a veteran to learn it or teach it to others; you just have to be a practitioner. So, go home to your three-year-olds, your eight-year-olds, your twenty-year-olds, your nieces, and your cousins—your beloved ones of every age and every name.

Go with the intention of teaching and learning together the marvelous art of perception! It's never too late because the gems of experience are the stuff of life. Collect them, study them, and learn from them.

I remember a night—long ago—after a day's walk of loving and learning.

It was 1:00 a.m. I slipped into little Cody's room. The room was framed with shadows because of the hazy glow of his lamb shaped night-light.

His baby-fat face, closed eyes, and dreamy smile looked like a doll in a Macy's catalog. He turned, and reflexes caused his smile to twitch and broaden. He stretched his legs and unknowingly tightened his hug around his favorite bear.

On this night, his world was safe and secure, not because of the provisions of materialistic things, but because his trust was locked firmly in the love of those around him. I have always loved him with all my heart, as I have all my children.

How he came to perceive my love is very important. If it didn't grow as he grew older, he and I would be poorer because of it. But the older he grew, the more he learned to perceive the depth of my love for him. And I would likewise perceive a deepening of his love for me.

Throughout his life, we learned to walk hand in hand, each equally but differently content. The years moved past us, and we kept walking and talking together. As we journeyed, we thought and thought a million times, "How deep is our love for one another?"

We didn't always say it out loud. We'd sometimes just let the memories pile up on top of each other, and eventually, our perceptions would have grown to such depths that the answer would come from all our memories, washing over us like the ocean's waves.

"Daddy, how deep is the ocean?" My son asked me one day. I didn't answer for a moment—just kept strolling along the beach, hand in hand, kicking the sand against the ocean breeze. I knew exactly how deep it was, absolutely and unequivocally.

I shot a shell out across the water and watched the massive waves blast it back at me. I picked him up cuddling him tight to my heart and whispered,

"The ocean is deep. It's as deep as my love for you."

He giggled, wiggled loose from my arms, and dashed defiantly toward the waves.

No, my son is no prodigy. There is no way his young mind can perceive how deep the ocean is based on what I said. But that's where I must begin. And together we stand on the shore and shout defiantly at the waves,

"The ocean is deep. It's as deep as my love for you."

Through the intensity of our shouting, his mind will craft the image of a deep ocean that is powerful, magnificent, and massive.

The older he grows and the more I challenge him to be intense with his mind and soul, the stronger his perception will become.

As we walk through life together, he will find that this is only one of a million experiences that will mold the quality and depth of his perception.

And when I am old and gray, maybe he'll come one day, and we'll walk over to the beach to reminisce. Maybe, just maybe, I might ask him,

"Son, how deep is the ocean?"

We'll laugh and recall old times as we continue our stroll, kicking the sand. Then we might stop to think quietly, leaning into the ocean's breeze. And he'll cuddle up close to this old, frail man and whisper,

"It's as deep as my love for you, Daddy."

The young maternal grandparents of the author, George and Birdie Hughes, appear with the author's much-loved Uncle Bo in 1908

SHRIEK LIKE A BANSHEE!!!

WARNING! This story follows no rules for storytelling. It starts at the end and dives deeply into the psyche looking for explanations about the existence of life. What that means is, this story requires you to wear your thinking cap for grasping its meaning. If you don't want to read a story like this, I suggest you skip forward to the next story so that you do not waste your time and subsequently blame me for it! (SMILE HERE.)

I have a bad back. It has been bad for a long time, and now the pain has inched its way upward into my cervical spine—close to my brain. Yes, my brain, which is my closest and most precious friend. After consulting with my neurologist, he suggested three epidurals, surgically injected directly into that delicate area that houses the critical fluids that rip up and down my spinal canal like Snoqualmie's Raging River. (Yep, it's a real river. Google it!)

Today, I had my first cervical procedure, which had been put on hold after a two-month delay. The hospital gladly blamed their new computer systems as the culprit, and I can quote them, though this may not be a full quote, but it goes something like this, "bibbidi-bobbidi bibbidi-bobbidi-boo."

So, the big day had finally arrived. And I am more than excited to tell you what happened because it is the most unbelievable thing to happen in a hospital operating room that you have ever heard. If not, I promise you can get your money back. Please just fill out the form at the end of this story that is reliably provided by my hospital.

This event can, however, be boiled down to only three little things.

The 3 things:
1. The Good
2. The Bad
3. The Weird

THE GOOD

First, I must take you on a time shift to the ending of this story. It's quite an unorthodox way to tell a story by beginning at the end, but in this case it's way more fun. So, AFTER the surgery and upon returning home, I was already aware of a feeling of intense invigoration, obviously caused by the injection. Such a feeling can sometimes be mere euphoria, falsely created by high expectations of feeling healthy again.

The early evening overwhelmed me with a strange presence. Yes, I realize that sounds like the beginning of a Hemingway summer in Spain. But I really, truly felt remarkably strange—I couldn't quite put my finger on it—everything pulsed around me inside and out—the sensations were like iconic ricochets of something of my past, things unattainable, ungraspable.

Why did everything feel so incomprehensible? I was frustrated because I couldn't even think of the right words to describe it. There must be something to compare it with. So, with uncanny persistence —no, it's not uncanny; yes, yes, uncanny is the word. Uncannily seizing a forgotten force, I suddenly recognized it. I couldn't believe it. It was so ancient but real, so forgotten but reemerging. I never dreamed this feeling could have ever left me, but it had. Now it was back, and yet I had never expected to know it again. I guess by now you want to know what the heck it was.

It was the physical sensation of "youth." I don't know how to describe it, and you probably think I am just being ridiculously verbose. Yet I am writing about it in this manner because there is something almost sacred about the sensation. Something eternal. And I really don't worry whether anyone thinks I am just making this up because, for me, it is impossible to make up something that is eternal.

Youth is eternal—and yet, that feeling of eternity is often missing in our lives, even though we know in the deepest part of ourselves that it is never forever gone. Perhaps it is a mistaken relic of our past, imposing itself and, more so, revealing itself as something different. It imposes (or reveals) itself upon us at times merely because we have lost our ability to identify it the older we become.

And so, it must, if it ever has a chance to come to us again. How can anyone be so reborn inside and out to reclaim the sensation outside of youth's allotted time? In other words, how can anyone truly get to feel like they are young again after they have used up all their "youth tokens?"

I have always been either young or old and have never qualified as being young after becoming old, nor have I felt truly old when I was young. So, I possess no measuring stick to define such feelings that I may have had previously in my life. Can an old person really "remember" the scent, tone, and depth of feeling that come with youth? Such an attempt might sound beautiful as it is recalled in a nostalgic poem. But in reality? I don't think so.

How did that strange, forgotten force seize me to recognize that sensation of youth? First, I felt it when I was washing my face before dinner. The sensation was quick and gone in a second. The water touched my skin unrecognizably, making me laugh and flinch simultaneously.

Again, I felt it just moments after dinner as I was thinking of how to hang a new painting that I had recently bought from a museum gift shop. Oddly, I was excited about it, just like a kid would be. I looked at the wall, and the paint seemed to shiver or shake when I positioned the painting to hang. So what? Really, I don't know what that was supposed to mean other than that time was moving and shaking a lost possession. Something that was lost was now surging into this space, which was literally making me feel new and fresh.

And then it hit me hard. The air was full of a melody that sounded like a children's song. I felt like a kid who wanted to burst out singing. I felt youthful. I smelled youthful; my skin felt tight; and as my shoulders suddenly and spontaneously broadened out, I felt the surging strength of a young man. It's like a long-lost friend picked me up and demanded to know, "Where the hell have you been all these years?" But would it last?

Hours later, it was all I could think about. Would it last? I'd know for sure when morning comes. Maybe by then, this indefinable feeling would taste differently or define itself more flavorfully. But for those invigorating moments, that's all I could think about this long-lost friend, and for sure, I would be prepared to tell anyone and everyone if it had magically become eternal. But for that night, for sure, I could say that I felt **AWESOME**!

THE BAD

Because the procedure is considered dangerous due to its delicate position between the brainstem and the spinal cord, it required a full *gowns-up*, knockout anesthesia process. So, it began for me thusly: Firstly, LIGHTS OUT. Secondly, I WAKE UP... to shrieking sounds like the banshees of prehistoric Ireland. OH! Wait, I was the one doing the *banshee-sha-sheeing*. The shrieking sounds were coming out of my slumbering mouth! Artillery shells were bursting inside my *ganglion banglion*. "What's wrong?" the other *shriekers* shrieked!

My doctor, who just happens to be the chief of anesthesiology at this rather large hospital, suddenly distorted his face with contorted torsions. (I really worked on that word play.) He quickly did a morgue-like inspection of my head, ears, nose, and mouth, ferociously twisting my face quite aggressively. He finished his kindly assault with a rather ungentlemanly yelp for a gurney!"Gurney, somebody bring me a god-xxxxxx gurney." Something like that.

This gurney was unceremoniously (and most furiously, I might add) attained by four Nurse Ratchets, who duly heaved me onto its hard steel surface as if I were merely a loaf of bread. (I think there's a gym in that hospital.)

There was nary a misstep in their motions as the four, in unison, began their trek. With two astern, two aft, and me leaning to starboard, the gurney rolled out of the surgery bay area onto the tarmac of the hospital speedway that led to Nuclear Medicine. There, the panicked bystanders watched as the room housing the C-Scan mechanical contraption opened its doors (as if for Ali Baba himself) for the examination of my brain and neck.

Calm down! Not to worry. I'm writing this, aren't I? It can't really be bad, right? NVM!! What they found was just some juicy juice from the injection squeezed loose from the cannon that had elegantly pierced my neck. Microscopic mists tarrying too long in the spaces between my inflamed discs had "let loose" my inner banshee.

"It happens all the time," my doctor assured me. "But normally, patients don't respond so loudly." Hmmm, was that an indictment? The nurse filled me up with some fentanyl and two CCs of Versed; maybe I would forget the entire incident (if not, I might later think about suing). Hmmm... but here I peacefully lay, and I do not forget how good it feels in the here and now! But I do not sue the hospital because my neck feels **AWESOME**!

THE WEIRD (And I mean weird)

So, I have to take you back to the beginning of this event, as I'm

lying on this soon-to-be runaway gurney, and I'm all "gowned up."
The presurgical knockout drugs have yet to be administered. It's
that smart time during surgery when doctors, nurses, and other
suspicious attending participants stand in the corner, holding
notepads, and make small talk! Before gently helping me to sit up
and bend at the waist, the head nurse (her name is Celine, and
you'll want to keep track of all the names in this section) insists I
remain atop the gurney with my feet dangling over the, er, starboard side.

She exudes her confidence, I suppose, in such overdosed
measures, hoping they will positively infect my obvious jittering,
flitting, and spastic movements. Almost motheringly, she hands me
a fluffy pillow and counsels me to hug it tightly—my very own
white-encased, surgery room teddy-bear.

My anxiety abruptly terminates the moment she compliments
my cologne. I thought that this was obviously a devious nurse's tech-
nique to stroke my fears. "Oh, my goodness, your cologne is really
something," she blurted out, giggling quite professionally (?) in the
process. Before I can address her professional giggles, I am cut off
from addressing the compliment.

The doctor, who had appeared to be self-absorbed across the
room, shuffling what appeared (no doubt) to be critical papers pertinent to his imminent success, speaks out. Almost tauntingly,
regarding her giggles about my cologne, he says, "Hey, Celine, it's
not that *Whiteabaster* or something, or druthers, or whatever it is
that your fiancé wears, is it?"

More eerily professional giggles gushed from all the nurses, as
well as from one of the suspicious alternate participants who was
fiddling with some menacing, shiny, steel gadget in a back (nonde-
script) corner. She's standing far enough away from the operating
table not to worry me too much...yet!

ENTER THE PATIENT: Into this small game of surgery room talk
that usually leaves patients feeling like slathered chunks of meat
gristling with sweat on the butcher's block, I speak!

"Nope, it's not that *white-bastard* stuff your fiancé dazzles your pheromone glands with!"

I didn't say that, but it should count as credit that I even spoke up at all. By speaking up, I was admitting I knew all about their little, smutty surgery room game. Let me continue with what I really, well, mostly said.

"It's called *Sauvage* (yep, it's expensive, but I'm not humble when it comes to how good I ought to smell in public places), sponsored by Johnny Depp," I commented with a bit of *touché* in my voice. But my Kentucky pronunciation of *Sauvage* automatically came out as **Savage**.

Why so forward? Why? I decided to inject myself into this dialogue because I knew something they did not and that is once I jump into something, I'm a talker, and often, a braggart!

So, I thought to myself, *"Yep, Johnny Depp, he's savage, expensive, and smutty—just like your fiancé."* And, as we don't know yet, but will all soon learn, so is my SURGEON," who suddenly interrupted as if on cue.

"Hey, Celine, what's going on with that crazy character, Johnny Depp? You know what I'm talking about? That ridiculous story about his wife's birthday party where somebody pooped in the bed—first it was a dog or dogs—then a new boyfriend—then Depp—then the wife. But she's insane anyway, right? Who knows? She's French, right?"

PZZZZZZZZZZZZZZZ. The room filled eerily with silence, followed by the bizarre and the weird.

While the room filled up with a moment of "the awkward," and while you're taking a breath with this story, let me point out that Kentucky-born Johnny Depp often lives in France for extended periods (don't all Kentucky-born boys?) And often, in the past, he lived with his French *girlfriend* from many years ago, who happens to be the mother of his children. Her name is Vanessa Paradis, and she is an innocent victim in my surgeon's story.

However, *from* the very excellent country of France, Johnny's birthday-famous flawed wife *is not.* She's from Texas! Yeehaw! Her name is Amber Heard, also known as Mera, Princess of Atlantis, and she is the main actor in the poop-found-in-the-bed scandal and thus the star of the banter in my operating room.

Keep in mind that I am the one who introduced poor Johnny into our *professionally* charged Surgical Storytime. I was merely extolling the benefits of my cologne. My testament ostensibly declared quite aromatically that I preferred it. It was obvious by the fact that I was freaking wearing it on SURGERY DAY! (Well, you know... any surgery day is potentially your last day, so why not smell your best?) Since I brought Depp's name along for the ride, it's up to me to put this scoop about poop to bed.

Thus, in a brazen attempt to rearrange the conversation by providing a note of the positive (and I might add the unexpected retort, as you will agree), I slyly said in my very best early 20th century British working man's accent,

"Now, 'ole up ther,' guvnah... ee's got sev'ral youngins,' ee does, and they be a-turnin' out to be gud actors therselves, guvnah." (Repeat *guvnah* as many times as you like if you're really fired up and feeling old *tyme* British.)

Okay, okay, the Cockney accent was never spoken in the operating room, nor was there any deference to the doctor as a Cockney version of Kentucky Governor Andy Beshear, who was governor at the time of my surgery and his office has put out a disclaimer that, indeed, he had nothing to do with my surgery.

Nevertheless, I did point this out, using such hijinks to take the edge off the stink in the room (no pun intended, but yes, it was). You know the kind of stink I mean! It was the stink of weirdness that was filling up the story in my head and right before your shocked reading eyes here and now.

My doctor was preparing to cut holes in my back and inject me with chemicals galore while simultaneously discussing the unknown "poop" found in Johnny Depp's bed. I mean, really?

The suspicious girl with the shiny samurai sword in the back of the operating room moved about cautiously (and it appeared surreptitiously for the purposes of this story, but most assuredly not) from her corner as Celine laid me gently back onto the altar, er, table, and the last thing I heard before passing out was the doctor saying, "Alrighty now, give him 2 CC's of..."

How did the surgery go? I don't know, because when I woke up, I remember all hell breaking loose, and somebody was shrieking like a banshee, and it was ME! LOL.

The author is hotdogging it in Southeast Asia

A MOTHER'S DAY STORY

When I was living in Omaha, Nebraska, I attended a seminar about what was then a hot topic—the war in Nicaragua. I was hungry to learn more about the world of the warring factions of the *Contras* and *Sandinistas* that had caused both Presidents Reagan and Bush such heartburn. On this day, I was going to hear the story of persecution from the mouth of a real, live refugee.

He entered the room quietly and unimpressively; I assumed he was in the wrong place. He was a boy wearing a simple sport shirt, fashionably torn jeans, and unlaced sneakers. He looked like the boy who threw my newspaper in the bushes every morning. But this boy had a haunted look about him.

With studied concentration, his strained eyes seared across the surface of the hardwood floor as he searched the room for a strategic place to sit. Once he was seated, he continued to burn holes in the floor with his glassy stare. Fear did not transfix his gaze, but rather a seasoned, determinative spirit. His name was Maxwell.

The year was 1990, the beginning of a new era for this Central American teenager. A teenager? It was not a fitting category for one of such fervid presence. I kept making the simple mistake of judging him by his young appearance before hearing the narrative of his ageless story.

What could a kid have to say that would possibly interest me? Once he was introduced and stood before us, he never looked at the floor again.

Gently, he began to speak about his homeland, the conflict, and the distinction between economic and political refugees. His words were heavy with the homesickness of a fifteen-year-old.

Then he told us the story of his prodigious flight to the United States. The story he told would be worth a fortune in the hands of any Hollywood director. He had escaped through the jungles of Honduras and Guatemala, snuck into the south of Mexico without being seen, and traveled hundreds of miles to San Benito, Texas.

Finally, Maxwell arrived in the land of the free and the home of the brave, only to be arrested by immigration officials, who immediately informed him that he would be deported back to his home country.

His story was filled with thrilling events and impassioned descriptions of herculean efforts involving perseverance, struggle, pain, hunger, humiliation, and a sense of hopelessness. This young man had my attention, and I felt emotionally exhausted listening to his soft intensity.

Yet for all the adventure, it was the part about his mother that overshadowed all the rest. His mother had been the guiding force that engineered and made possible his successful escape. She refused to let him attempt his brave escape until he turned 12, the age of mandatory induction into the communist Sandinista army. She kept him close until the midnight hour.

It was a simple, ageless story about the primitive instincts of a mother protecting her offspring. She did all she could and gave herself completely, as it were, for the life of her son.

Aspiring to be an attorney, she had dropped out of school during the Ortega dictatorship and taken a job to make the necessary money to adequately fund her son's daring escape. She worked as a travel agent on the side keeping track of travel conditions and possible routes.

And then, one day, he must have kissed her goodbye like a million sons have kissed their mother goodbye for generations. Then he began the yearlong journey that culminated with his detention in a Yankee lock-up facility.

Uncertainty, fear, doubt, suspicion, anger, apprehension, hate, and love—all these things and countless more must have dominated the minds and hearts of both he and his mother for the duration of that beguiling journey. Uncertainty ended in disappointment, as the prospect of his deportation seemed unavoidable.

Miraculously, in steps this American lady, with the heart of gold and all that. You know the type—the one with the desire to do something and the ability to pull all the right strings to get it done.

Well, she boldly intervenes and adopts this boy and says, "To heck with this," to those whose job it is to ensnare the righteous in the strings and tapes of governmental bureaucracy.

Vicariously proud of the lady's success and hoping to make moral as well as ratings points, the news media rallied around her and created a video for national broadcast.

They said, "We'll tell this story to everyone, and it will warm our hearts and prove to those communist thugs that they can't always win."

And so, the boy's story was aired on national television, having a passionate but passing effect on the conscience of the American public.

Within a week, it was safe to assume most of the American public had forgotten this story or simply filed it away as another one of those sad, but unpreventable, tales of the "trodden upon."

But the Sandinistas would not forget the mockery American newscasters had made of them.

The report came slowly and vaguely, but it came. Maxwell's

mother—a young mother, a healthy mother, a heroic mother—had suddenly and mysteriously died. Why? No one knows.

It was a little-known and baffling disease that seemed prevalent only among those who exasperated political order. It is especially known to afflict those who publicly and internationally embarrass dictators.

In this case, the disease became fatal because of the unquenchable, eternal love of a mother who did all she could and gave all she had so that her only son could be free.

It's an old story, isn't it? The love of a mother is supremely expressed in the very throes of death.

I did not experience the humiliation of a communist regime while growing up, nor did I wander the jungle with the encouragement of a supportive mother.

My mother never had to sacrifice her career, her ambitions, her future, or her life so that I could be free.

Maxwell's story is an old one with precedents throughout history. These mothers of history always do the same thing when they must.

And you know what? So would mine. I have no doubt. It's that eternal maternal instinct. She would have given it all she had. If it were necessary, she would have risen to unrecognizable heights, propelled by love.

I know this because I am her son. Because I am her son, that is reason enough for her to have loved me for my entire life. I know this because it's one of those ageless, eternal things.

I know another thing too: I loved my mother just as much as Maxwell loved his. I just wish I had told her more often.

You probably know this about your mother as well.

So, take a break from the hectic journey of life's daily grind and go tell your mother that you realize how much she loves you, and for that great depth of love, you can say no less than, "Mother, I love you."

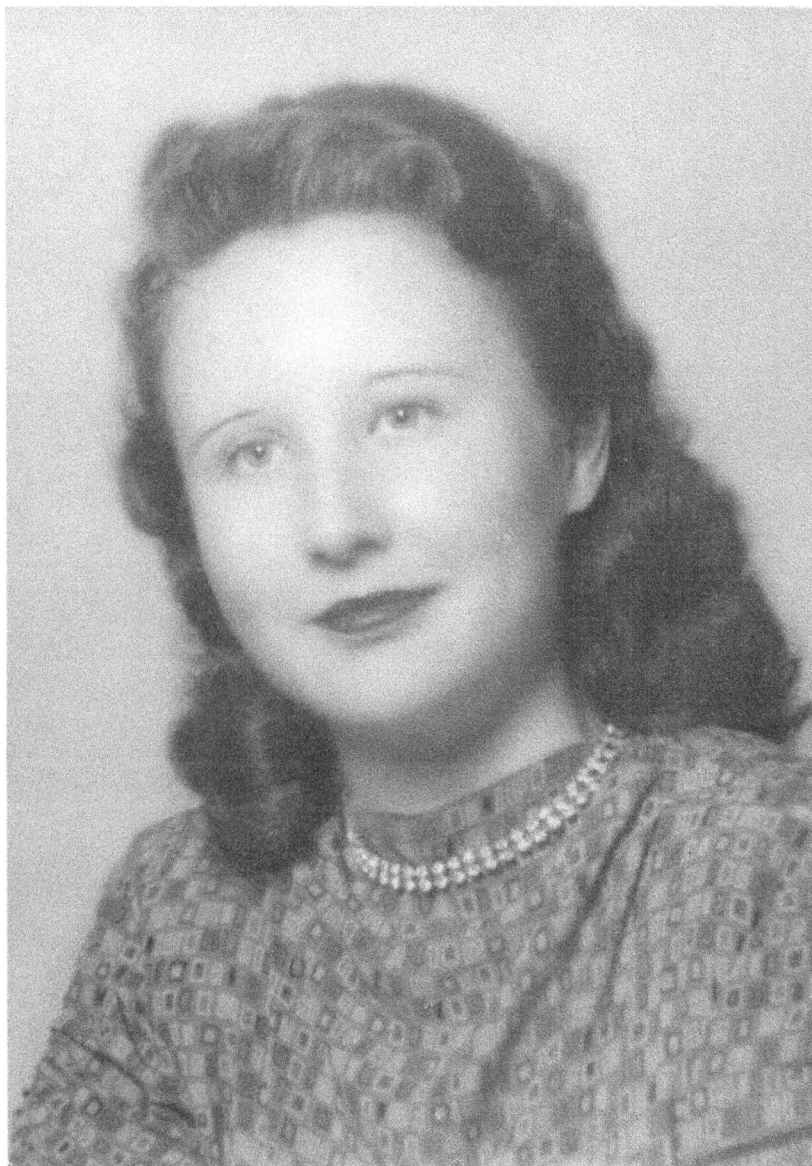

VonCille Naylor, my sweet mama, born on Valentine's Day, at age 22

WHEN GOD CALLS, WE FIND OURSELVES

I was eleven years old when I made a public decision to become a minister. Baptist folks call it "surrendering to the call." The call, of course, comes from the living God of the Judeo-Christian tradition.

We were living in a picturesque Tennessee postcard town called Charleston. It was 1965. And Tennessee living was a lazy Sunday afternoon spent swinging on an old tractor tire hanging from a fifty-foot-tall White Oak tree.

I don't suppose those folks knew much about the heritage of that little "spot in the road." Weary pioneers had traveled over the Appalachians all the way from South Carolina, looking for new lands to plant new dreams. In a pretty little valley, thirty miles from the mighty Mississippi, they had cast their lot in a new world.

Someone invariably thought of home, and hoping to ease the pain of severed roots, they chose the name "Charleston" with a slight spelling variation due to inexplicable reasons. Back in the Carolinas, the original "Charlestown" had been named for a king, His Royal Highness, Charles II. But as frontier trails were transformed into superhighways, people forgot all about old King Charles.

(And, BTW, that was the last King Charles to sit on England's throne until this newest one, who was crowned King Charles III, last spring, one day after my grandbaby Finn's second birthday; May 6, 2023, for His Royal Highness, Charles the Third, and May 5th for His Not-So-Royal Highness, Finnian the First.) It's important to know these kinds of details—there are a lot of numbers in this beautifully textured parenthesis—but why else write a book about memories without details, right?

Anyway...

As for my charming Charleston, it's doubtful anyone had ever stopped to think that their quaint southern village had been named for a British king three hundred years in his grave.

Charleston will always be special to me. It was there that my mind was set to thinking, my heart was set to dreaming, and my soul was charged with a commission from a king of a different sort.

I haven't been there for many years, but my thoughts often travel to that precious place, providing new assurance and confidence with which to face the uncertainties of the present.

The innocence of those times and the vivaciousness of my youth would combine to produce in me convictions as solid as that old oak tree. I experienced one of those insightful leaps that all of us confront every so often in life in the storm of a June-dark night.

During the sacred mystery of that storm, I began a process of self-examination that culminated in "surrendering to the call" of a ministry I would pursue for almost thirty years.

But more importantly than all the theological mysteries of this heavenly call, I found myself.

The storm had been announcing itself for hours before it reached my valley. It was getting goosebumps-close. The rumbling thunder shook our home as if it were a miniature dollhouse. It was keeping me awake long after I should have been snugly asleep and making me feel half-terrified and half-angry.

I saw lightning flash brilliantly across the windowpanes of my tiny room. For a moment, everything was illuminated, and cryptic shadows danced their way along my bedroom wall until the blinding light vanished, plunging my room into darkness.

The timing of the next orchestration could be calculated precisely if I counted like Daddy had taught me to count the variables of lightning and thunder.

I waited patiently, counting, "One, two, three, four, five, six."

Again, the lightning lit up the sky. "Uh, oh," I thought, "this one's close."

The streaks of light shattered the blackness of midnight. Once more, the heavens bellowed forth with an awful groan. Now I knew that the storm was about to begin its real performance.

The eye of the storm would ring, chime, clang, boom, and roll forth a hymn both cacophonous and melodious.

There is something seductive about a storm. I cannot explain why or how. I do know that something deep inside of me has always succumbed to the fury of a storm.

That night, I remember shaking and trembling with fear. Despite the fear, I felt compelled to climb out of my safe, warm bed and walk out into the storm.

The mind of a child is truly a wondrous thing. Oh, how the mystique of that night captivated my yearning mind! I remember moving without detection through the darkened rooms of the parsonage (that's what Protestants call the preacher's home) and trying to keep my footsteps in time with the blasting echoes of the storm.

As I opened the back door and stepped onto the porch, a wisp of wind bitterly stung my face. Though it was the last days of spring, the rain was cold and numbing. Barefoot and pajama-clad, I walked through the puddles that had begun to form in our little gravel driveway.

The church that my father pastored was just a few steps away. A light of almost supernatural intensity blinded me when I turned to face the red brick sanctuary. My heart was beating quickly and hard as the brilliance obliterated the darkness.

The sleek, elegant steeple glimmered enchantingly against the illumination of the sky. To a little boy who had been brought up listening to his powerful preaching father, it was a vivid affirmation that God was on his throne, unleashing a demonstration of omnipotent power.

The God of Abraham and Moses repeated the display of his power over and over while I stood frozen before the altar of his church. One time the sky became as bright as the brightest day, and I thought that at any moment I would see a winged white horse bearing the returning Christ.

I ran to the steps of the church and began climbing my way upward, thinking the higher up I got, the better view I would have of the whole show. Now, my heart pumped fearlessly as I believed that I would be the first person on earth to see the greatest spectacle in human history.

The world slept, and I alone would welcome back the victorious king. After all these decades, I still remember thinking how strange it was going to be that only I would be witness to this extravaganza of the eternal one.

I was oblivious to the pounding wind and rain as a million thoughts

jammed up the circuits in my brain. I waited and waited and waited.

The storm quieted and slowly slipped away. All that was left were faint rumblings and tiny flashes that could just barely be seen in the hills far away.

What had happened? Why didn't Jesus come back, as all the preachers kept saying he would?

"Why?" I yelled angrily, raising my head to the sky.

I will never forget the emptiness, the confusion, and the warm tears streaming down my face, mixing with the cold droplets of rain.

In my mind, the manifestation of God was in the storm. He had summoned forth the powers of the universe and swept through my valley, awakening me, and calling me out of my dreams to witness the revelation of his might.

After all, he had flooded the face of the earth during Noah's day.

The children of Israel had seen the Red Sea miraculously divided for their benefit.

Jonah had felt the fury of God's storm upon the waves of an uncertain sea.

The disciples of Christ had witnessed the master of the storm both calm and walk upon the Sea of Galilee. I had heard my father preach this with unequal verve and zeal many times.

Yes, this God was most assuredly a God of the storm.

Entranced and bewildered, I returned to the reassuring security of my bed. I listened to the dying storm, tossing my head back and forth on the pillow, pondering new and exciting ideas. The ideas became dreams, and the dreams melted away before the deepest unknowns of my sleep.

The next day, I told my father about the unidentifiable feelings that possessed me and that maybe it was God's way of calling me into his service. He listened kindly to the wild banter of his eleven-year-old son, but he didn't know and couldn't know how the storm had transformed me. Only I could know that.

Was God really in the storm? Well, many of my ideas have changed over the years, and while I may not believe them the same way I did once, I believed them then with all my heart.

It wasn't necessary to relegate the Christian God to the status of Zeus, who indiscreetly and randomly hurled thunderbolts upon the earth. However, God is defined, he is not merely a hurler of chaos in the midnight skies. But in the innocence of my childhood, God did just that every time it stormed.

It's difficult to explain to a child in what way or to what degree one can have a spiritual experience. The difference is easily discernible by a mature mind that can distinguish symbolism from reality.

Just because one says that their God is the "God of the Storm," that doesn't mean that he is personally involved in the deployment of rain, lightning, and thunder.

But a god of any substance must be the god of our storms.

Sixty years after the storm of that night, I have a very different understanding of God. And however different he may be from the God of my childhood; he remains the God of that storm and every storm since.

The God of that storm in my life aroused within my heart an awe and reverence for the eternal, which in turn awakened a new depth of perception about the world around me. This personal experience invigorated the seeds of faith that had been germinating within me for a long time.

It was especially important to me because it started me on a life-long journey of asking questions, wanting things, and finding out for myself. The quest for life came alive that night.

I looked upward and was finally able to see inward.

In finding God, we find ourselves.

Whoever your god is, they become the enabler in your search for yourself. Such power may be in the storms of your life. Or maybe not. Something stands outside us waiting to be claimed in order that we may find identity within us.

It sounds like a dichotomy, I know. But to focus inward, we must first focus outward. We must look beyond ourselves to bring definition and recognition to what is inside.

It's the beginning of a journey that never ends until death brings down the final curtain of life's drama. I saw the real me for the first time that night.

I was a person with perception, heart, and soul.

I felt that God was leading me in a certain direction, one that I sought to follow for many years.

our thinking now and then. Old Mrs. Peters over in Paducah would suddenly start talking backwards sometimes. Often, my father would take me with him when he visited the sick and "shut ins."

Mrs. Peters was a regular shut-in because she had previously suffered a stroke and no longer did well in public. This was sad, according to Daddy, because she had once been a great Sunday School teacher and used to love to talk. The stroke had messed up the beautiful way with words she once possessed, causing everything she said to sound like a foreign language.

Our visits made her so excited, and she'd get to talking up a storm, and then out of nowhere would come pouring out the backwards stuff, making her red-faced and *"flustrated."* Folks over in Paducah would say *"flus-trated"* when they meant frustrated. This linguistic *faux pas* drove my finicky sister nuts.

Anyway, Mrs. Peters would get so *"flustrated"* with her derailed train of thought that she'd slam down her fist and sputter, "Forget it; I lost it." And we'd stay a little longer to comfort her while she sat there all red-faced and tight-lipped, refusing to open her mouth again with the embarrassing backward talk.

The old drunk had his sight and hearing turned around backwards. In his case, it was probably because too much vodka numbed too many brain cells for too many years.

Poor Mrs. Peters' brain cells were a little messed up too. But she didn't want to talk backwards. She processed her thoughts properly. They just came out backwards.

I get to thinking backwards sometimes. I admit some things can get out of hand, and I get so confused and anxious that everything seems to be turned upside down and turned around backwards.

Like the drunkard, I *hear* lightning and *see* thunder. Nothing seems to make sense, and I get downright *"flustrated"* like Mrs. Peters and feel like I've just lost it.

But in recognizing my own despair, I find good medicine. After finally having kids myself, I began to realize this when I let the kids drive me to the edge of my own personal Grand Canyon.

I still realize it today when my work becomes so out of focus that I hear things I should be seeing and see things I should be hearing—or when the daily news is so brutal that it makes grown people want to cry.

It's this backward processing that sets off a buzzer in my head that says, "Slow down, Buster, or you're going to bust." (I know it's "burst," but that doesn't go with Buster.")

And so, I do. Well, I try.

So, when I start hearing, seeing, and talking backwards, I know it's time to slow down a tad and stop getting so flustered.

It used to be easy to do when the kids were still kids. I'd put away the work, nuzzle my babies for a while, and smell life's roses. Nuzzling your babies is the best tonic for all that ails your soul.

After all, I want to get all I can out of life. I don't want to end up like poor, sweet Mrs. Peters. I don't want to find myself forever saying, "I lost it."

I want to keep all that life has to give me—all the memories, all the love, *everything*. I've learned to slow down because life has given me too many treasures that are worth keeping.

I'll take life moving forward, not backward, and try to keep it that way, thank-you!

When my understanding of God changes, it doesn't do so because he changes. Rather, it is because my understanding of God matures in such a way that new directions must be charted for my innermost to continue growing.

The power of the universe first called out to my heart in that Tennessee storm six decades ago. It is a power that continues to come to me through all the storms I've encountered in life—the storms without and the storms within.

And when this power comes, I always find more of myself.

Jeffrey Naylor's first public speaking opportunity at age 13 in 1967

DID YOU SEE THE THUNDER?

I was living in Lexington, Kentucky, when a drunken derelict taught me how to slow down and pay attention when I heard the *unhearable* and saw the *unseeable*.

He came into view about a half block away as I was walking along the little street where I used to take my daily "constitutional," as Great-Aunt Della used to call it. I always thought her 19th century sounding terminology was the epitome of grandiloquent speech—to call a walk "a constitutional!"

The old bum started to fall as he stumbled and swayed, just barely avoiding the shame of the gutter. His trench coat was soiled and shabby—a long-time companion, no doubt. It was too big. And it swallowed him up, reminding me of when I used to dress up in my father's clothes.

Stone-faced and disoriented, the poor fellow looked like a tramp right out of Steinbeck's "The Grapes of Wrath." A scruffy beard was sparsely spotted across his face, and his shoes shouted the testimony of many miles.

Miles of loneliness.

Miles of motion without momentum.

A bottle of vodka had fallen out of his pocket and rolled violently into the concrete gutter. It seemed strangely inordinate and almost comical in size. The whole scene could not have been staged better for Paramount Pictures.

There was just one thing missing. The stage. This was reality smacking me right in the middle of my daily health program. "Go away," I mumbled to reality.

The bottle of vodka had spoken to him, and he was trying to balance an approach to rescuing it from the gutter. He bent over to the same rhythm that all drunks know and stabilized himself against the concrete curb with the tips of his crippled fingers. The pinkie was missing from his right hand, cut off at the second joint. It didn't affect his balancing act.

Suddenly, as if he had been injected with a dose of sobriety, he stood up sharp and tall. When he did, our eyes met. He was startled by my presence, and I was entranced by the tractor beam in his eye that, for a moment, pulled me into his distorted reality.

Shaking his head, he tried to focus on my face. "I'm sorry, but hey, what was that?" he asked, turning an inquisitive glare toward the sky.

"Did you hear the lightning and see the thunder?"

"No, I didn't," I told him.

His glassy eyes seemed to sink into an impenetrable darkness, and he shuffled down the street, mumbling the words "thunder and lightning."

If anyone had looked at my face, they would have seen the same ghostly stare. My eyes lost their focus as I felt stymied by the old man's question.

I mulled it over in my mind: "Hear the lightning? See the thunder?"

The uncanny boom of a jet breaking the sound barrier sent chills up and down the spine of my conscience. It was eerie but appropriately timed.

I suppose we all get turned around and feel a little backward in our thinking now and then. Old Mrs. Peters over in Paducah would suddenly start talking backwards sometimes. Often, my father would take me with him when he visited the sick and "shut ins."

Mrs. Peters was a regular shut-in because she had previously suffered a stroke and no longer did well in public. This was sad, according to Daddy, because she had once been a great Sunday School teacher and used to love to talk. The stroke had messed up the beautiful way with words she once possessed, causing everything she said to sound like a foreign language.

Our visits made her so excited, and she'd get to talking up a storm, and then out of nowhere would come pouring out the backwards stuff, making her red-faced and *"flustrated."* Folks over in Paducah would say *"flus-trated"* when they meant frustrated. This linguistic *faux pas* drove my finicky sister nuts.

Anyway, Mrs. Peters would get so *"flustrated"* with her derailed train of thought that she'd slam down her fist and sputter, "Forget it; I lost it." And we'd stay a little longer to comfort her while she sat there all red-faced and tight-lipped, refusing to open her mouth again with the embarrassing backward talk.

The old drunk had his sight and hearing turned around backwards. In his case, it was probably because too much vodka numbed too many brain cells for too many years.

Poor Mrs. Peters' brain cells were a little messed up too. But she didn't want to talk backwards. She processed her thoughts properly. They just came out backwards.

I get to thinking backwards sometimes. I admit some things can get out of hand, and I get so confused and anxious that everything seems to be turned upside down and turned around backwards.

Like the drunkard, I *hear* lightning and *see* thunder. Nothing seems to make sense, and I get downright *"flustrated"* like Mrs. Peters and feel like I've just lost it.

But in recognizing my own despair, I find good medicine. After finally having kids myself, I began to realize this when I let the kids drive me to the edge of my own personal Grand Canyon.

I still realize it today when my work becomes so out of focus that I hear things I should be seeing and see things I should be hearing—or when the daily news is so brutal that it makes grown people want to cry.

It's this backward processing that sets off a buzzer in my head that says, "Slow down, Buster, or you're going to bust." (I know it's "burst," but that doesn't go with Buster.")

And so, I do. Well, I try.

So, when I start hearing, seeing, and talking backwards, I know it's time to slow down a tad and stop getting so flustered.

It used to be easy to do when the kids were still kids. I'd put away the work, nuzzle my babies for a while, and smell life's roses. Nuzzling your babies is the best tonic for all that ails your soul.

After all, I want to get all I can out of life. I don't want to end up like poor, sweet Mrs. Peters. I don't want to find myself forever saying, "I lost it."

I want to keep all that life has to give me—all the memories, all the love, *everything*. I've learned to slow down because life has given me too many treasures that are worth keeping.

I'll take life moving forward, not backward, and try to keep it that way, thank-you!

PART 1: BROKEN HEARTS

Most protestant ministers are not like the stereotypes portrayed by the entertainment industry. It's not just the movies that give ministers a bad rap. Some high-profile televangelists have helped construct the distortion.

Their Hollywood-style telecasts, podcasts, and other media events have spawned the creation of a new breed of preachers who, with the aid of bright lights and dazzling sideshows, have helped change forever the way American society will look upon their profession.

Since the days of the frontier, Americans have loved a good foot-stomping revival. People have doubts about the clergy, though, because of how impersonal modern technology has become.

When I was growing up, the minister was treasured as one of the most respected citizens of the community. They might have had high academic credentials, or they might have been equipped with only the testimony of their special calling to serve God. But once they had been affirmed by the community as a legitimate representative of the Kingdom of God on earth, their acceptance as a leader was guaranteed.

No one made fun of that generation of ministers, and even Hollywood churned out some great movies about the lives of Peter Marshall, Norman Vincent Peale, J.D. Grey, and Billy Graham.

Back in the late spring of 1993, my father only had four days left before ending his many decades of work as a faithful Southern Baptist minister. He'd already gone a few years beyond that arbitrary retirement age of 65. This was not a day he'd been looking forward to, and he didn't really want to quit.

The congregation he had pastored for almost fourteen years didn't want him to leave either. For almost forty years, he had been the kind of minister who brought dignity and honor to his profession.

Fresh from the killing fields of World War II and the Korean Conflict, he experienced a new level of conviction for serving the needs of others. His pastorates had been small and large, but never anything like the big-budgeted evangelist's empires of today—just the stuff of small-town America.

He had spent his whole life laboriously feeding the poor, visiting the sick, and making other people's lives easier. There was never a midnight doorbell or phone call that went unanswered. Never an outreached hand went away empty.

Many were the times when I saw him reach into his own pockets to help somebody like Billy Joe Sanders buy milk and bread for his wife and three little children or give Johnny Goldfinger the extra twenty-five dollars needed to pay the rent one more time. He traveled the miles and put in the time, and now his work seemed to be ending.

He wasn't gullible, though. I was with him one time when he gave a suspicious-looking guy twenty dollars for groceries. (That's almost two hundred today.) The fella wiped his greasy hands against his hand-me-down shirt and slowly reached for the cash as if he were taking holy money.

"Thank you, reverend," he said shyly, "now I can buy my babies the milk they need."

Daddy always blushed a little when someone called him reverend. He felt a little uncomfortable with the title.

I remember us driving that man down to Brown's IGA supermarket and watching him go into the store before we pulled away.

"Daddy," I quizzed, "ain't we going to wait for him?"

"No, he'll find a way home," he said.

"Well, Daddy, what's to keep that man from spending the money on something besides milk for his kids?" I asked with a hint of disbelief.

"I'll have to trust him this time," Daddy said, wisely shifting his eyebrows in a way that told me that he knew exactly what he was doing. He knew the risks as well as the rewards.

I don't know if he did this every time he helped a stranger, but after we finished our errands and were on the way home, we stopped along the street in front of the stranger's house. Maybe he did it because my inquisitive innocence ignited a spark of doubt in his mind.

Dusk had slipped into the first good darkness of the evening, and we could see the man through the front window pacing back and forth. I never thought of us as peeping toms. After all, anyone could have seen him if they were passing by. Daddy certainly had the right to check up on his investment.

I remember thinking how neat it was to see this intrusively bold side of Daddy. We were like godly spies as we sat there idling in Daddy's spotlessly clean 1964 Ford Custom 500. There was no mistake in what we saw.

With each stride across the floor, the man was vigorously "wetting his whistle" from a giant bottle of whiskey. We could see the little kids running through the room.

Daddy had that Sunday morning pulpit look on his face, and I was afraid he was going to go up to the door and jump all over that fella. I didn't want him to do that. What if that guy had a gun?

"What are you going to do, Daddy?" I hesitantly whispered.

As Daddy began to shift the gears and pull away, he just smiled and said, "Next time, I'll bring the milk myself."

That was 1965. By late spring 1993, the vigilant warrior was showing signs of wear and tear.

For decades, he had worked long hours, seven days a week, and, for days at a time, skipped sleep—a bothersome interloper. He worried over the problems of others until they rested squarely on his own shoulders. Now, the unrelenting toil had taken its toll upon his body, and he was about to leave this work of the heart as a debilitating shadow of the mighty fortress he used to be.

Finally, his heart broke beneath the load, and when it did, mine did too. He had always been a vigilant caretaker of his health. But his careful diet and regular jogging weren't enough to make up for the damage he created by taking on other people's problems. He took care of others just a little bit more than he took care of himself.

Just a few months before this crisis, Daddy had appeared to be the epitome of good health. People admired the unwavering health regimen he had established for himself. No one was prepared to hear that his heart had grown diseased beneath the load of his faithful work.

Initially, when he halted momentarily between life and death, one of his parishioners lamented, "If your health-conscious father could develop heart disease, then there's no hope for anybody else."

It was a beautiful sentiment, but it doesn't take into consideration other factors that lead to heart disease, such as the effects of one's emotions or genetics.

"It must be genetics," someone said.

But my ninety-three-year-old Granddaddy Clyde, who, at the time, was still cultivating beehives and chopping down Tennessee oak trees with a hand ax, couldn't think of anyone in the family branches who had ever suffered from heart disease.

I suppose it was permissible for this son to believe that an over-burdened heart had created the disease that was ravaging his mighty father.

Mama had called to tell me the bad news just a few days before his surgery. He'd had a sharp chest pain while out on his daily jog, and his physician had demanded he come in for tests to determine the cause. He had failed the blood tests and the treadmill torture run, and there was just one more test standing between him and open-heart surgery.

Later that afternoon, she called to say he would need to have surgery within forty-eight hours. The secure tones her voice always possessed were replaced with vibrations of desperation.

"I need you," she pleaded, "I can't face this alone."

I didn't know that I could face it either. It was a scene right out of my childhood nightmares. The prospect that my father, the physical and spiritual giant of my life, could be cut down so quickly and cruelly seemed unfair.

He might not be able to be a minister ever again, and that possibility might depress him fatalistically. Without his ministry, he wouldn't know what to do with his life.

Furthermore, his physician had explained to him how imperative it was that he have the surgery as quickly as possible. This overwhelmed him. What if he didn't survive the surgery? What if he did, but would never again be able to speak before his congregation?

Shouldn't he be able to end his career with one last, great moment before the people he had served so completely and before the God he had served so dutifully?

NO! That seemed to be the blasphemous answer, and he placed himself in jeopardy by becoming depressed at the thought.

Gathering up my whole family, we journeyed uncomfortably to an uncertain tomorrow. It was a thousand miles to the flat, swampy land of West Kentucky. We traveled with hope and hopelessness.

I never liked the scraggly, inhospitable McCracken County landscape. Dismal. Too rainy.

That's probably why the nineteenth century leader, Chief Paduke gave that swampy river bottom to the white man. As I traveled from Princeton, New Jersey, through the twisting mountains of West Virginia, I prayed for sunshine. By the time we reached western Kentucky, the sky was a dismal gray.

We went with the brightest expectations but prepared for the darkest of circumstances. Staid and crestfallen, we drove all day and all night. What little optimism we had waned with every turn in the road. Our sanguine spirits sagged before emotions that were evasive and obscure.

Fearful of the present, we refused to consider the future.

I had forgotten how differently Kentucky compares to the East Coast. Superficial differences are always evident.

The accents are slow and soft.

The food is fattening and multifarious.

The pace of life is placid and measured.

The geography is flat and swampy.

It was the deep, foundational differences I had forgotten. These were magnified for me at the kaleidoscope of a hospital where Daddy was to have his surgery.

I had become accustomed to hospitals in the East with their hurry-scurry atmosphere.

Too many patients, too few physicians. Too much need, too little space.

Under-budgeted, understaffed, and overwhelmed.

Some East Coast hospitals have evolved into indifferent and complacent institutions that provide little solace for the sick and even less for their families. Don't get mad, Yankees. I suppose it's nobody's fault in particular, or maybe society's fault in general.

It's always better to blame ourselves collectively because the guilt gets spread around a little more equally, making it easier to accept. Or excuse.

Daddy had been admitted to the hospital immediately after Mama's last call. This hospital was a hospice, indeed. It was a place for finding rest, hope, community, and fellowship, as well as medical care. His surgery took place at the Western Baptist Hospital, Paducah, Kentucky.

Paducah (named in honor of the legendary Chief Paduke of the Chickasaw nation) isn't a town most Americans are familiar with, but it's big enough to have two large hospitals.

With over 1,400 employees in 1993, the Baptist Hospital was the largest employer in the city. This fact alone seemed to be on everybody's list of hot topics. I think they were proud that the biggest business in town was one that cared for people. Thirty years later, it's still the largest employer, with over 2,000 employees. It seems that in Paducah, caring for people is an ever-growing business.

The lobby was overflowing with the families of the sick. They were closely bound by mutual fears. The crowds hung out in separate groups, but passionate messengers moved from one group to the next, sharing words of comfort and hope. There were no thumb texters in those days. Spreading news meant getting up and moving!

At times, the crowd grew so large, one would think there had been a regional disaster. But no, this was normal. The ties that bind are made of steel in this little town.

On a few floors, there were more waiting rooms that were like miniature versions of the lobby. On the fourth floor, between the cardiac and intensive care units, there was a very special waiting room.

Stern-faced matriarchs guarded the entryway, manned the phones, and soothed the frayed, edged nerves of the anxious. They served as volunteers, but they served with intrepid doggedness and were tenacious to the core.

This room overflowed with the tired and bleary-eyed, twenty-four hours a day. These folks were settled in for the duration.

What about work? To the devil with that! Duty called. Family called. Many had been there for days, even weeks, sleeping upright in stiff-backed chairs made tolerable by pillows brought from home.

Everyone spoke softly there. Whispered sounds filled the air, lending dignity and reverence to the room, which made me feel like I was in a most holy place.

There was always a full complement of free coffee and cakes available.

Homemade.

From the heart.

By the trays full.

The Sunshine Sunday School class from one of the Baptist churches had brought in the last batch. Some people discussed how well they compared to the previous batch that the Methodists had brought in.

Tempered with love, they all helped alleviate the knot that roped itself around my gut every now and then.

I really didn't want to talk to anyone during this family crisis. I preferred to be left alone with the misery of my uncertainty. Over the days, however, I was drawn back into that world I had been so anxious to leave twenty years prior.

I got to know some of the workers from "down at the plant," who fussed in muffled tones about the new, foreign management team.

Then there was the Sunday School teacher from a church way out in the country who remembered that I had dated one of the girls out there twenty-two years ago. She told me the girl had three kids now.

"Tell her I've got five," I bragged. (Eventually, six.) The politics of overpopulation lose their focus in small southern towns.

I sympathized with the tobacco farmer, who coughed his way through every conversation so hard that I thought they would come any minute and take him back for oxygen.

The lady, who worked in women's shoes at the J.C. Penney store in the Kentucky Oaks Mall, told me what type of shoe would be best for my daddy to wear during his recuperation. She talked positively and vigorously about everyone's future. I liked that.

All the room's hushed insecurity was suspended by her unimpeachable belief that there was enough hope to go around for everybody. Everybody would be okay, and everybody would be comfortable wearing the right pair of J.C. Penney slippers.

Sinewy.

Emotional.

Faithful.

There was solidarity among that bunch in the fourth floor waiting room. Everyone seemed to know everyone, but I learned that most of them had never met before this unsolicited crossroad in their lives.

By sharing a loved one with a broken heart, our fears became apportioned and, thus, sufferable. Coffee and cake weren't the only nourishment I received in that room.

It wasn't just the huddled families that created this nurturing oasis. Everybody on the hospital staff was a chaplain. From the ladies in the cafeteria serving fresh baked buttermilk biscuits and sausage gravy, to the young boys outside providing free valet parking, everybody wished us well.

From solemn, smiling, respectful voices came, "We'll be thinking about you" or "We'll be praying with you."

It wasn't "praying *for* you," but "praying *with* you." What if some people didn't believe in prayer or didn't know how to pray? That was an idea that their faith would have considered impossible.

Everyone kept a distant, watchful eye on everyone else, and when someone looked like they would break from the strain, a body moved swiftly to their side and provided uplifting commiseration.

Now it was more than spiritual sustenance that was rendered. Folks felt at ease jumping in and offering help for any reason. If I looked like I was lost or couldn't find something, all I had to do was stand still for a couple of minutes and put a question mark on my face. Invariably, somebody would come up to me and offer to help.

. . .

Not talking to strangers suddenly seemed criminal.

The hospital's large cafeteria could have easily seated 300 people. One day I sat at my table and realized I wanted some vinegar for the fresh Kentucky mustard greens I hadn't tasted in years.

I glanced around the huge room for a condiment stand and focused on the "fixins-bar" a few yards away. I looked over the supply but didn't see any vinegar.

As I turned to go back to my table, an elderly man spoke up and said, "The vinegar's up under the top," while his cheerful wife pointed eagerly.

Taken off guard, I asked politely, "I'm sorry, what did you say?" Even though I knew, I couldn't believe I had heard correctly.

"You're looking for the vinegar to put on your greens, ain't you?" he asked.

How did he know? I thanked him, took the vinegar, and sat back down at my table, nearly twenty feet away. Assiduous old fool, why does he care whether I find the vinegar or not? I guess it was everybody's concern to keep an eye on everyone's nutritional intake as well. How about that? It was a nice touch, I suppose.

Maybe he wasn't a fool. I had lived here once and took all this southern kindness for granted. It was a pure and golden time. My nostalgia made the greens taste a little sweeter. Now, I'll remember the old man every time I eat mustard greens.

When I first arrived at the hospital, the idea of seeing Daddy in a hospital bed seized me uncomfortably. He had devoted almost half a century to visiting the sick but had never been admitted to a hospital. He looked great and said he felt good, but he knew he had a difficult path to travel.

The day before, he had thought he would be able to continue working for several more years. Now he felt demoralized by this forbidding fork in the road. The fact that it was Sunday and he yearned to be at church—a place from which he had not missed a Sunday since World War II—only made his depression worse.

He told me that later in the day he wanted to call the church leaders and inform them of his decision to resign as pastor, effective immediately.

If he survived the surgery well enough to continue working, it might be six months or more before he would be capable of handling the demanding workload of such a large church.

His well-intentioned but misguided reasoning had deduced that six months would be too long for them to go without a minister, and with his resignation, they would be free to find a replacement.

As depressed as he and I both were, I knew I had to get off my emotional roller coaster and help him find a more positive game plan. For him, it was something that had to be resolved before he went under the surgeon's scalpel.

"Hold on here, Daddy," I thought. "Now you're going against everything you ever taught me."

When I was about four years old, I left my favorite stuffed animal outside on a rainy night. When I found him the next day, he was terribly weather-beaten and water-logged. Not listening to Daddy's advice that he could be dried and repaired, I decided tearfully that he would have to be thrown away.

In an emotional funeral, I commended my purple and white bunny to the local garbage pit. You know, dust to dust, etc. I cried for days and wished I had listened to Daddy's reasoning. It was too late for repentance; my bunny had been hauled away.

My father had tried to teach me that, despite my bunny's appearance and condition, my deep love for him would be adequate for appeasing my fears.

Now, thirty-five years later, we played role reversal, and I was able to convince Daddy that the tremendous love that existed between him and his congregation would be strong enough for them to confront an uncertain future together. At the very least, he should give them an opportunity to minister to him.

He agreed that instead of making a phone call, I could meet with the leaders and explain to them his desires. Besides, he didn't need to experience the emotional task of quitting his job, ending his career, and preparing for open-heart surgery all within a half days' time.

Not many people make themselves confront such stressful issues all at once, at least not on purpose. Why in the world would anybody want to do that? Most people wouldn't, but for Daddy, the issue had to be settled regardless of the consequences.

The appointment with the leaders was set for five o'clock that afternoon. When I arrived, I was directed to a room full of shocked and somber southern gentlemen. Their loving strength and courage enveloped me. The deep lines in their faces and the rough thickness of their handshakes told me that they were hard-working folks.

Many were quite a bit older than my father, but they spoke of him in tones replete with reverence and awe. The unfavorable news about their respected leader had startled them in just one day. Their love and devotion to my dad hung thickly in the air.

As I spoke to them about some of Daddy's concerns, they were as silent as lambs, and their rugged faces melted softly under streaks of shameless tears.

When I was finished, they sat stone-faced and motionless. After a few moments, their leader rose and whispering almost secretively, he asked me to step out for a moment so that they might talk among themselves.

Less than five minutes passed before they asked me to come back into the room. I could see that in those few moments, their emotions had overflowed. Their reddened eyes, wet cheeks, and faces drawn tight with sadness were an affirmation of the depth of their love for my father.

Amidst sniffling sounds, their leader spoke to me with a quivering voice as we both stood before the group. "We want you to go tell your daddy, that he has been our minister all these years; he was our minister yesterday, and he's still our minister today," he firmly stated.

With that said, the sniffling increased as he went on to explain that no one who spends their whole life serving the needs of others should expect anything less than boundless love and loyalty in their own moment of greatest need.

"You tell your daddy that we will not let him take away from us this opportunity to take care of him," he intoned in a "there, take that" attitude. They also informed me that he was to think of himself as taking a sabbatical until he got better, which was defined as "for as long as it takes."

I had seen Daddy cry only a couple of times in my life. I had forewarned him before I met with the leaders that, as much as they loved him, they weren't going to let him go through this alone. He should have anticipated how he might react to such an outpouring of love and support, but he hadn't, and it overwhelmed him beyond even his own expectations.

Perhaps he didn't need to become this emotional before his surgery, but it purged his mind and enabled him to get himself ready for what was coming in the morning.

PART 11: BROKEN HEARTS MENDED

The alarm clock sounded like a train whistle when it went off. It was 4:20 a.m., and the room was so dark I thought I had gone blind. I pulled the curtains back for some moonlight to help me find the light switch. The sky was painted thick with that inky blackness that so often precedes dawn.

It all felt like that first bleak morning when I awoke in Boot Camp twenty years ago. I felt ignorant, empty, and afraid of what the day would bring.

Our family arrived at the hospital about 5:30 a.m., and the technicians were already poking, pricking, and prying all over my father. It was an indignant moment when they announced we would have to leave the room while they shaved his entire body.

I could not process my feelings as I stood outside the room, waiting for this to be finished. They were in his room! The unknowns were touching, maneuvering, and shaving Daddy's naked body. This mighty orator and mover of people's hearts was lying in bed, exposed, and denuded before strangers.

It was this unexpected and humiliating necessity that gripped my mind with fearful speculations about the day ahead.

The gurney was wheeled into the room, and I panicked. My half-sedated father was placed on that flat slab of a table and quickly moved out of the room and down the hall to the elevator. Mama stayed back while my sister and I flanked the rolling makeshift bed as it moved between walls that seemed to press in against us.

I held his hand while we stood waiting for the elevator that would take him to the operating room. As the door opened and they whisked him away, I blurted out, unexpectedly and firmly, perhaps too firmly, but like a child, "You guys better take care of my daddy."

My sister hushed me for being so disrespectful to the surgeon and his team of experts. But I was not afraid of my boldness. Yet they had looked at me curiously, stunned that anyone should say such a thing in such a way. As the door was closing, into the last crack I shouted, "I love you, Daddy," and moved to the wall far from everyone and cried.

A crowd had begun to gather early in the lobby, and by 8:00 a.m., the place was filled with people. Soon, I began to realize that most of them were only here because of Daddy.

The receptionist, who sat at the oval-shaped desk in the middle of the room, began to field phone calls from people asking about Daddy's condition. Many were calls from former parishioners in other cities and states. I was numbed in the presence of so much love. There were so many phone calls. In those days, no one was tethered to a cell phone. Hopefully, the younger generations can come to understand what it means to say, "The phone was ringing off the hook." It took a great deal of effort to demonstrate love with a phone.

They had previously told us that a critical stage in the surgery would be reached when he would "come off the bypass." The bypass machine, that indignant but marvelous lifesaver, would become Daddy's heart while they laid his own out for mending. Once that had been accomplished successfully, our apprehensions were supposed to be eased.

And so it was that, after several hours, a nurse came into the lobby and loudly, almost triumphantly, announced, "HE'S OFF THE BYPASS." In response to that, a veritable roar of joy went up among the crowd of more than one hundred, which caused my excitement to accelerate to a degree I hadn't anticipated. People stood up to embrace each other and shake one another's hands with broad smiles and tear-streamed faces.

It was like an old-fashioned revival worship service. I wondered how Daddy would approve of such a thing in the moment of his deepest peril.

It was well into the night before they allowed us to hover for a few precious minutes around Daddy's bed. The huge, open room smelled of sickness and strong medicine. The large staff moved about the room quickly and purposefully. I knew that they took seriously the task of caring for so many who lay at life's edge.

For the first time in my life, I realized that our culture works with great intensity to hold on to those who are slipping away from us. We can't accept the fact that they are crossing over—into death. It is a dimension outside the realm of research and evaluation, and it frightens us.

It is a void that no one really understands, and we do all we can to keep pulling the dying back to us. We pull and pull until the tug-of-war with death is stronger than all our efforts, stronger than all our medicine, and stronger than all our love.

My father was a mighty representative of his God. With a voice of thunder and a heart of gold, he had always been the measuring stick for almost everything in my life. I don't mean that I always tried to measure up, but I have looked and looked, and I have never found anything better.

They had whispered reverently for us to come into the critical care unit, where he was. "Who was this man that lay before me?" I thought. A technological octopus entangled him.

His face was ashen and bloated, and I knew the thick bandage covering his midsection concealed a huge scar that marked the spot where surgeons had opened the diseased heart of this saint, who had loved to the breaking point. And my heart felt broken as it heaved within my chest until I thought it would burst.

Within three months, in September, Daddy had made a miraculous recovery. He had begun to plan his return to work and was convinced that he would not have to retire from his work of the heart. Yet he suffered a frightening relapse, and for a few days, we were confronted with the possibility that he might need open heart surgery again—a prospect with fatal implications.

We all knew it would be too soon for such a demanding surgery, and the possible outcome could be devastating. Please remember that this was a time when surviving open heart surgery wasn't given high odds. Five years would have been considered a very assertive goal.

But the crisis soon passed, and once more he reluctantly planned for his retirement to take effect as soon as possible. His retirement "celebration" was supposed to take place on a late September Sunday afternoon, just a few days shy of five months since the entire crisis had begun.

I had already started to grieve at the thought of how to record this story of a broken heart. Even worse, how could I possibly celebrate the day that would be his last for doing the godly work that had so dominated his life? He was only 66 years old. He was too young to stop his life's work but too young to die.

All the doctors had cautioned him that he could never again use the forceful, passionate oratory that caused so many people to consider him Jack Calvin Naylor the Great.

Again, he felt depressed and uncertain about his future. His yesterdays were so full and rich, and he feared his tomorrows would be so empty and meager.

But the royalties and dividends he would reap after years of sowing so much love would not leave him emotionally bankrupt after all. As it turns out, Jack Calvin Naylor was a recipient of second chances, and soon he would have lots of time to appreciate and cultivate the love that so many wanted to give.

At the time, I believe it was his poor health that prevented him from realizing what wonderful things the future promised him just over the horizon's edge. Soon, he would be surprised at how fast the love of others could mend a broken heart.

My father's courageous life did not end here with the Great Heart Crisis. I have much more to tell you about his ferocious comeback. And I will, I promise. For now, I will tell you that he did finally retire, not in 1993 but in mid-December 2021, at 93 years and 11 months and two weeks of age. He pastored full-time until he was only two weeks away from his 94th birthday, eventually living almost a century, refusing to quit almost until the time his body decided to release his soul back to his God.

During those many years, he suffered from and defeated prostate cancer and throat cancer, fully recovering each time. After each life-threatening illness, he returned full-time to his work. He retired on his own terms. He was blessed with those kinds of opportunities that allowed him to continue working, and he was humbled by their significance. Not only did he outlive open heart surgery by five years, but only one year shy of thirty.

I loved Daddy for every day he lived, and when his heart faltered, causing him to briefly pause between life and death, the fear of losing him almost left me shattered. And, during subsequent pauses near death when he fought prostate and throat cancer, I again froze with the fear of losing him.

But it is an unbreakable love that tightly ties the eternal threads of our connection. We may be vulnerable to the unexpected turns that life throws at us, but each crisis changes us and makes our relationships better and stronger.

Often, people will say obnoxious things to give comfort to others in their moments of grief. "He's at peace now; he was ready to go." I dislike that one the most.

Daddy may be at peace, but he was never ready to go. He loved life and struggled to hang on to every breath until the very last breath. I should know because I was there in the days before he took his last breaths.

Do you want to know what he was talking about in last days? He was curiously pleased to know that he had outlasted Queen Elizabeth, who passed away on September 8, 2022. He chuckled in barely audible whispers about how much he despised Prince Charles' queen-to-be.

He was suffering greatly, and he could barely move, even with help, but when anyone mentioned Queen Camilla's name, he could not stop himself from making a vindictive smile.

At the end, he was blind and barely capable of comprehensible speech, but if God wanted him to leave, He would have to wrest him from the grip of Mother Nature herself like he did when he grabbed the Old Testament prophet Elijah up, allowing him to ride his chariot into heaven's gates. Daddy's Dodge might not be ready for such melodrama. But so it was that, in the night, against the hope of his dreams, his body literally failed, and he was gone.

Just like the blowing winds of autumn outside his hospital window. He was there and then he was gone. How could that be possible? The physical link between us is severed, but the journey continues.

Our journey as father and son will never end. Together, we were always able to confront the uncertainties of our futures. Because of his life, I am fortunate to have found genuine wholeness despite all my brokenness.

And what if one day my heart breaks again? I will remember the ancient poem that variably states,

> *"Blessed be the tie that binds.*
> *The mortal ties that poorly bind.*
> *My earthly heart will be perfected,*
> *And bind me once more in eternity."*

Jack Naylor, Daddy preaching at age 93. He preached 3 times a week until he was 93 years and 11 months old. He left the living at 95 years and 9 months old.

ROLL CALL

The thought came to me the other day that if I dropped dead right where I stood and my funeral was held a couple of days later, who would come?

I've moved around so much since the day I was born and lived in more states that I should be cautious to mention it and half a dozen countries as well. My family would have to send out invitations across the world so people would know where to come and weep or laugh!

Death is not something that threatens me because I have a strong belief system that has already taken away its sting and pangs and tossed them onto the garbage heap of human fears.

A much greater fear of mine would be, "Who wouldn't show up for my funeral?" I want it to be a time of celebration and happiness, and Americans are so used to being miserable at funerals.

If word got out that the funeral was going to be a party, people might get scared and stay home.

I've always enjoyed having lots of friends over for food and a bit of craziness. It's a sure thing that part of me will be at my funeral, the other part engaged in loftier matters. But if part of me is going to be there, then I want all my friends to be there too.

Maybe I can talk my family into taking my body on tour. We'd go to places all over the country (and maybe other countries) where I've got a lot of friends stored away. I think a six-stop tour would do, and I would feel properly celebrated.

At each stop on the tour, people would know in advance that we were coming because we would advertise in all the different media. The idea is to lead people to believe that someone important is coming. This way, everybody would get confused and think this might be something significant. The herd always follows wherever the media leads, right?

The ad would be short, sweet, and right to the point:

"Jeffrey Naylor died this week, and his funeral will be in town tomorrow night. Everybody's welcome."

All I ever wanted was a bleached pine box, and lately I've been thinking that a nice Grecian urn might be the best thing. Keats would approve of its simplicity.

"Beauty is truth, truth beauty—-that is all,
Ye know on earth, and all ye need to know."

(Come on, a little classic poetry never hurts anybody.)

Well, whether it's an urn or a box, we could take the money we'd save on a fancy, silk-lined, copper coffin and use it to make the ad go viral!

But this story is about the Roll Call of invited guests. While, to some degree, everyone is invited, I must admit that there are some special folks whose invitations cannot be neglected. I'm afraid that if they were left off the guest list, I'd be singing off-key with regrets for the rest of eternity.

So, I made up this roll call of names in advance and expect those listed to pay attention and be prepared to honor my request.

If you don't see your name on the list, please don't feel like you're not a valued friend. There are some names I am compelled to list because we've covered a lot of ground together in this life, and we might as well cover it in death as well.

Of course, it goes without saying that I'd want my kids to show up. Their presence would serve as payment for all the years I had to watch them slouch around like corpses on lazy Saturday afternoons, driven by the conviction to remain motionless.

Yet, really, this roll call isn't intended for family and such, but for longtime friends who have stayed with me through the decades, always accepting me for who I am and tolerating me for all my shenanigans.

Now, I'll call the roll randomly, so no one gets jealous.

Alyssa and Nathan Donner get called first, and rightly so because I've known them longer than all the rest. Nathan is a successful attorney and owns a couple of businesses that have always seemed a bit shady for a lawyer. But he's got to do something with all the money he's been making.

Nathan was probably the smartest guy at my college, and I decided it was my responsibility to make sure he chose the perfect career to make the most of his genius. So, I had his career path all laid out, but he was too stubborn to accept my advice. I'm not happy about it, but after all, it is his life.

We spent a lot of time together doing stupid adolescent things—the kind of things that build friendships made of steel.

One day we skipped class and hid out in my '68 Camaro Rally Sport (with hideaway headlights) just so we could smoke the green cigars that we had purchased the night before at the Convenient Mart.

The night before, we had walked into the store with the confidence of mature young men, quite successfully concealing our true, eighteen-year-old selves. Both of us were just above six feet tall, and that meant we were probably going to be the tallest people anywhere we went. At least in this state.

As we approached the cashier, we announced with our deepest voices that we wanted a particular brand of little cigars that had been advertised on television. (We were in the second bass section of the collegiate choir, so we sounded older than the cashier guy.)

Standing resolutely there, we didn't budge from the strength of our confidence. We had put the ball in his court, so we waited. But without hesitation, the cashier took the bait of our con, and "there you go," or as the Brits say, "Bob's your uncle." (You should look that one up. Yeah, google it.)

We jumped into the Rally Sport with its 327 V-8 engine and took off like we had robbed a bank. That car could burn up the rubber. (Guys everywhere love to make the tires squeal, even though we know it means we'll have to buy new tires very quickly.)

Motor Trend magazine TODAY reports that my Camaro had a "fuel-injected 327 engine that was a high-winding screamer." I wish I had known that 50 years ago. I would have driven everybody nuts talking about my car, the "high-winding screamer." Wow!

Well, my "screamer" kidnapped us with its 375 horsepower, taking us to a secret, out-of-the-way spot where we could become REAL men, like Clint Eastwood, smoking high-quality fermented Kentucky tobacco. Well, we weren't sure if these little cigars were Clint's special blend. It didn't matter!

But we quickly discovered why it's illegal to smoke these tiny bombs in cafes, grocery stores, and, well, pretty much all public places. So, after about five agonizing minutes, we gave up, wiser and paler.

Nathan has always been there for me, and I suppose he understands my peculiar sense of humor better than anybody. His beautiful wife, Alyssa, complements his family with grace and charm. If ever you're down Paducah way, I invite you to call Alyssa and let her talk to you.

Listen to her sweet southern accent as she talks about something as mundane as grocery shopping, and you'll be ready to tackle Wall Street, the national debt, crime, and Kim Jung-un. Honest! Let me give you her digits. Well, remind me later.

Nathan's enduring stickability to friendship through the thick and thin of my ins and outs and Alyssa's soothing, uplifting rhetoric earn them a spot at the head of the pine box or the urn. I want them right up front so I can keep an eye on them, whether I am flesh or ashes!

Billy Joe and Peaches Biltmore file in next, and there ain't nobody (oops! a southern *faux pas)* who can make melodies any sweeter than these two. Listen. Can you hear it? No, you can't hear my memories, but give me an hour some Friday night, and you'll think you are at the opera listening to Peaches' spellbinding voice singing romantic arias.

She'll have to sing at one of my funerals since nobody else in the bunch, except Billy Joe, can even sing worth a hoot. Sorry to my other friends who always thought they could sing.

And oh my, how Billy Joe can sing, but that's not why he belongs on the list. Many centuries ago, in simpler and poorer times, Billy Joe and I sold used cars together at Hillbilly's Chevrolet in Lexington, Kentucky.

That's not meant to be an advertisement. It's more of a testimony to the fact that if we could sell cars successfully in the middle of a recession, we shouldn't ever forget it or let anybody else forget it.

I was trying to finish graduate school, and Billy... Well, I don't know what he was trying to do, come to think of it. But we were the "cream of the crop," as Daddy always used to say, and the memories from those insufferably happy times cascade down upon me with biblical intensity.

I've never known a person who Billy Joe couldn't totally mesmerize, or is it metastasize? with his sales pitch. Deadbeat snotty-nosed and sour-pussed know-it-alls generally drove away in a new car after Billy Joe got through with them. Ha, ha! They just thought they knew it all.

"Billy Joe, you, and Peaches can stand behind the pine box or hold the urn and sing for me." I'll rest more peacefully, I'm sure.

"Loretta and Oggie Hatfield, come on down and stand down by my feet."

It's an appropriate spot for these guys because many were the times they stood by my side, encouraging me to stay on my feet when all around me was nothing but darkness and uncertainty.

Oggie's a *braincracking* name, but an Oggie by any other name just wouldn't be Oggie. Loretta's giggling in the middle of foreboding adversity has always served as an invigorating tonic for me when the days get long and hairy.

Cutting down trees was about the only job me and Oggie could find during one desolate and interminable recessionary season. What in the world did we do together to build such an enduring friendship? Most of the time, we did nothing together. But there's some real philosophy in doing nothing with your friends.

Doing nothing together is the stuff of persevering relationships. It's not everybody you can sit around with and do nothing with. None of us had any money, a real job, or much of anything else, for that matter.

Creativity flows blood-rich when you must wake up every day and face the challenge of doing nothing.

But our nothings evolved into something of an eternal substance. It's called friendship, and the hours, days, and weeks spent together made us almost inseparable.

Because you guys enjoyed our friendship so much in life, you should enjoy it in death. "Oggie, you and Loretta come and stand at the foot of my box and do nothing, but, Loretta, don't you dare start giggling."

Tim *Theide* or Tim *Thiede*, whoever you really are, it will be your responsibility to make sure the box holds up on my six-stop tour or the urn doesn't slip someone's grip and is broken. You fixed every-thing I broke and broke everything I bought. We spent too much time doing a lot of insanity together.

I don't guess I have done as many things with anyone as I have with you. We've driven all over the world together—or rather, I drove. I never trusted your driving. The hours we put in together doing odd and bizarre things ought to qualify us for some kind of category in the Guinness Book of World Records.

You are a lot younger than I am, but I've managed to teach you a few things. You will probably never achieve everything I want you to. But without your lazy, ho-hum, let's-not-get-too-excited attitude serving as the counterweight to my gun-ho, king of the mountain approach, I'm sure I would've had at least two or three heart attacks along life's journey. To have achieved that makes you an endearing friend who will never be forgotten.

"Tim, you sit on the floor and make sure my box doesn't fall apart or, er, the urn is broken."

Ash Zakinsky knows why she comes last because most people don't even know anybody whose name starts with a Z. Zorro's sword ripping Z is a fitting symbol for you. Your silly, winsome ways have always hit me kind of zigzag-like, leaving me confused but always laughing.

You did make this special roll call, but what in the world will you do at my funeral? I don't want you to sing, and nobody could possibly hear your whispery voice if you tried to give a eulogy. But you are one of the best friends that I have ever had, so maybe you can quietly encourage everybody to avoid celebrating too heartily. "Shhh."

I have always loved you for how much happiness you used to give all our family, but on the flip side, I hated you for moving away and making us miserable. You were a second mother to my babies, and you deserve an extra star for putting up with them, especially Cody-Man.

On second thought, Ash, I do want you to offer my eulogy after all. Just stand up there and whisper your loudest. It will make me happy knowing that everybody will spend the rest of their lives trying to figure out what you said. "What *did* she say?" They'll be asking that question until their own funerals.

Well, the roll call is complete, and everybody's got a job to do. Don't let me down. At least not until you get to the cemetery. (Oh, sorry, that's what my kids call a dad-joke.) And please, let me down easily if I'm in the box, and place me gently on the mantle if I'm in the urn. You all know how paranoid I am about something going wrong.

Dear Readers, as "Dear Abby" would say, you may wonder what purpose this silly little epilogue has served. Deciding how to end a book of memories was proving too difficult a task for me, so I figured I'd just write something about the end of my life.

Don't misunderstand what I mean when I say I have no respect for death or the grave. That is certainly not my aim. (Nor is this the end of this book, as I have tucked the first chapters of the book at the end for those who cheat the ending all the time.)

It is my aim to make it known that I value love, trust, loyalty, and fellowship as the stuff that adds pizzazz to life. But I also know that death is but a mere rite of passage, transporting our lives into a greater and more definitive level of existence.

The truth is, I've known you here, and I'll know you over yonder. (Read yonder as there.) Over yonder in "Beulah Land," friendships will re-group, never to be separated again. Variables of all kinds of past experiences fuel memories, and it is our friends who add spice to those memories, helping make life worth the effort.

The truth about friends and families and all the memories they create is that even though we are but sojourners in earthen vessels, we are vessels that are richly endowed and adequately prepared to live, die, and live again.

That's the truth... and it's the kind of truth that makes you free.

FINDING THE FUTURE
(OR READ ANY GOOD BOOKS LATELY?)

The inner search of my soul is a quest that takes me on a journey into the past as well as the present. From the two pictures, I cast a mold of the future. Undeniably, destiny entices me when I seek meaning in the past and present. I fool no one, least of all myself, when I deny this fact.

The total sum of who I was once and who I am now can only be fully realized as it stands in tandem with who I will become.

I look at the past from the perspective of the present, with an eye on the future. After all, it's the prospect of the future that functions as the dynamo for the present.

By the time I have learned all I can from my past, I will have moved beyond the present and into the future.

What I hope to glean from looking backward will serve me only in the future. Why? Because the time it takes to realize the past, apply it to my life, and claim or deny the results may take months or years, I'll always be behind.

The purpose of examining the past is to find some meaning for my tomorrows. It's a never-ending task. I can never keep up with what the past must teach me. The present is becoming the past with every tick of the clock.

Since the present is always changing, it's up to my past to give my future a clear sense of meaning and purpose.

In 1993, one of America's greatest novelists, Wallace Stegner, died. And the world was robbed of a great genius of introspection. Many Americans are unfamiliar with the tutelary shadow of his influence. I honor him here not because of the lack of notice his passing generated, but because his death elicited a response from many.

I didn't know him personally, nor was he ever conscious of my existence. But the empty space his death has created within me echoes loudly with regret. I loved all his writings, but it was one work alone that pervasively changed my understanding of time and inspired me to put this book of memories together.

Stegner used the device of the historical novel to illustrate how an examination of the past can bring order to the present and hope for the future. His book, *Angle of Repose*, is a beautiful journey into the complicated nature of time that gives meaning to the search for one's true self.

The main character in Stegner's book is a sad person who gives up in the face of life's cruel circumstances. Ditto for a million Americans. This character is physically crippled when he gets cancer and must have his leg amputated. This is a surprise setback for his future.

How many of us will fall under the weight of the unwanted, unanticipated scavengers of the future?

When his wife leaves him for the pitiless and pitiful surgeon he had trusted with his health, this man's mind starts to break down. In one despicable stroke, his humanity is incredibly and unfairly debased.

Disquieting reality often uses the same hand that rocks the cradle to cast us into the crevices of defeat.

Stegner's sad misanthrope fights for his life until he is almost dead, but then he gives up and gives in to a miserable life of loneliness, helplessness, and pain. His life degenerates uncontrollably from order to chaos. A lifelong historian engrossed in the study of all that once was, he's now fixated on the decrepit creature he's become.

Introspection through reflection becomes the impelling impetus that forces him to journey back to his roots. When he goes back to his family's estate, he is determined to write a book about his family. He believes that if he can write such a book, it will serve as a vicarious potion of rejuvenation.

And so he begins:

"I'd like to live in their clothes for a while, if only so I don't have to live in my own," he mawkishly laments.

But I am here yelling into the pages of that book that the clothes of yesteryear's memories can only help him, and he will function more effectively with the wardrobes provided by both today and tomorrow.

I suppose there are a thousand ways to count the value of a work of love like *Angle of Repose*. There are magnificent affirmations inherent in this Pulitzer Prize-winning novel.

Stegner's dialectic interweaving of the past with the present is beautifully rendered. I use the term "beautifully" because I was moved sweepingly and majestically into the midst of historical periods that are too often portrayed with mundane statistics and facts. This is a story crafted with a prism that is brilliant and vivacious.

His story takes his readers to the Black Hills of South Dakota, representative landscapes of American beauty. The memories of my trips to this mystic place took on new dimensions with Stegner as my guide.

When I was there, I tried to look past the suffocating commercialism and imagine the struggle of those determined gold miners. Stegner inspired a salubrious qualification of my memories.

Stegner's crippled historian tells the story of how his grandmother came to live in that desolate country. He describes in pulsating detail the violence and grimness of an era that most people today think of as unrealistically noble and rural. I merged the images of my South Dakota memories with his and found my heart racing to the beat of an unrelenting reality.

I rode with Stegner along the treacherous, gullied roads. I felt the cold northern blasts of numbing winds, smelled the odors of dirty towns filled with weary, stone-faced adventurers, and regretfully sensed the finality of the hangman's noose.

When I put these images together with what I've seen and done in my own life, I got a fascinating and unforgettable sense of how completely unfair life is.

Stegner's tale moves back and forth from the wild west to the civilized east. Long, arduous journeys are tainted with breathless uncertainty but, more accurately, filled with boredom. Each trip necessitates an insufferable and lonely layover in Omaha, Nebraska.

If I hadn't lived in Omaha several years ago, I might not have known that it was the headquarters of the great Union Pacific Railroad. I might not have known that, almost without exception, railroad travelers experienced burdensome delays in that city.

Since I did live there and knew some of the popular lore about the Omaha station, his depiction of their stops made me feel the visceral guts of history. I guess you could say that I closed my eyes and waited with Stegner's imagination on that cold and forbidding platform.

Even though I have no reputation as a literary critic outside of myself, I found some characterizations to be endearing and worth remembering forever. At first, his character, who tells the story, is a display of everything that is offensive and unwelcoming about people.

This ugly, twisted, helpless, bitter, doomed, and miserable historian was not a person I wanted to be drawn to immediately. I frowned at him for nearly a hundred pages before I decided I would like him. Whether I could read the book without dread hung in the balance.

I realize it's not necessary that I like every character in every book. For me, however, it's just shy of being necessary. Like an old, nasty dog, he grew on me. The old, ugly historian drew me in, and I began to understand the depth of Stegner's intentions.

He unfolds the history of his family by writing an interpretative narrative gleaned from his grandmother's published articles and personal letters. Sometimes the grandmother speaks for herself; other times he speaks for her. Sometimes I'm caught up in a bristling narrative of the nineteenth century; at other times I'm listening to the historian philosophize about his own dilemma in the twentieth century.

In allowing his character to find meaning in the stories of his family's past, Stegner teaches the inherent value of our past as creative constructs for our present and intuitive blueprints for our future.

Gradually, information emerges about the character's father. At first, I see his father as a child wagging about the country with parents who are more interested in their own goals than the welfare of their firstborn. With great emotion, I attach myself to his father, who, as a child, lived through several near-death encounters.

Eventually, beautifully, I see a different picture develop in the historian's mind. It's a way of thinking that lets him accept his father's lack of interest because he knows more about how he was raised.

The mysteries of human conduct are eradicated by focusing.

But wait! During all this alternating from past to present, from retrospect to introspect, I'm introduced to the historian's son. Father and son's opinions of one another are thrashed about violently, and, at the very least, I have a picture of mutual apathy.

Suddenly, I realize that four generations are brought into sharp focus because of the painful searching of one generation. Because of what Stegner tells me, I feel as though I know the first three generations of this family, but I don't like how he treats the fourth generation, which the historian's spastic, thoughtless, and emotionless son represents.

Because of this tension, I must look at my own life as a member of the same generation. This has given me a great understanding of what it takes to find meaning in the connections between generations. My own family history takes on a connectedness that I hadn't seen before.

Angle of Repose will mean many different things to different people. I believe it's a philosophy about defining the future and the approach to finding that definition. Stegner's historian is searching for his future as he examines his past. His past is inclusive of those who stand before him as well as himself. By examining them and himself, he will find the keystone that will allow him to secure his future.

In the beginning, the historian's son questions the validity of searching for the past. "The past isn't going to teach us anything about what we've got ahead of us," he tells his father.

Even though the crippled historian claims to want to live the lives of the past so that he does not have to face his own, that is not what he accomplishes, nor will any of us. His search centers on finding the meaning of the phrase "Angle of Repose."

At first, he believes it's "the angle at which a man or woman finally lies down." This answer is too simplistic, and Stegner shows us that discovering the keystone, or "meaning point" that intricately connects the events of our past, present, and future can only complete the journey of introspection through retrospection. That point of meaning lies deep within us.

The angle of repose is that which brings unity to time and space, providing definition for that which was, for that which is, and for that which will be.

Stegner's main character found out what his present and future meant by thinking about his family's past. By doggedly following the trail of their relentless struggles, he found the definition of their repose to be different than he had imagined. He found their differences to be unacceptable but honorable.

Respecting each other is a brave way to make up for the fact that you can't get along with someone.

The pathetic teacher also found resolution in the dissolution of his marriage. During his trip through time, he realized that they could talk about their broken relationship and fix it the right way. But would he have the inner strength to take what he had learned and put it into motion? He pondered:

"Could I?

"Would I?"

This thorough examination of the past placed an indictment on his future. Would he do it? Would he learn from all his digging, all his agonizing, all his heart-wrenching introspection?

Digging through the soil of the past is fertilizer for the soul. And I've been preaching that all my life. There are so few who listen.

What will any of us do once convicting discoveries force us to confront the meaning of our past as it relates to the totality of our lives?

If we learn anything from our toil, we learn that the cumulative events of the past, examined amid the yearnings of the present, must be used to presage, and anticipate hope for the future.

It's what all of us must do when we accept the gifts of the past to navigate the present and chart the future.

In my search for meaning, I begin my journey first looking inward, now looking backward.

I'm like Stegner's crippled, searching, and hungry protagonist. I look backward and inward to find the future.

Don't we all?

Professor Dr. Jeffrey Hughes Naylor. I am 50 years old in this photo. Unbelievable, right?

HORIZON'S EDGE IS THE FUTURE

Eighty-nine years to the day after Robert E. Lee surrendered the Army of Northern Virginia to the Union commanding general, U. (unusually) S. (sympathetically) Grant, in the prosaic and silent surroundings of the wooden and brick Courthouse of Appomattox, Virginia, something fantabulous happened to me. I sucked in the harsh, thick chemicals of the planet's atmosphere for the first time.

That first breath of life was a tasty entree of 78% nitrogen, 21% oxygen, and 1% carbon dioxide, carbon monoxide, helium, argon, and a bunch of other bits and pieces that have been floating around the universe forever.

My first meal of life was deliciously inflating, and I beamed with joy until somebody ruined the party by whacking my naked backside, setting me up with an edgy disposition that I still wear loosely today.

Dateline: April 9, 1954. I was born in Orlando, Florida, to Jack Calvin Naylor and Flossie Voncille Hughes Naylor. Dickens couldn't have said it any better than that.

Jack was short for John, and so you might think he was named for John Calvin, the great Scottish Presbyterian minister, but he wasn't. Well, maybe you weren't thinking that, but I thought that for about twenty years.

Daddy was born in the year 1927, when Calvin *Wholidge* (I mean Coolidge) was president. This lackluster approach to naming children was an offshoot of Huey Long's Share the Wealth plan, called the Share the Wealth of Famous Names plan.

It couldn't have branched off until 1935, but it's not important to know when it happened, is it? Trust me, eventually, it happened. How, why, and under what circumstances could it possibly make a difference to anybody? Or would it?

My mama was named after her Aunt Flossie, who spent thirty years in what everybody in those days called a "crazy house" because she had a disease of her memory that no one knew what to call it except "crazy."

It's such a crazy disease, you know. Nobody knew about Alzheimer's disease in those days. Ignorance is such an unfortunate burden. It seems like this kind of thing happens a lot in life. When people don't understand something, they simply label it as crazy. It's easier that way and doesn't call for any inner reflection on their moral conscience.

But let's move happily along because, from the earliest times, Mama strictly prohibited anyone from calling her Flossie. She declared war on anyone who attempted it! You can imagine what I'm going to tell you next. Yes, everyone called her by her first name, driving her insane. Eventually, the battle for her name was lost to time and my mother won in the end by becoming known using only her middle name.

It is my mother's middle name that defines her inner and outer beauty. It's a name that makes me smile when I say it. *VonCille* is a French name that means something we've never been able to validate, and it's better left unmentioned. But it's a beautifully seductive name when you give it that old *Pah-rhee* inflection.

It's a name that stands tall and strong, with two domineering caps of V and C. VonCille, the Victorious and the Conquering. How? Well, she regularly cheated when spelling her name, taking liberty to capitalize the V and C quite illegally, but no one knew the difference to debate the issue. Or, I should say, dared to debate that and many other issues. Such actions as this served like a dynamo to her indomitable spirit. VonCille Hughes was a force of nature her entire life—all ninety-one years.

So, anyway, she did well for eight consecutive years in Miss Gingham's one-room schoolhouse out at Sycamore Grove. It was located so far out in the West Tennessee bottomlands that even the mosquitoes had to use the U.S. Government Survey maps to find it. Chuckle, chuckle, chuckle.

That was a joke you would have heard back in those distant, forgotten times. I'm sure it got a lot more laughs back then than my teenagers are willing to give it in the 21st century. They gave it a dismal negative 10 and feigned nausea when they heard it. But what do they know? Kids!

They won't know anything unless they learn from the past. And they can't learn from the past unless they listen to the tales of family memories and take notes on every day that passes.

Well, this collection of thoughts and memories is for the six living treasures that are my children. It is a labor of love intended to portray their father and all those things connected with his life in a way that is true to his eclectic, unpredictable, and undefinable personality. I think that's how all kids see their parents.

Next question. Why did I write this book the way I did? These stories aren't meant to please anyone's taste for a particular organizational style or genre. What's all that worth to me a hundred years after I'm dead, buried, and *moldering* in my grave like old John Brown? What good is it to be a slave to the vacillating dictates of a fickle and flickering American public?

STOP! Okay, let's have a Culture Break. Speaking of Old John Brown moldering instead of molding, you can sing this poem to the tune of "The Battle Hymn of the Republic." You know it. It's the "glory, glory hallelujah" song. Go ahead, try it! I know you don't want to, but we're going to anyway!

"Old John Brown's body lies a moldering in the grave,
   While weep the sons of bondage whom he ventured all to save;
   But though he sleeps his life was lost while struggling for the slave,
   His soul is marching on.
   Glory, Glory, Hallelujah!"

Every few years, the standards change course in response to the whims and whiffs of ephemeral impositions. Please excuse me; I didn't mean to leave the frustration vent open.

Oh, I realize some do it for money and don't mind giving their minds over in servitude to the literary boundaries established by others just to make a couple of million bucks. After all, somebody must.

Outside of money, what would it matter if I wrote a Pulitzer Prize-winning book and everybody between here and *Foundation's Edge* read it?

What if I wrote an unsolvable mystery, a suspenseful inveigler or a quantum-leaping sci-fi? Who knows, even my great grandkids might like reading it. But what will this tell them about the real me —the one whose genes pulsate within their cells? It might make for good reading, but it wouldn't be reality.

I want my descendants to read the history of my memories—my interpretation of who I was and how I related to the world around me. These real pictures are sent into the future and given to other people without taking away from who they are.

They will be portraits that show how colorful and different my life has been. They will be painted on canvases from the purist school of art, which have lots of empty spaces.

With the bold, unbounded strokes inspired by the mystical blue lights of my mind, they will be able to learn about my past, present, and future. If they know their roots, they will have a strong foundation for understanding the reality of their own time.

Only through a retrospective alignment with one's roots can anyone experience a reality beyond the inventions and fascinations of our brain; everything else is virtual reality.

I hope my children will discover their own reality and pass it along to our descendants who wait for it in the undiscovered country.

They wait over there, where the horizon's edge is the future, separated from us merely by the indeterminate oscillations of time and space.

These ideas and stories about memories will nourish the bond of family, regardless of how many years make up the gulf of time that separates us. But I'd be honored even more if you read them too. Perhaps, the commonality between them will give you some food for thought as well.

This is a collection of memories about some things I like to think about, some people I have known, some places I have been, and some things I have done. Well, at the very least I thought about doing them. My kids probably won't forget where I was born or who my parents were, but their kids might and that bothers me!

Somebody needs to write the "stuff of families" down and pass it along. And the way I see it, since none of my ancestors were willing to assume the role of patriarch, I will.

I'm the last Naylor within my clan; therefore, I nominate myself as patriarch. I ought to be able to restock the clan with the four sons and two daughters I have managed to produce by the grace of God and through the labor of womanhood.

And speaking of womanhood, my daughters will be taught to keep their given name and not trade it in for a hand-me-down substitute twenty-five or thirty years from now. Anyone who's going to be the first female President of the United States needs to keep her own name.

I don't know which one of them will fill that role. It's just 2024; eventually one of them will do it. Don't think I'm crazy. I'm their father, and I'm allowed to dream for them.

What's in a name? Memories center around names. Names of places, names of events, names of ideas, and names of people. They are the starting points for discovering where we came from, where we are, and where we are going. My name is Naylor. I hope you enjoy my memories!

VonCille Hughes Naylor in 1950, married 1 year

THE BLUE LIGHTS OF MEMORY

I was born in the Orange County Hospital that was in downtown Orlando, population 40,000. We lived in the burbs in a white stucco house stylishly accented with the mesh wiring of a screened-in back porch framed in Longleaf Pine.

Elegant enclosures of this type were popular in the area and were locally referred to as the "Florida Room." It's a relaxing hideaway neatly tucked at the rear of the house and strategically designed to catch every whiff of stagnant-free air that was able to blow by in spite of the summertime heat.

Mama was a typical homemaker of the 1950s, dutifully staying home with the kids while Daddy brought home all the bacon. It was bucolic, but belittling. The bacon came by way of the United States Air Force, where Daddy served as a Master Sergeant.

While living in the city of lakes, Daddy allowed his enlistment period to expire, thus ending his ten-year career in the military. (Five in the Army and five in the Air Force, World War II, and the Korean Conflict.)

My memories of that time find their existence in the glossy black-and-white photographs my parents took with their boxy brown camera. Its coarse-grained finish is etched faintly within the tactile memory banks of my brain. This memory of touch is there for a reason. Patiently, I wait to retrieve its meaning.

As I grew older, I developed a liking for reflecting upon those pictures, and thus the memories of that time are based upon the conjured imaginations of the wishful years of my youth.

I see myself fat and happy, playing in the yard dressed only in cloth diapers and cotton t-shirts. My sister is running across the yard clad only in panties, which was permissible for three-year-old girls in 1954.

Her "Prince and the Pauper" haircut and bandaged chin are the extent of my images of her three-year-old self. I look at the old photos today and remember this time as the happiest a young family with a new baby and toddler could possibly be.

The only verifiable memories of family life during this time come from my parents' tales about Pepe, our Siamese cat, and Daddy's decision to become a minister.

Pepe loved to run and meet Daddy in the driveway every day when he would return from the air base. Generally, the Florida weather was moderate enough for Daddy to keep his window rolled down, enticing Pepe to jump into Daddy's lap even before the car would stop.

One day, Pepe ran into the street to reach Daddy before he started turning into the driveway, and a different car hit and killed him. This was my first tragedy by association. This one in particular caused great sadness every time it was told to me.

For me, the story ranked right up there with Bambi. I made my mother tell it to me many times. Over the years, I grew accustomed to her familiar narrative in such a way that it began to sound no different than the other make-believe stories she would read to me at bedtime.

I imagine this is how myths are born.

Daddy had always been a spiritual person, having served as Sunday School Superintendent of the Antioch Baptist Church in

Tibbs, Tennessee, at the invigorating age of sixteen. That's inspiring. When I was 16, I was burning up the rubber of my Camaro Rally Sport every day and choking on nasty, nickel cigars in the woods. Now, there's a bit of a difference.

Tibbs was a conservative little farming community located ten miles outside sprawling Brownsville and fifty miles from metropolitan Memphis. His grandmother's quiet piety inspired Daddy to want to devote his life to serving God, but a note from President Truman during World War II put an end to that.

After ten years in the military, he finally gave in to the seed of a more dedicated and focused spiritual life that had been growing deeply within him. The first year of my life was the last year of Daddy's military career, which proved to be an anxious-provoking year for him, making him hungry for new beginnings in deeper spiritualities.

Memories of Daddy's capabilities as a minister grip my mind with multi-variegated awe.

Awe of his power.

Awe of his fluency.

Awe of his supreme, analytical mind.

His swift and novel interpretations of truth were magically cast as spellbinding oratory. He, however, tells a different story rooted in humble beginnings.

Daddy was not known as a quiet man but as a man of repose. There is a difference. Thought to be shy by most, his unimposing personality was simply germinating until the time it would blossom. Yet even the most brilliant mind must have time for experimentation.

A local pastor, who was delighted that another soldier would leave the service of war for the service of God, guided his first preaching experiments. This kind pastor encouraged Daddy to "work up a sermon" and try it out on his very own congregation.

Five minutes was all Daddy could manage, claiming that he stammered and mumbled himself into public embarrassment. Such a catastrophe oftentimes turns off shy and reserved people. Calm people would persevere despite the embarrassment that comes with a fresh start.

He fine-tuned his skills and succumbed to the force that propelled his heart to master this deeper spirituality. His oratory skills soon surpassed those of his local pastor and most pastors, for that matter. He was a gifted giant of expression, and his genius touched everyone who heard him throughout his career.

Those folks in Florida would have never dreamed in 1954 that this "five-minute" preacher would one day change the lives of thousands of people.

People from all walks of life were interested in his ministry, from ditch diggers to CEOs, from farmers to plantation managers, and from city councilmen to governors. They would all seek him out one day and experience the transformative power of his oratory. But when I was one year old, he could only preach for a bumpy five minutes.

There's not a whole lot more that can be gleaned from the memories of one-year-olds. Like I said, my inventive imaginations are responsible for most of the affirming memories I later clung to as reality.

The nascent imaginations of my youthful innocence slowly turned into true, blue memories that I treasured throughout the rest of my childhood.

They are imaginings of surreal blue skies as clear as the sunny dawn on the first day of spring, of soft rippling lakes wafted by warm coastal breezes and palm trees full of coconuts, and of the ancient sounds of innocence that ring crisp and resonant.

Inherent within our memories are the whisperings of indistinct but soothing sounds. That's something we don't often think about, but the sounds of the past subconsciously color the way we remember.

The sounds of my imagined Florida were smooth, low, and mellow. What else should a baby expect to hear but the harmonious melodies of nature? To complement the serenity I had created, they could be nothing less than blissful symmetry.

If sounds were colors, these would be pale blue mixed with soft streaks of white. If sounds were tangible, these would be fluffy, like the first cotton of the summer's yield. It's irresponsibly fun to make up the past, and certainly more poetic.

From this place, like all places in paradise, we moved. The year was 1955, and Daddy was sticking to his dream.

Johann Wolfgang von Goethe said, "Whatever you dream you can do, begin it!"

Daddy began it by enrolling at Union University in Jackson, Tennessee. It's a county seat town that's 63.7 miles from Memphis. You'd have to pass through Brownsville, as well as Tibbs, to get to Memphis.

The geography of it all made it a nice place to live. It was close to home but far enough away to have some time and space to grow. That's a reassuring place to make new beginnings for anybody.

Daddy completed college in only three years. At the same time, he worked one, sometimes two, full-time jobs, took care of a growing family of four, and graduated tenth in his class. As soon as he graduated, he was offered an officer's commission in the U.S. Navy.

I like the ring of that story. I've been telling people about his academic accomplishments for years with such an egotistical kind of zeal that one would think I had done it myself. I wish I had his zeal and stamina.

At first, we lived in the city. There are tiny flashes of "real" memories from these days, which were almost seventy years ago. Wait! What? Seventy years? Those times seem timeless.

I like to think that I am the same person I have always been. I mean, I have the same bullheadedness now as I did when I was six and was driving everybody nuts, yet there's something peculiar about those Jackson days.

There are bits and pieces of that time that just don't seem to fit in with reality. They are like slightly distorted triangles whose sum never quite adds up. They float in and out with a purity and whole-ness that tease me, flushing my chest with polar-cold uncertainty.

The way these memories make me feel is so different from the way other memories make me feel, which is more like a moderate sink-flash. (You can watch TikTok videos about the meaning of sink-flash.)

These whirling adventures linger hard in my emotions, and I often think that they are the surging choruses I have been looking for as a "searching" adult. If only I could lasso these emotions and make them stay alive in me forever.

These anchors of depth and permanence would rekindle the fires of meaning in my life. But I can only hold on to them for a few flick-ering seconds when they surface from time to time.

Unexpectedly and gracefully, they make a whistle-stop journey through the thick of my soul. I try to reach out to them and hold on to them, but they slip away like the awakening dreams of midnight. It's frustrating.

It's hard to put into words how those fleeting moments felt. In fact, it would take the holiest litany of all the beautiful words from every language that has ever existed and from every language that one day will exist. Maybe that's being melodramatic.

What's wrong with having a little melodrama with the intro-spect of retrospect? The world certainly makes me process enough rot every day.

There's nothing wrong with sprinkling a dash of the splendid and the heavenly in my nostalgia. And so, I indulge myself. To heck with the critics of melodrama!

The nagging feelings of the past wear me out mentally and phys-ically, making it hard for me to understand them and impossible for me to say what they are. I walk down memory lane quite often, hoping to stumble upon those feelings.

The lightning images are bathed in mystery blues. From hidden black holes, they emerge, and there is no match for an earthly comparison. I can look at every kind of blue all day without finding the hallowed hue that splashes about within these memories.

With the force of cosmic streaks from another dimension, my memory is teased with neural cells of color that only appear real to my inner vision. Is it all an invention of my brain?

What about those reports of people's near-death experiences? I hear about them on television, and my phone is a whirling, beeping monster, providing me with hundreds of these stories every time I pick it up. (But I only really read them when I'm bored out of my mind standing in line at Kroger.)

Mysterious blue lights are supposed to mean something, aren't they? Exposure to these unfathomable lights goes hand in hand with being close to eternity, the *unknown*, and that which is beyond mere mortal existence. Isn't it?

Maybe it's a glimpse of paradise after all. Maybe the innocence of two and three-year-olds is encased in this mysterious providential blue light, swinging by looking like a Halley's Comet of the soul and originating from imperceptible sectors deep within the numinous pulsations of the Creator's universe.

Maybe I am meant to remember this otherworldly Providence through the eyes of childhood for a reason.

They are like shadows of light from heaven, dancing across the spectrums of time and space. The eternal blue light of my childhood periodically reaches out to remind me that the tranquility of what was is the tranquility for which I search and will have again one day.

Maybe it's the celestial blue light that many talk about so engagingly, causing the rest of us to listen so covetously.

"Sounds great," you say, "but I don't believe those kinds of things any more than I believe I can teach my dog Brunhilde to speak German." I don't know what to tell you. Some folks have lost the fire of divine imagination in the dregs of elitist skepticism. The boring sophisticates of the 21st century would rebut with uppity impunity with something like:

· · ·

"This kind of teary-eyed philosophy is nothing less than waterlogged rhetoric indiscriminately spewed out by anybody's and everybody's guru who tries to place the mantle of God-like immortality on insufficient old *Homo sapiens sapiens*. It's just a flash of blue light because blue is probably your favorite color, and therefore your brain has a synaptic fit of ecstasy every time it gets turned loose with one of those whizzing, wheeling memories. A neuron makes bubbles in your head and makes your chest flush cold and fast. It feels good. You like to feel it, and you like to experience it as much as possible. Euphoria is an affirmation. A lot of what you know about your past was told to you in countless family reminiscing sessions. Those stories are just that. They are not the flashing, flushing memories of a dimensionless holy place of eternal substance."

(*An imaginary imagining of somebody somewhere, probably me, but not what I really think. Gosh, somebody had to write it!)

Swerving noses of urbane condemnation work overtime at taking all the sacred out of life. They can turn up their disbelieving noses in yuppie frenzy if they want to, but I'm going to cling to the redemptive power of my memories.

Whatever happens in anyone's past only serves to enrich their ability to accept the present and their agility in confronting the future.

The innocent faith within my memories feeds me, clothes me, shelters me, and protects me because they are stories that are intended to live forever.

These are stories that will always be a part of processing every detail of every day for all my days. So, what does it matter if the hues of blue mean nothing other than my predilection for blue? It's my life and my blues.

If the hallowed feelings they bring can rejuvenate, motivate, and restore me, then such memories will always be the greatest treasures I could ever hope to find.

And so, they are precious memories gleaned from stories that have their greatest meaning only to me. They are stories about the people whose beer cans Daddy swept out from under his car with a street broom every morning before he went off to the preacher's college.

Or about the people he met at the little country church that he pastored during his last year at Union University

Or the schoolteacher that saved me from the pit of ravenous wild pigs

Or my own child, who got lost once in a sea of cartoon characters.

They are stories about people and events that are locked neatly away in my brain's cryptic storage centers.

These are stories based on memories of almost seventy years ago, forty years ago, twenty years ago, last year, and even just yesterday. They are golden, heavenly treasures.

If you think about it, your memories are also rich storehouses full of very similar stories. The difference is that they are your stories, and their meaning finds validity only to the degree that you will allow.

Reading the stories of someone else's memories may help you remember your own. And the wealth reflected in both will hopefully give you a greater *ump*! for today and more *pow*! for tomorrow.

Daddy used to preach it mightily; he's gone now, but I still believe it.

"Look back to the rock from where you were cut; joy and gladness shall be found there, thanksgiving, and the voice of melody."
–A dude called Isaiah

Jeffrey Naylor reflecting while walking along the shore of Lake Michigan

A FOXHOLE FRIENDSHIP

This friendship first blossomed one zero-dark-thirty morning when our company moved out to a live fire shooting range... with orders to advance and recover. (To recover, I assumed, the lost terrain of disadvantaged lizards, desert lilies, and prickly things unknown heretofore by us men of civilization.)

The only thing this day was supposed to mean to me was that I was once again on a highly significant training mission, whether I wanted to be or not. I would move forward cautiously, but I felt more frazzled than cautious.

As I moved forward, I had been instructed to fire my M-16 semi-automatic rifle with confidence and authority. It was my objective to wound helpless metal dummies as they innocently popped up between the cracked rocks and innumerable cacti, their swords drawn to halt my advance no matter the cost.

When I was in the R.O.T.C. (Reserve Officer Training Corps), I felt as if I were on the mission of a lifetime. This new little civilization I had joined needed me and my group of brothers to learn skills that would make us the first line of defense for *homeland security*. (That would have been a strange sounding phrase indeed in 1974.)

In this world, I would find out the true meaning of foxhole friendship. Such a friend might possibly be the best friend I would ever need in battle. They would not become just *a* friend but quite possibly my best friend, my "foxhole buddy."

A "foxhole friend" is someone who will not unfriend you regardless of the circumstances, whether bullets or bombs fall around you. It wasn't like unfriending a Facebook friend. These friends became lifelong friends after spending weeks of grueling training in the dirt and mud.

They would not desert you or deny you, and if you became wounded, they would either secure you to safety or remain by your side no matter the circumstance. This friend was the kind of best friend who would kick and rattle the sides of my bunk bed every night, purposely denying me sleep.

That doesn't sound like a best friend, does it? But this friend would do that to be the first one of us to get up in the very early morning to make sure I would not make us late for company formation. He didn't do so out of rivalry but out of camaraderie.

His name just so happened to be Mark Marvel from California, and we lived through our army times together like two un-twistable strings, indefatigable in our desire to never be pulled apart. Our friendship was the kind that would dazzle like an "almost glorious" and lofty moment in the fleeting nanoseconds of battle when the only thing any outsider could see would be the dichotomies of good and evil, or right and wrong.

The only black spot in our special friendship was the constant little lie about Mark's grandfather. He would spin the tale quite convincingly that his grandfather owned Marvel Comics, which I genuinely believed because I was too green to know any better. After all, Mark was from California, and that was enough credentials for me.

But would a foxhole friend still be your friend even if you almost accidentally killed them? Nevertheless, on this day, in these dark moments, I almost succeeded in completing a crossfire hit that zipped directly toward the path of my very best friend on that foreign island of basic training.

In that loft of friendship lore, my weapon discharged a fateful flare of metal, heat, and an imperceptible flash of fire. At that moment, I knew what had happened. What is strange is that at that moment, I understood the event in its entirety, seeing and realizing its significance for the past, present, and even the ungraspable flashes of the future. And so, I froze. My heart froze. My feet froze. Everything was frozen with heat. A heat so hot I could hear my heart being seared on the anvil of my conscience.

And then I realized he knew it too. My bullets missed the dummy, and they missed the best friend I had ever had during my long and honorable twenty years on this salty, grimy desert and water planet.

Yet, barely missing them both did not permit my throat to swallow the brittle dust with any less grievousness, nor did my soul feel any less bereft of this newly found and most distasteful, indelicate grief. Grief? You betcha,' grief!

Grief for what could have been, grief for losing my friend, grief for losing my soul—grief that would gather me up and pour me back into the pathetically unapproachable thing that I had been before I knew such a friendship existed.

Our drill sergeant knew when it happened. He was always watching. All that did was stir up more shame. My heart knew it so emphatically that it began severing the arteries of my morality—my ethics for existing. And they were all cutting so deeply into me that I thought I would never breathe again.

But we all did breathe again, and Mark and I remained the closest of friends for all the time we were in training together. And then, as quickly as we had become foxhole friends, we were separated. He had gone back to California and I back to West Kentucky, leaving our chances of following up with one another in the uncivilized era of stamps that needed licking and envelopes that did not properly fit any paper known to man.

So, in a day of sticky stamps and crumply letters, correspondence was not an appealing prospect. In that bygone era, even a telephone call cost almost as much as a call to the third moon north of Jupiter's furthermost ring (and it's the thickest, I am told).

Nevertheless, in my mind and in my heart, he is still my very best friend, whom I will never forget, regardless of how great the foment that Mother Nature or the laws of men will prey upon us both. In the meantime, he is my foxhole friend in that together we drummed haphazardly but faithfully at the soulful heart strings of our existence on that day, in that moment, of the flashing nanoseconds as those lively bullets zipped around us.

And so, in reality, we were just kids in grown-up bodies, being soldiers of the American desert, digging foxholes not for war, but for friendship. Though we were only kids, indeed, we were playing a grown-up game that drenched us with something new and unrecognizable.

There was a melancholy within us both, speaking to our growing minds in languages of war and peace—daring new languages for us both. The world was making us grow up fast as we learned quickly to discern the meanings of strange and inexplicable ideas.

Such as, for young recruits, the former criminals of who we are and what we will become were growing as soldiers of men; a newly discovered belief that war is a far greater creation of the "otherly"... of both gods and men; and that those real things of war have always, however slyly, attempted to mislead us into an indiscernible, eerie world.

It is an unbreakable, ethereal law, an undeniably ethereal beauty that enslaves our freedom with a gravity unseen, enabling unperceived chains of ownership to keep us bound, albeit unknowingly, but hold us bound to never disqualify war or enable us to break free from its ideology, but rather to succumb to its almost exotically possessiveness, from which we become in the process as they would turn us against our natural selves, making us soldiers of the realm, soldiers of the fight.

Yet, I think we did not allow that to happen. We left as stronger friends than we had begun, even without ever seeing one another again, because after we had fallen into the "foxhole" of our fears and had rallied together, we bonded with a new kind of courage found not only on the battlefield but also in faraway places.

Now, many years later, I am confident that the battlefields we walk on every day to get here and there can follow no greater model of friendship than what we learned on that day in the briny desert of our just desserts.

"Greater love hath no man than this, that a man lay down his life for his friends." A fella said something like this about 2,000 years ago and I think it's still a kind of love worth having.

A CONVERSATION WITH CHELSEA

C helsea and I exchanged two emails on December 1, 2009, while I was teaching in South Korea. It was exactly one month before I would be beaten and left for dead and subsequently spend four months in a South Korean hospital.

Dear Daddy:

What am I supposed to do, Daddy?

I feel so lost and helpless all the time. I can't seem to care about anything anymore. I'm letting people and things walk all over me.

—Chelsea

Dear Chelsea,

You are an adult now. You are responsible for your own movements and decisions. No one can make decisions for you. Becoming an adult makes you feel like you have suddenly landed on another planet. It is you who is now in charge. You are responsible.

That feeling of responsibility can feel burdensome, unfamiliar, and so odd that it allows guilt to creep inside your mind, making you feel like you have abandoned some essential part of your life—that you have abandoned the strictures and safety of childhood. Don't feel lost and helpless before this unwarranted guilt.

You have a challenging new plan now to finish the last four months of high school and begin college. You have been preparing for this time all your life. Already, you have firmly charted out these goals and dreams. Your beautiful courage will move you through the years like fingers sliding into a glove, pushing through to find the end. And the end will be the beginning—the beginning of your whole life of wondrous living.

You have dreamed of this time for many days and nights. Your dream is my dream for you. You are a beautiful girl who will find many great friends in college. They will change your life.

You say that you seem to not care about anything anymore. But I don't believe that you don't care about things any longer. As your daddy, I know for certain that you care passionately about things.

You have given much of your time and effort to caring for all manner of things throughout your life. You just need to be patient and realize that the cold winds of December wrap us in apprehension as much as they do with scarves and coats. It makes us feel dubious about everything we are, were, and still wish to be. So, don't let it stop you; just understand it as a newness of feeling and that this feeling is a part of your life—not to be ignored but to be experienced.

You are in control of all your tomorrows now, but they will not come quickly. As you build this extra foundation for your life, the days will seem to come slowly—one month after another, years fighting back the months. When you have finished preparing yourself, you will be more than ready to accept what life gives you, or rather, what life expects from you.

Stay busy with your dreams and focus on your goals. If I had the time to sit and worry, then I think life would drive me crazy. Sometimes, I think that I just need to make it to bedtime and that if I rest, tomorrow will come sooner and more peacefully, making it easier for me to say, *"I have made it one more day."*

I refuse to allow myself to believe that life is worthless because life is all that I am. There is no life outside my own existence and experience, so I must push myself through the hours, through the days, through the weeks, through the months, and through the years. For me, life is a process of pushing myself from one point to the next. Sometimes it makes me feel a little lost, but I refocus and remember that I am what I choose to be. And I choose to exist and not stop the joy of living. That is what gives me the courage and strength to go through each day.

Just remember that somewhere else in the world, you are making an impact without even knowing it. Have you ever thought about that? Somewhere, sometimes, someone is always thinking about you or talking about you. That is proof enough that your life does make a difference. I am sure there are countless moments in each day that Pop thinks about you and wonders what wonderful things you are accomplishing.

Also, your brothers, too, and Meme in her convoluted ways! Without you knowing it, they are thinking of you in moments during which you are fretting that there is nothing left to feel. Chelsea, they are not moments of nothing because your life is always making a difference, played out in an abundance of memories and thoughts.

I hope the same will be true in my own moments of solitary confinement. I make myself believe that somewhere, someone is whispering my name—in a thought, in a dusty memory—someone is feeling and thinking of me, enabling me to have positive feelings for life.

For you, it will be the same, I promise! Just like today, already hundreds of students in my English classes have spoken your name when I showed them your elephant and tiger photos. They were amazed that you would let an elephant step over you and hover his giant foot above your head. So, they busied themselves looking at the photos over and over, simultaneously repeating your name aloud:

"Chelsea. Chelsea. Chelsea. Look at Chelsea and the elephant." You didn't even realize that people halfway across the world were thinking amazing thoughts about you.

How many other times and moments do others speak of you, think of you, or pause to reflect on you? It is the same for everybody, isn't it? Truly, this is the cure for loneliness and despondency. People need only sit and meditate on how others are remembering them at any moment.

This phenomenon is not particular to any individual; it happens to everybody. Therefore, everyone can build up structured and qualitative value each day. Somewhere, many times a day and night, someone is seeing your face in their minds, reading something you wrote, or hearing your name from a friend.

It is impossible to know as many people as you do without having a positive effect on them, and they in turn influence so many others. It is impossible to be so connected and be forgotten. So, in that sense, you are not lost. What you are, who you are, and what you make others feel each day mean you have a purpose in life, and therefore, it is impossible to say that you are lost.

Because you are the point of focus for the thoughts of others, you know that you do make a difference. Knowing that you make a difference in life demonstrates that others care about you, and subsequently, you too can reciprocate and show care for them with your thoughts and memories.

So, contrary to what you thought, you do care about something. I believe that you care deeply about life, people, and the past and the future. Sometimes we may shiver in a lonely moment and feel too much separateness, causing that coldness to fuel our feelings of isolation. These are normal feelings, and we must learn to make the most of them and not allow them to serve as points of depression but rather as points of rejuvenation, knowing that they are what they are for a purpose. And that is just one of the characteristics of a life that matters.

You matter! You matter to others. You matter to me. You are

constantly in my thoughts, quite literally. You are never alone or without value.

You were my most precious treasure when I held you in the trembling moments of your first breaths in this world, and you will always be my treasure.

Love,

Daddy

Jeffrey and daughter, Chelsea Naylor

A BEDTIME POEM FOR MY CHILDREN
MECHANIZED EAGLE—AVICUS METALLICUS

The Great Bird tilts gently from side to side,
A mechanized eagle is rising in the sky.
The higher we go, the slower feels our stride,
But gravity is something our ascension cannot deny.

Gracefully we soar above mountains majestic.
Not as operose as those who journeyed first.
Just cruise with me on wings simplistic,
For they are mere wrinkles of time that make the earth.

The higher we climb, the more the tugging planet disappears.
Clouds rush forth like the evening tide.
Dressed in white covers, earth's canvas smears,
As the great bird claws skyward on its heavenly ride.

There are no mountains now to see; the world is a cottony terrain.

Dazzling figurations transform the clay, becoming in a way
A land mystic, showered with sunshine, never rain.
An ethereal creation bathed in beams of beauty in full array.

A vast, Crystal Ocean now lies below,
    With furrows and rivers of a ghostly pale.
    Their pattern, designs, and symmetry bestow
    Upon the traveler's heart a magnificent tale.

It's a tale of ascending and descending in a chariot of steel.
    Riding the airwaves with imaginary sails,
    Lower then higher, slower then faster over river and rill.
    Liquid fire sparks the sky, as *Avicus metallicus* never fails.

Jeffrey and Jeramie Naylor and All My Children

Afterword
MEMORIES ARE THE LIVING TREE OF LIFE

THE MECHANICS OF MINING MEMORIES AND CRAFTING STORIES

This book is a collection of stories that are drawn from the memories of my life. It came into existence as a hiding place where I could share my life stories with my children and friends. I hope the telling of these stories from my collected memories will positively contribute to the development of my growing and loving family and friends—and maybe have an impact on your family too.

Before the first human story was ever written, people gathered around sacred places to listen to interesting and life-influencing stories told by great storytellers. We don't do that much anymore and have unfortunately lost the strength of human connectedness, which is the elemental foundation of our civilization. My stories have grown from a hodgepodge of memories tossed about, shifting, and growing through the years, providing people with some suggestions for facing life.

My maternal grandfather and Mama were thrilling storytellers that people eagerly sought out, sometimes traveling great distances to hear their "tales." I may not be "cut from the same cloth," as Mama ALWAYS used to say in her critique of fellow humans, but I try.

Understand, by no means am I claiming to be a great storyteller. But I've learned a thing or two about life and cultivating the art of storytelling, specifically by mining the priceless memories stored in my mind.

Through storytelling, I hope to inspire an atmosphere of equality both inside and outside of my family, illustrate positive models for leading a healthy family life, and emphasize the significance of confronting common, everyday issues like racism, homelessness, social injustice, and the democratic maze. These goals are achieved through gathering and crafting my memories into meaningful stories.

By sharing what I have learned from my own memories, I also hope to bring attention to health issues such as Alzheimer's, innumerable cancers, neurological dysfunctions, psychological concerns, as well as the many, many other ailments that plague the Human Condition.

I enjoy telling stories based on the events of my life and the lives of others, which, if you stick around and listen to them, eventually will touch on every subject in the world. You could most definitely say I've got something to say about anything and everything to anybody anywhere. I'm a talker. Memories emerge from sharing and talking. Good storytelling is good talking and good talking is enthralling.

The fundamental requirement for being a collector of memories and storytelling is to be a talker. [When others don't, can't, or won't speak up, I always did! I have always been a talker.] Just now, several memories entered my mind when I wrote the words in the parenthetical sentence above. I was thinking about memories and how they emerge as stories. And you might well ask, "How do they become a narrative or a story worth telling?" Well, let's get into it.

In the previous paragraph, I connected storytelling to talking and

I confessed that I have always been a person who enjoys talking. The simple expression of this truth inexplicably caused a memory to open in my mind. It's always been there; I simply haven't had a need to think about it before this moment. Memories never leave. They wait for you to open a space in your thinking that allows them to emerge.

Let's follow this unexpected memory and discover where it takes us. This memory resurrection has two stories in it—two gems of truth.

I remember in the far-off days of high school; periodically, the faculty would "convene" the student body to assemble in the gymnasium and listen to the most boring and abstruse speakers imaginable. I think this was a common form of torture in high schools everywhere fifty years ago.

At the end of the speaker's torturous presentation, they would invariably ask the student body to present questions. Nobody wanted to ask questions because nobody knew what the guy was talking about anyway, and nobody wanted to be there in the first place. Or the last!

Without somebody venturing a question we would sit there trapped in an interminable vortex of mindless space—a place of no hall passes, no preferences for teacher's pets, no chance to goof off in the coach's office, but there we sat, veritably shoved up against students whom we hated. High school at this level sucked!

After a couple of semesters of this encore gimmick for student "entertainment and enrichment," I decided to "take the bull by the horns" and come up with a carefully orchestrated question that would express the angst of us all.

While the guest speaker thrust his words mightily into the air and students continued to languish in the bloody bleachers of higher learning, I spent my time scribbling out the most outlandish, convoluted question I could think of (if it was somewhat consistent with the speaker's grievous topic, anything was acceptable).

When the time for questions arrived and the minutes passed without any student responses, I paused the silence a moment longer and then raised my hand, waiting to be anointed with the task of engaging the enemy...er...speaker.

"Okay, yes! The young man there in the middle. Yes, you! The one with the tie. The only one wearing the tie." (Furtively whispering under his breath, "the *weird tie*.")

Not everyone knew my name, but upon seeing the guy with "the" tie, the student body moaned, and one day groaned appreciatively because they would grow to know over the years that "the talker" would soon put their unwanted assembly to death! Their rescue! (Try a little *suspension of disbelief* with this paragraph.)

There would be only one question posited in the gym this day and it was *my question*, which was always received by two responses: 1. total befuddlement by the speaker (and the faculty) and 2. uproarious laughter and applause from the students. They applauded because it brought things to an abrupt end, not because they liked me.

Heck, I wanted the speaker to stop the insanity as much as anyone. If by asking a crafty question that had the appearance of understanding and appreciation the speaker would tuck his feathers neatly under his coat and leave the building, then mission accomplished!

The spontaneity of interpolated cheers very nearly brought an Apophis orchestrated *Chaos* to its proverbial, lofty edge in the Reidland High School gym that day. And as it were, it was merely the first of what would be many more such days at future dreaded assemblies. Higher learning—achieved! Forever afterwards, I was the high school assembly disrupter.

Next, the second story from the same memory.

Toward the end of my senior year, they called us all up to the gym for an unscheduled, unknown assembly. In rueful lines, marching out, class by class, with dangling arms shifting back and forth through the long hallways like circus monkeys we moved in dreaded unison.

Ah! No worries. There wasn't a guest speaker. Thanks be unto Zeus and all the high school gods of relief! It was a men's civic association awarding certificates to chosen individuals for being community minded (the most baneful award ever devised by adults to embarrass high schoolers in front of their peers).

One by one, around half a dozen students were called to face the crowd, and one by one, the substitute Mayor in charge called out the names of the students to receive their award. At each presentation, he asked, "Would you like to say something?" And at each presentation, the recipients parsed out a few barely audible sentences of gratitude. Why, what could they possibly say? This was an unexpected ceremony in the middle of Biology I frog dissection!

No one knew they could or anyone else might be honored on this day or even what the purpose of all of this was anyway. It was an enigma. The entire matter. Might there be refreshments? Nobody knew. With the conclusion of each student's remarks, the student body would respond with the soft, boring clapping of hands expected in such events as these.

Inexplicably, I was the last recipient called, presented, and queried with the same ineluctable question: "Would you like to say something?" A switch went off like an explosion in my brain, reminding me of all those high school years devoted to speaking up, bringing *Chaos* at the approval of the entire student body. I had always had something to say and this incessant talking of mine had upon innumerable occasions rescued the entire school from the reprobation of the so-called *guest speaker*!

As the microseconds passed and the infinitesimal specks of brain dust settled, I leaned over the microphone and firmly and crisply said, "No, thank you." And I stepped back!

In that same instance, the student body let up a thunderous roar, stomping their feet on the bleachers and screaming Bob Ross' *little happy screams.* That's right, they were so uncontrollably ecstatic because I had chosen to be quiet.

When the storm abated, the municipal presenter leaned into the microphone and said, "Wow, you must really be popular. We've never had such a response for anyone receiving an award before." Of course, with that statement, a bomb went off in everybody's head and they laughed even louder. What a charade!

Okay! Those are the memories that came alive in my mind just a few moments ago. What message are they supposed to have for the reader, the listener?

The storyteller crafts these memories into stories by sharing/talking them into significance. These stories are rich and fertile memories which if remain unshared cannot benefit me in any manner. Shared memories hold forth truths that spell out the essence of an individual, giving purpose and foundation to life. Memories evinced, pureed, cultivated, shared, refined, expanded, and outwardly manifested become the guidepost of my life.

Memories shared **might** enable others to develop better thought, but most assuredly memories **will** enable me toward personal enrichment through better thought.

Without an appreciation for memories my life is lessened from what it can become. If I cherish and elevate memories to a place of honor and appreciation, I demonstrate that I want the best from my life. Sharing and telling stories about my memories is a way to integrate them into the very fiber of my existence. Shared, they live. Unshared, they lie dormant. Shared, I live fully. Unshared, I waver, incompletely. Is storytelling important? Yes! Why?

STORYTELLING EMERGES AS PROOF OF LIFE.

The stories I share emerge from personal memories that have coalesced around my beloved ancestors, grandparents, parents, myself, my children, and grandchildren's lives, and of course, the precious friends that have come and gone against the horizon of my life.

The stories in this book are not presented in any order because memories do not emerge in any order. The genesis for this book came from the realization that every day I am bombarded with images, ideas, and many different events and periods of my life.

Do sudden memories in the middle of the night come in chronological order? Of course, not; that would be insane. So, in that sense, my stories are presented in much the same way that memories come to us—not in order! One chapter may be rooted in something that my grandparents told me that happened in their lives in 1940, and the next is from something that happened with me and one of my kids in 2023!

Sanguine and melancholy, bitter and sweet, all rolled up together —the stories are intended to be humorous and serious uniquely composed.

Hopefully, you will experience a unique blend of humor and seriousness—a veritable Portuguese salad bowl of *saudade*! In other words, it is the dream of every author like me, who hopes readers will come away laughing and crying.

The distinction of this vignette of my life is that the stories are told from the viewpoint of a "Southerner" in common everyday life. There might be lots of little cliches unfamiliar to some people, but they shouldn't detract from comprehension. The sweet dialect of people from the Midwest and South of the US is often endeared in movies and books.

This book is not meant to be an academic paper or an apology of any kind. I've finished writing all the academic papers I have a desire to write. Hardly anyone wanted to read them yesterday and certainly does not want to hear what I have to say about arcane topics now.

I have written in a tone that is meant to appeal to an average, casual reader who wishes to read something that doesn't require all 100 billion, billion, billion neurons of the brain. Read it on the train, on the beach, on your break at Amazon or while resting on the side of a vertical climb in the Rockies. You are elevated but the vocabulary is not as elevated as I might use in an academic paper or in other genres.

I don't want to write in a way that might cause you to slip and fall from a sudden neural snap! I want you to read one chapter or two chapters at a time...relax. More of us need to relax and find peace through simplistic concentration. That's not because I think my audience has a low level of intelligence. On the contrary, it is because I have faith that my audience will grasp the deepest meanings of my stories expressed with greatest simplicity.

The deepest meanings are often understood through the simplest expressions, ideas, or images. Simplicity breeds depth. It is my hope that from my simple life you will find a little something of value.

And then, you'll decide it's time to harvest your own memories and feed your children from the bounty of your life.

Often when I write, I place a photo or image taken from the thousands in our family library in front of me. It allows me to think with greater clarity about the past. Sometimes the photo ends up becoming a story.

I wrote this afterword while focusing on the picture I had taken in October 2018 near one of the winter camps of the Five Civilized Nations of American Indians who suffered during the march of the Trail of Tears in the 1830s, in Livingston County, Kentucky.

I took the photo, but only because my dearest friend, Karen Quertermous, showed me this place by guiding me and my wife Jeramie into an almost forbidden and sacred terrain at the confluence of the Mississippi, Ohio, and Tennessee Rivers.

At the time (2018) very few people had ever seen the rock formations of this sacred place. It screams with beauty, ugliness, freedom, slavery, love, hatred, legalism, justice. The blood, sweat, tears, and whispers of death that left many of these travelers buried here is the causality of the sacred nature of these formations. True high spiritualism can be drafted into one's soul from this place.

I've always thought of this photo as a representation of the Living Tree of Life. From the Living Tree of Life come our memories, our inward nature, through our dreams, our memories, and our spiritual focal points.

I have used this photo many times as my mantra for honoring my memories and the importance they have for my existence.

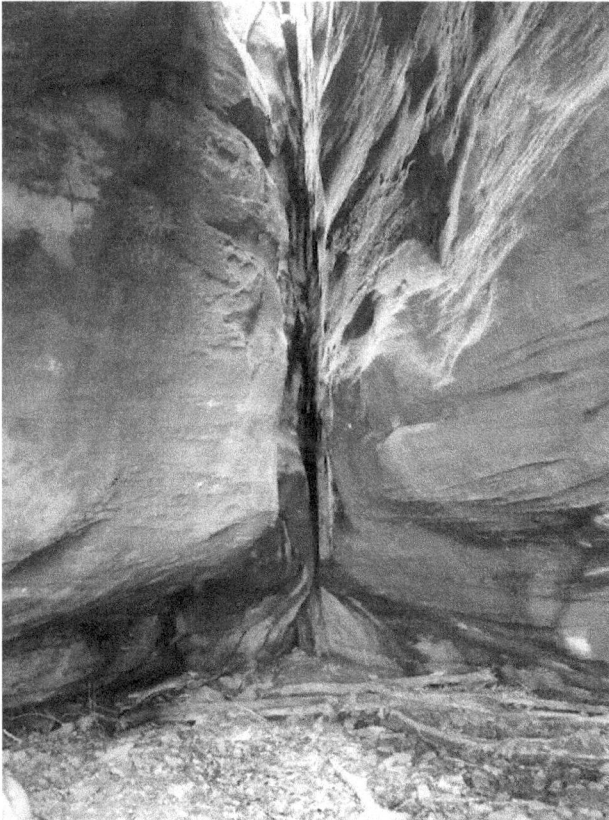

Afterword Dedicated to Karen Quertermous, my dearest friend with an ancient heart.

Jeffrey and Jeramie Naylor with Karen Quertermous

Acknowledgments

Who should one attribute acknowledgment to when writing a book? Who should be considered partners in obtaining the final product? It's impossible to name everyone who has enabled me to see this book published. Why don't I just thank everyone I've ever known? Well, I can't do that. So, I'll do this instead.

I want to thank every member of my family that has loved me and tolerated me over the years—all my grandparents, my parents, all my children and their spouses, and all my grandchildren.

More specifically, I want to thank my son, **Joshua Alexander Naylor** and my daughter, **Chelsea Danielle Naylor** for lending their ears to my midnight emails and last-minute texts requesting help with my narrative. To which they provided immense and artistic responses that have contributed enormously to my ability to create.

Finally, I save this last acknowledgment for two of the most intelligent and imaginative people I have ever known. The senior most editor at Winterwolf Press, **Christine Contini**, is a genuine seeker of the truth in all she says and does. I am honored that she took a craftsman's care with my narrative in preparation for publication. Christine understands writing as a craft and a gift, and I am thankful that she is my friend.

Laura Cantu is the creator and publisher of Winterwolf Press. She is an artist, a writer, a great lover of all people and I am immeasurably blessed that she opened up her life to share her gifts with me. And for that, I am most humbled. I am thankful and amazed for her many considerations and suggestions that enabled Winterwolf Press to publish this book.

This book's release date is Valentine's Day, 2024. This needs to have a separate kind of acknowledgment. The book is about love for family, friends, and life and it seems fitting that I acknowledge the power of this day of love. In a more personal way, it is special to me as the day my paternal grandmother passed away and the day my sweet Mama was born.

Valentine's Day is the greatest day in the year to celebrate LOVE with everyone around you and I hope by reading my book your love with and for others will blossom anew.

Alice Barton Naylor, Jack Naylor's sweet mama, passed at 32 on Valentine's Day

About the Author

JEFFREY NAYLOR is a bit of a Renaissance Man in that he has dipped his mind into many adventures throughout his life including a creator of stories, songs, and poetry, and instrumentalist.

He is a former professor of philosophy, ancient history and religions, modern Christianity, literature, cultural studies, archaeology, creative writing, and American history, teaching in the US and abroad.

He has served his country as a Chaplain in the Veteran's Administration Hospital system and as an officer in the United States Army Reserve.

He enjoys drawing, painting, theatrical directing and acting, especially musicals and has appeared on the stage high school through community theater levels, as well as appearing almost invisibly in the Paramount Picture, "*I.Q.*"

He is a chronicler, holding private interviews with many cultural, religious, and political figures, including Teddy Kollek, fighter of Nazism, founder of modern Israel and Mayor of Jerusalem. His greatest interview was the life-long interview with his father, Jack Calvin Naylor, a Southern Baptist pastor until he was 93 years old.

He is the father of six children and six grandchildren and has a thing or two to say about family!

ALSO BY WINTERWOLF PRESS

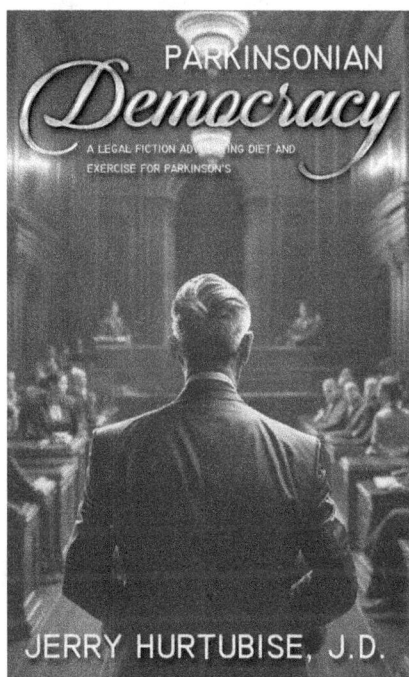

We at Winterwolf Press are thrilled to announce that our latest publication, authored by the talented Jerry Hurtubise, has made a remarkable debut, receiving outstanding reviews since its release on Black Friday.

In a glowing endorsement, a respected physician has awarded the book a 5-star review on Amazon. He highly recommends it not only to individuals battling Parkinson's disease but also to their families, praising the book for its insightful and engaging content. His review highlights the book's fun, approachable style, making complex topics accessible and enjoyable.

For these and other titles, go to https://winterwolfpress.com/

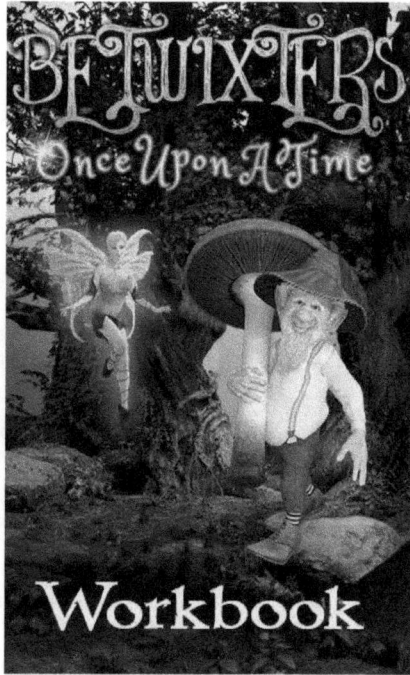

The importance of social awareness and inspiration to change what can be changed is not lost when it comes to Laura C. Cantu and her work.

This complementary workbook contains lesson plans and activities that teachers and parents can use to engage children as they read, *Betwixters Once Upon a Time.*

Each lesson plan was designed by a Licensed Professional Counselor who has been a school counselor and has worked with children and teens for twenty years.

For these and other titles, go to https://winterwolfpress.com/

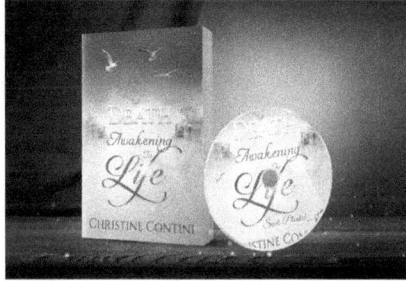

At the young age of thirty-seven, Christine Contini experienced a sudden cardiac death. Over forty minutes later, she returned from the other side, carrying the keys to unlock profound understanding and seemingly supernatural abilities. Dying allowed Christine to awaken to humanity's natural energetic potentials and pierce the veil between the physical and energetic worlds.

She began working with the recently deceased, the dying, and those in comas. What she learned from these experiences formed her foundation of 'Energetics'—a complete system of awareness, balance, and understanding.

In Death: Awakening to Life, Seeds Planted, Christine takes us on a journey through life, death, and rebirth. She presents fascinating information about what happens after we die and describes, from first-hand experience, the many pitfalls that can entangle the dying and their loved ones during the death process.

Christine also shares heartwarming stories about gifts from the dying and their successful journeys to the other side.

These true accounts will captivate and inspire readers to question life and reality.

For these and other titles, go to https://winterwolfpress.com/

SUBMISSIONS
Book Submission & Acquisition

UNLEASH THE POWER OF YOUR STORY WITH THE STRENGTH OF THE PACK!

Join our pack and submit your fully edited manuscript today to see your vision come to life. Together, we'll create howlingly great books that readers will love!

Winterwolf Press and Shadow Wolf Press are thrilled to be growing faster than we ever imagined possible! Our commitment to publishing high-quality books has struck a chord with readers, and we're excited to continue expanding our catalog.

As we grow, we want to ensure that we're providing the best possible experience for our authors, which is why we only accept books that are already fully edited and ready for publication.

When you join the pack for support with editing and proofreading services before submitting your work to us, authors can ensure that their manuscript is polished and free of errors, ready to be transformed into a professional, high-quality book.

For more information, go to https://winterwolfpress.com/submissions/